AF316993

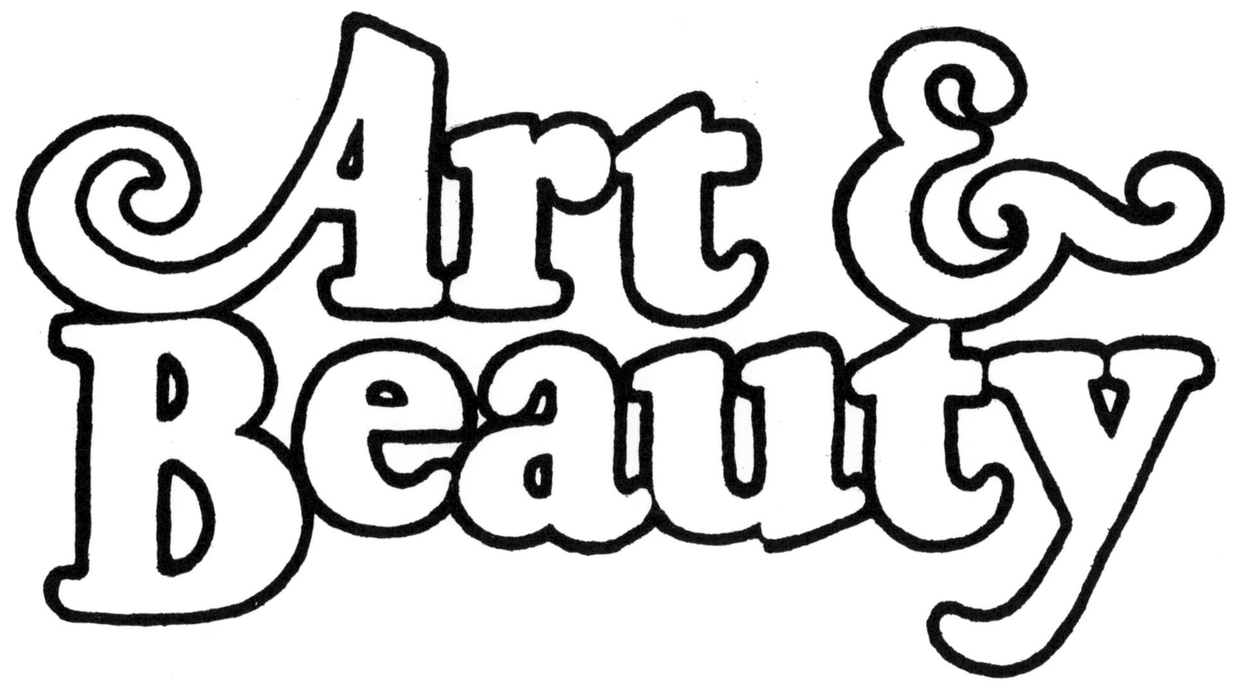

Drawings by R. Crumb

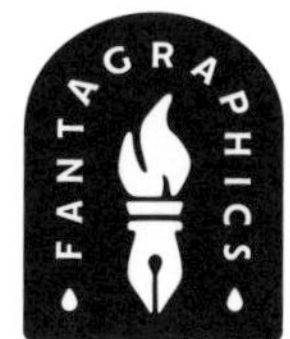

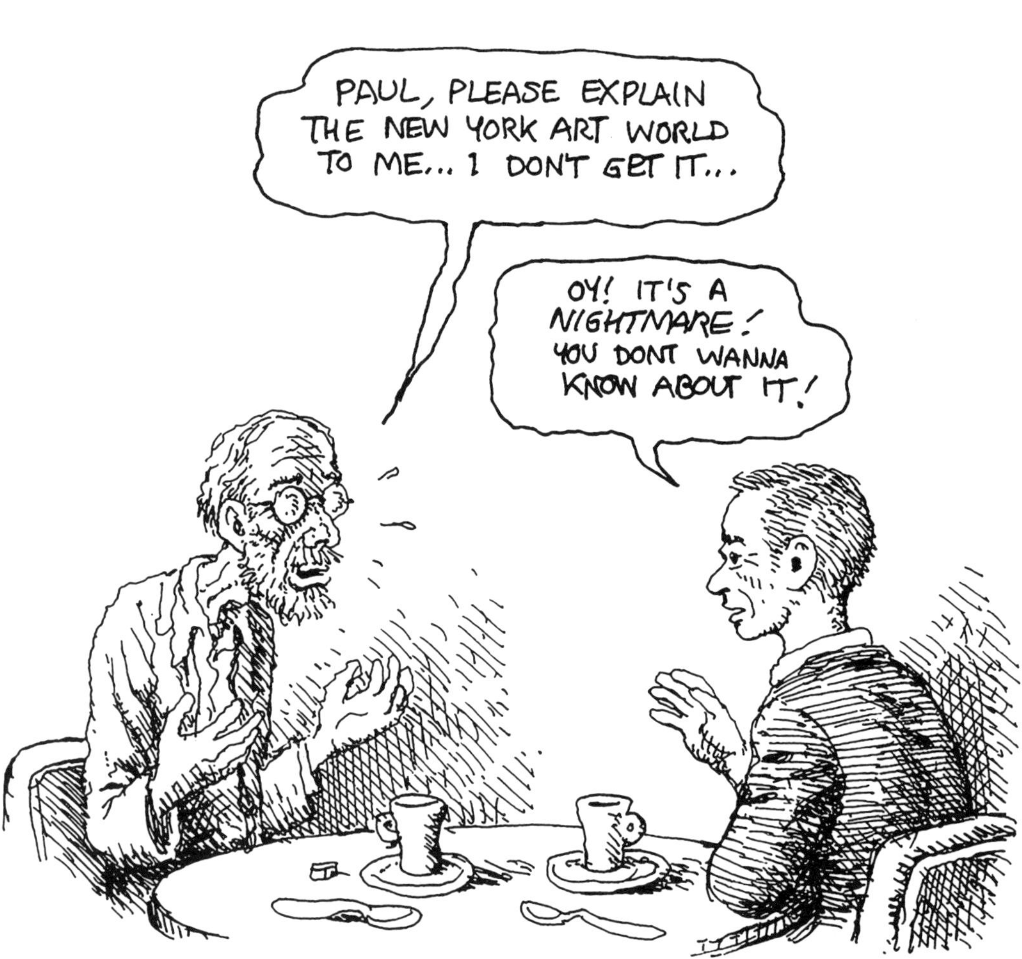

PAUL, PLEASE EXPLAIN THE NEW YORK ART WORLD TO ME... I DON'T GET IT...
OY! IT'S A NIGHTMARE! YOU DON'T WANNA KNOW ABOUT IT!
R. CRUMB
LYON
SEPT. '05

INTRODUCTION
by Paul Morris

In a strange way, it's fitting that I should be writing an introduction to this body of work—
Art & Beauty—since it is through these two subjects that Robert and I developed the deep
friendship we have—a friendship that has expanded to include my husband, Sam, along
with Robert's wife, Aline, and their daughter, Sophie.

In terms of Art, Robert and I have very different backgrounds. Perhaps differences can
make for the best and most productive relationships. Robert comes from a lineage of
comics, cartoonists, commercial illustrators, and graphic artists. After thirty years as a
contemporary art dealer, I have much more experience with modern and contemporary
artists, and admittedly little with comic artists. With regard to these differences, Robert
once said (in *The New York Times Magazine*, no less):

> The fine-art world knows very little about the cartoon world. Even my pal
> Paul Morris, God love him, he knows nothing about the cartoon world. He's
> very knowledgeable about fine art but has no idea who Krazy Kat is, and he's
> like the Leonardo da Vinci of the cartoon world.[1]

The next time we met face to face, Robert asked me if what he said had bothered me and I
replied: "No, my ignorance is entirely your fault—you didn't teach me enough." Over time,
though, Robert has taught me a great deal about his wonderful world, and I have come to
know and appreciate a long list of comic artists and their works.

As far as Beauty is concerned, our differences part only along gender lines. Robert and
I both seem to like a "built" physique, but as a gay man my taste also includes beards,
whereas Robert is attracted to beautiful women who are also strong athletes, like his wife
Aline. (If you take one of Aline's extraordinary aerobics/yoga/Zoomba/dance classes,
you'll get a sense for how fortunate Robert has been.)

Bodies aside, our opinions on Art and Beauty (both shared and opposed) promised
a long relationship in theory, but it was in practice that we have successfully built a
bond as dealer and artist, and as friends. I was initially drawn to Robert's work through

the drawings themselves; it was only later that the narrative pulled me in. Robert is
a remarkable draftsman whose subjects are shockingly honest and revealing. I have
discovered a broad spectrum of styles from the breadth of his practice—from his early
works, drawn with a languid thin line, to the more charged subjects of the later years,
rendered with a heavier mark. I became an even bigger fan of his as I saw the tender
portraits and romantic landscapes that have appeared over the past few decades. But
being a skilled draftsman was only the beginning—I think what made me a serious
student and lifelong devotee were Robert's fiercely unapologetic stories. I have never
worked with an artist who I knew so intimately, and over the years we have talked a lot
about his evolution. He explained how his older brother Charles, through the sheer force
of his dominating personality and obsession with comics, made Robert into a diligent,
hardworking cartoonist by age ten, and that Aline (who was making groundbreaking
comics well before she met Robert) pushed him into telling stories about himself—stories
whose honesty can make readers a bit uncomfortable, even when all they want is more.

I think Robert's deep, almost unnerving honesty is one of the truly unique qualities that
has created his enormous and loyal fan base. He gives his readers permission to admit
to their own desires, even if they verge on taboo. I have witnessed dinner parties where
people open up to Robert as if he were their psychologist because they sense his innate
acceptance. If hitting a nerve and inspiring people is the sign of a great artist, then Robert
wears the mantle as well as any other.

And yet, Robert is not keen to be compared to contemporary artists and doesn't encourage
me to describe his work in terms of a vocabulary that I'm more comfortable with—one
that draws on other artists. But from the start, I wanted to broaden Robert's audience
without ignoring his place within the comic-art world. Perhaps what I really wanted was
to drop the labels altogether and let Robert's work be seen as the great art it is.

I initially showed his work in a 1999 group exhibition with Barry McGee's sad-sack street
characters and Philip Guston's lumpy smoking figures. Soon after Robert agreed to a solo
show. Fortunately for me, he sent his placemat drawings. When Robert eats at a restaurant
he tends to draw on the paper placemats, and over the years he had assembled a body of
work large enough for an exhibition. These drawings are very much like pages from his
sketchbooks, but they can be surprisingly elaborate and complete, considering they are
made over the course of a meal. The initial show was a success on many levels: for comic
fans it confirmed Robert's expert draftsmanship, and for an art-world audience,
it channeled a looser and more "contemporary" feel, as the images were not framed

in a grid. Shortly after our first shows together, it became clear that we had made an impact with a generation of curators who also appreciated Robert's work: over the past fifteen years, he has had major presentations at the Museum Ludwig in Cologne, the Carnegie Museum of Art in Pittsburgh, and the Musée d'Art Moderne de la Ville de Paris.

In 2007, Robert had his first exhibition at David Zwirner. Around the time we started working with the gallery, his production of single drawings slowed as he tackled his largest and most elaborate body of work to date, *The Book of Genesis Illustrated by R. Crumb*, which is Robert's graphic interpretation of the first book of the Old Testament—two hundred pages that he not only illustrated, but also included every word of the original text. Since 2009, *The Book of Genesis* has made several stops at important venues in Europe and the United States, including the Hammer Museum in Los Angeles and the Venice Biennale. I think Robert is still surprised to see people looking at the pages on the wall—as *art*—since almost all of the work he has ever done was conceived to be read or looked at in print.

With that project behind him, I was thrilled to see that a third volume of *Art & Beauty* was the next piece to come out of Robert's studio. These volumes are interesting for both the drawings—which include some of his strongest portraits—and the extensive quotations that Robert collects for each issue. These scattered texts give a glimpse into the way he thinks as he draws his subjects, and they allow us to see his interior world in a different light.

I visited Robert and Aline several times as the work developed and was delighted, not only to continue my comic-art education, but also to learn more about music from Robert, who has over seven thousand 78 RPM records at his home (not to mention an encyclopedic knowledge of certain periods and musicians).

The stories behind the people he draws and the musicians he admires underscore Robert's unflinching appreciation for the truth. He has taught me many great lessons through his work and our friendship, but probably the most important is to be very honest about who you are, and always to tell the truth—desires and all.

1　Robert Crumb, interview with Lisa Eisner and Román Alonso, "An Eye for the Ladies," in *The New York Times Magazine* (March 30, 2003).

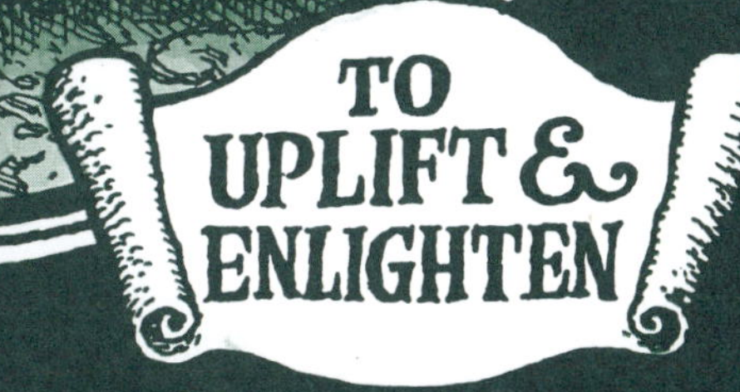

Art & Beauty
Beauty
magazine
NUMBER 1
TO UPLIFT & ENLIGHTEN

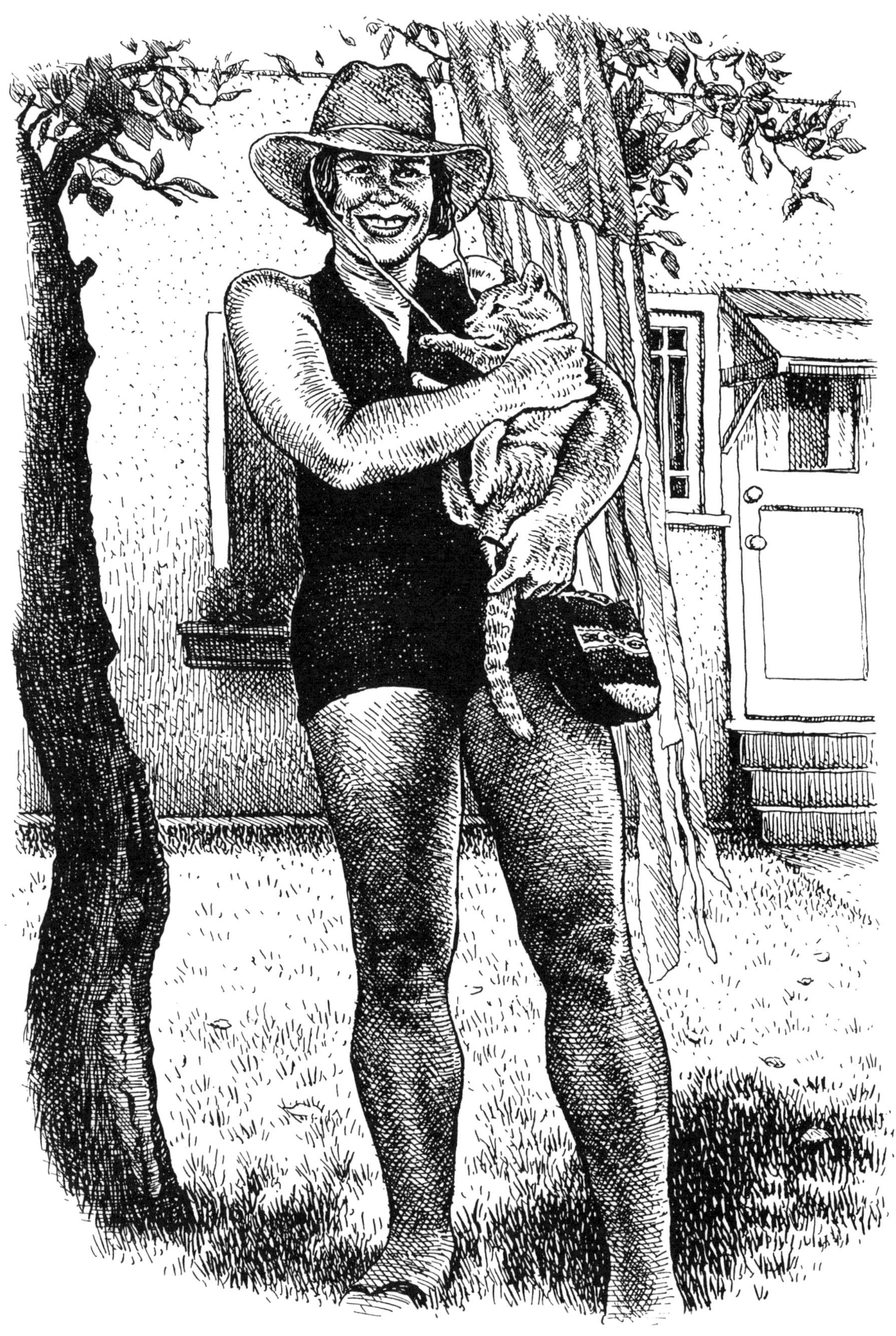

In this pose the sweeping curves of our model's long, magnificent legs combined with subtle shadow effects form an intriguing study reminiscent of the ancient Greek goddesses.

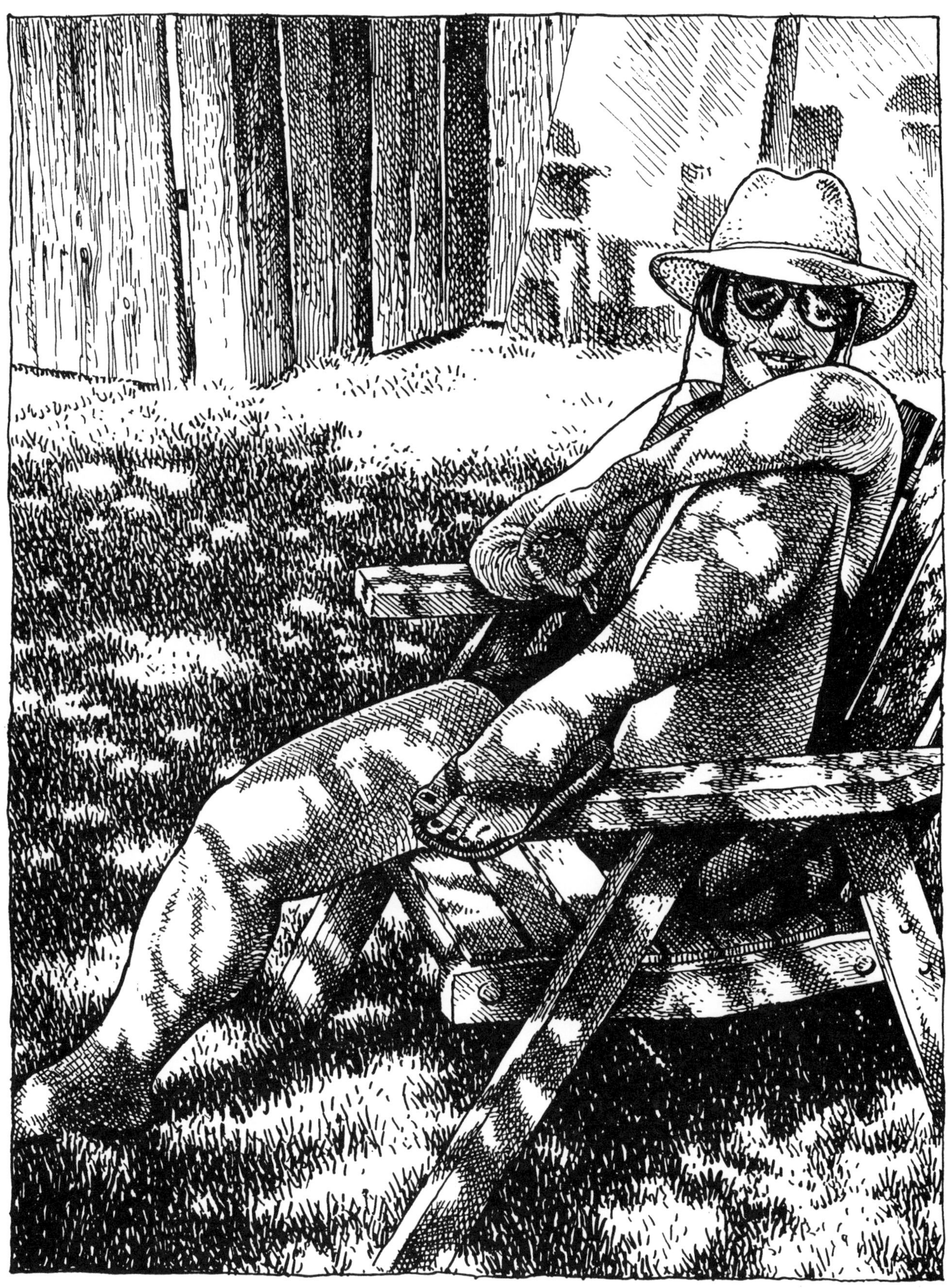

Taken under specific conditions of light and shade, this study is a demonstration of the striking tonal effects that may be obtained by camera, pen or brush when bright sunlight is filtered thru leafy foliage onto the gorgeously curvacious limbs of a lovely model.

Art & Beauty
MAGAZINE

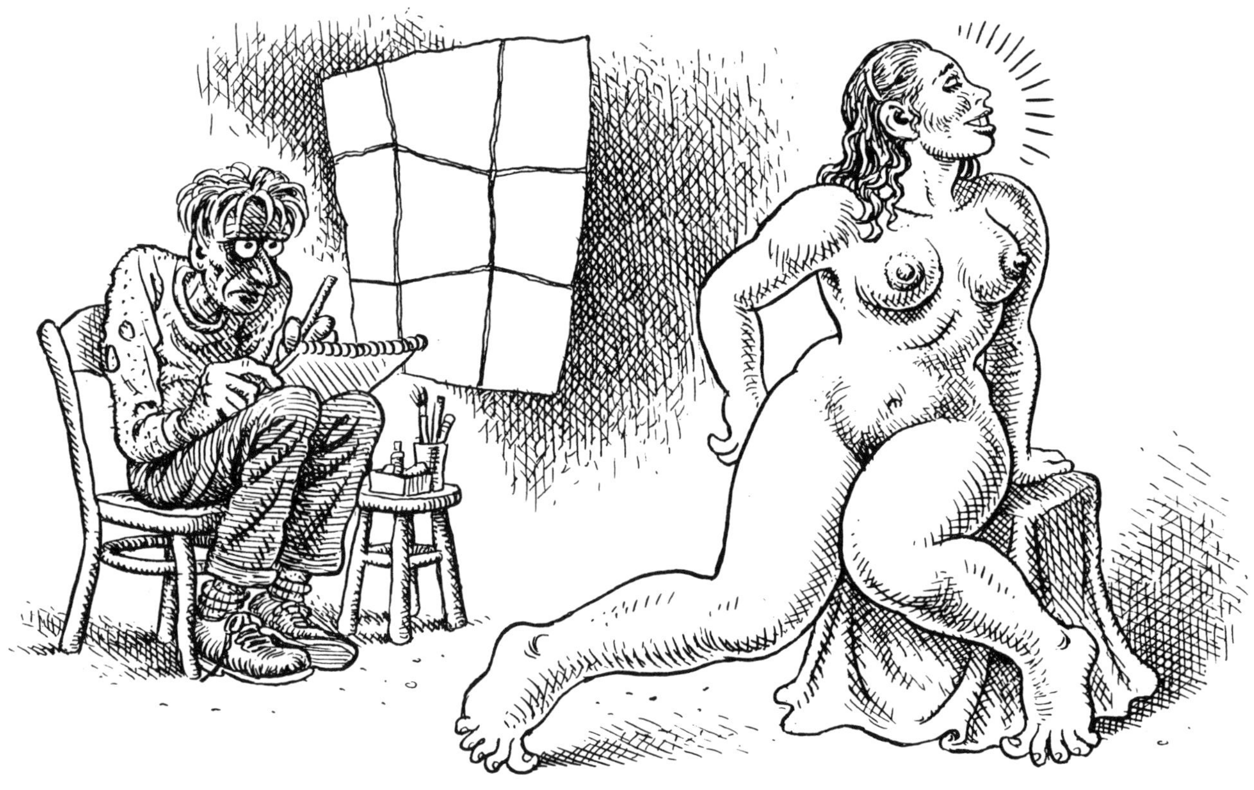

SHE: Don't you think that Postmodernism is an inclusive aesthetic that cultivates the variety of incoherence?

HE: Hey, I love my wife but OH YOU KID!

"ALL MEN ARE IN SOME DEGREE IMPRESSED BY THE FACE OF THE WORLD; SOME MEN EVEN TO DELIGHT. THIS LOVE OF BEAUTY IS *TASTE*. OTHERS HAVE THE SAME LOVE IN SUCH EXCESS THAT, NOT CONTENT WITH ADMIRING, THEY SEEK TO EMBODY IT IN NEW FORMS. THE CREATION OF *BEAUTY IS ART*."
—— RALPH WALDO EMERSON

"THE PEOPLE WHO MAKE *ART* THEIR *BUSINESS* ARE MOSTLY IMPOSTORS."
— PABLO PICASSO

"NO ARTIST OF ANY PERMANENT ACHIEVEMENT EVER THINKS OF MONEY ONE BIT MORE THAN IS ABSOLUTELY NECESSARY."
— N.C. WYETH

ART & BEAUTY MAGAZINE, Number 1, ©1996 by R. Crumb. Published by Fantagraphics Books, 7563 Lake City Way, N.E., Seattle, Washington, 98115, U.S.A. Visit our website: http://www.fantagraphics.com/
Printed in Canada

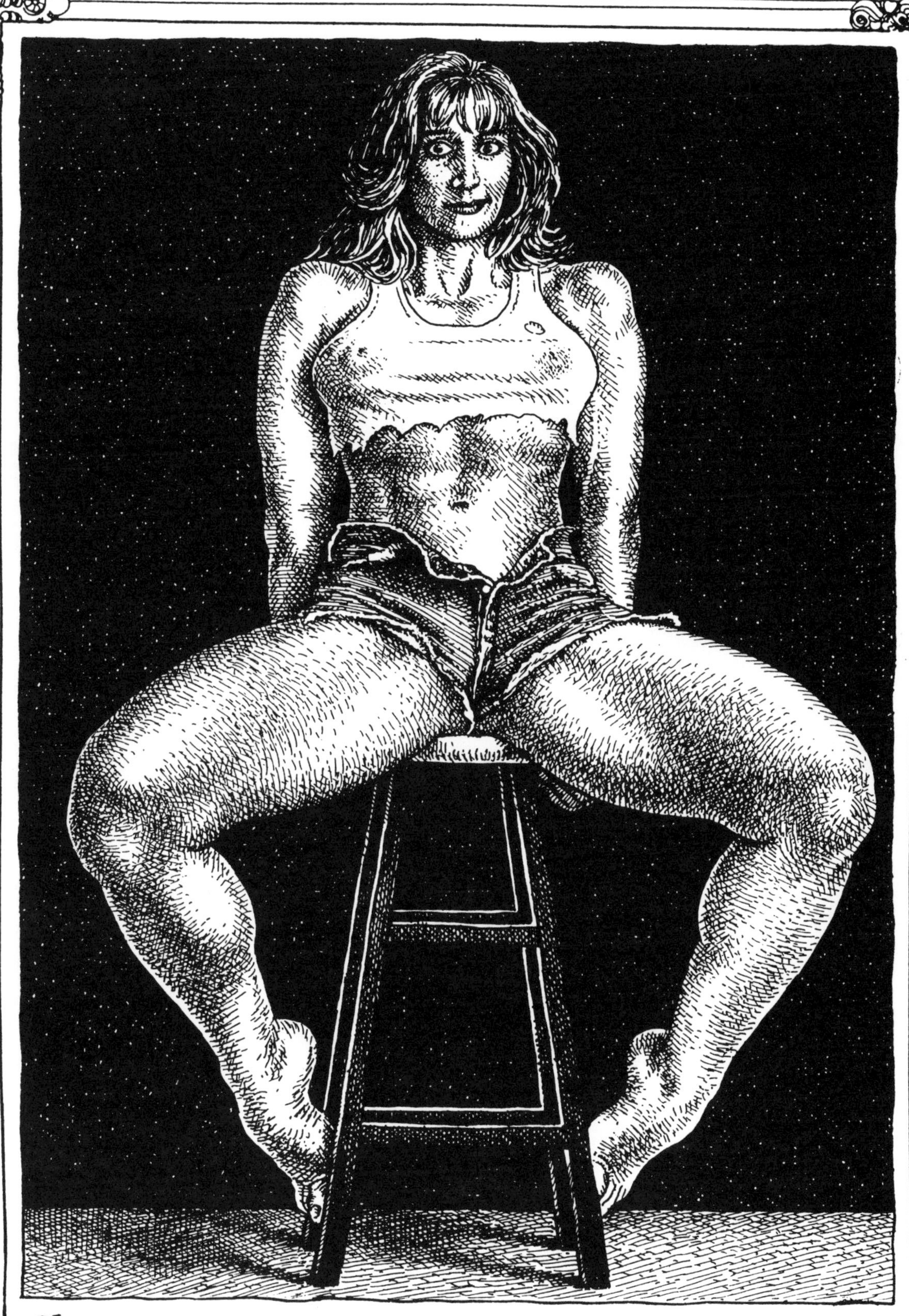

NOTE THE SEDUCTIVE CONTRAST BETWEEN THE SENSITIVE, DOE-LIKE FACIAL EX-PRESSION AND THE MAGNIFICENT BOLDNESS OF THE POWERFUL PHYSIQUE. A MORE SPLENDID MODEL COULD NOT BE FOUND BY AN ARTIST.

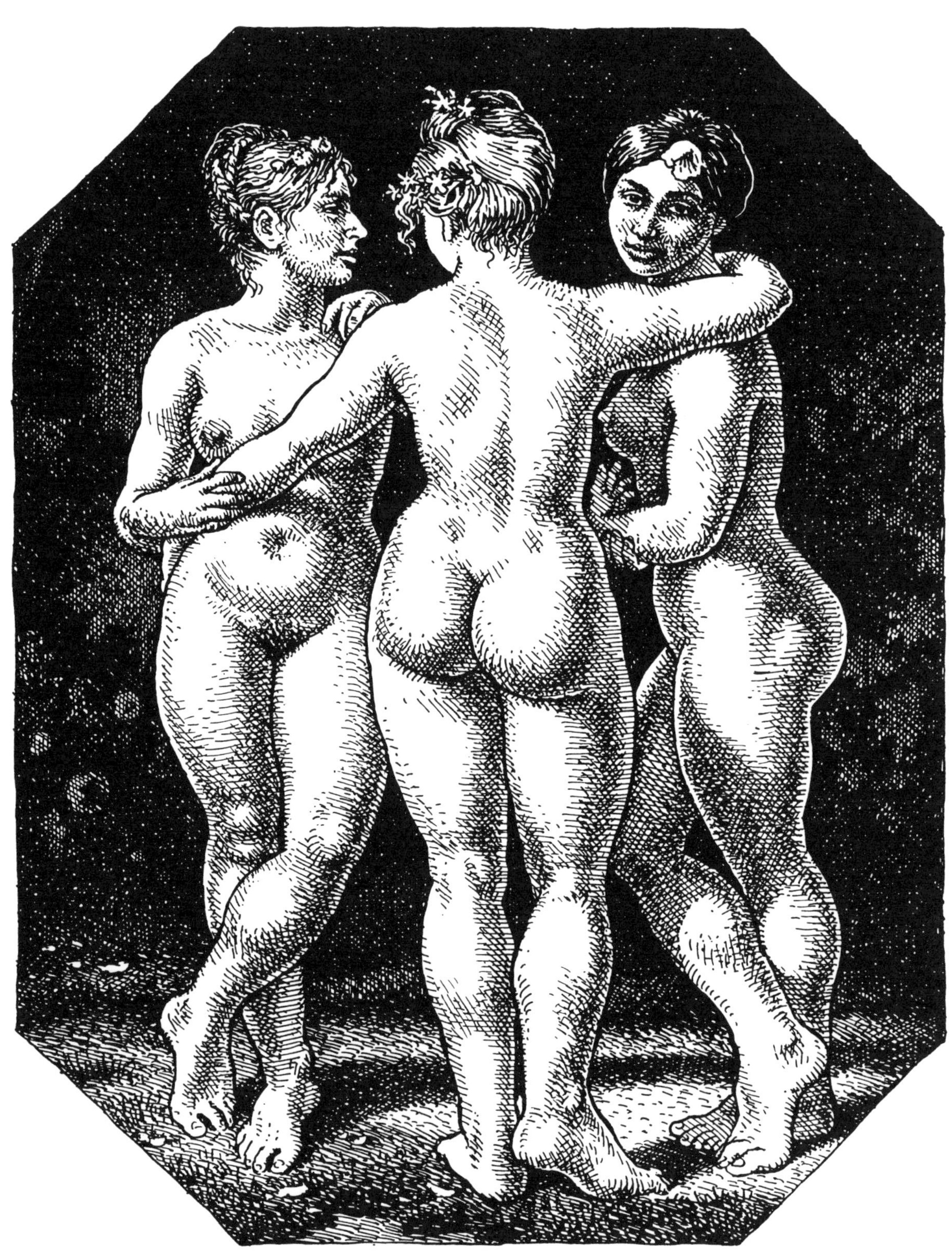

THE THREE GRACES — *Copied from* REGNAULT

WARMTH OF SOFTLY MOLDED CONTOURS IS ONE OF THE CHARMS OF THIS EXQUISITE CLASSIC COMPOSITION OF NUDE FIGURES.

"**A**BSTRACT ART: A PRODUCT OF THE UNTALENTED SOLD BY THE UNPRINCIPLED TO THE UTTERLY BEWILDERED."

> —AL CAPP, creator of the
> popular comic strip "Li'l Abner"

"**M**INIMAL ART IS MAXIMUM PROFIT."

> —ISAMU NOGUCHI, Minimalist sculptor

"**A**RT IS ANYTHING YOU CAN GET AWAY WITH."

> —MARSHALL McCLUHAN

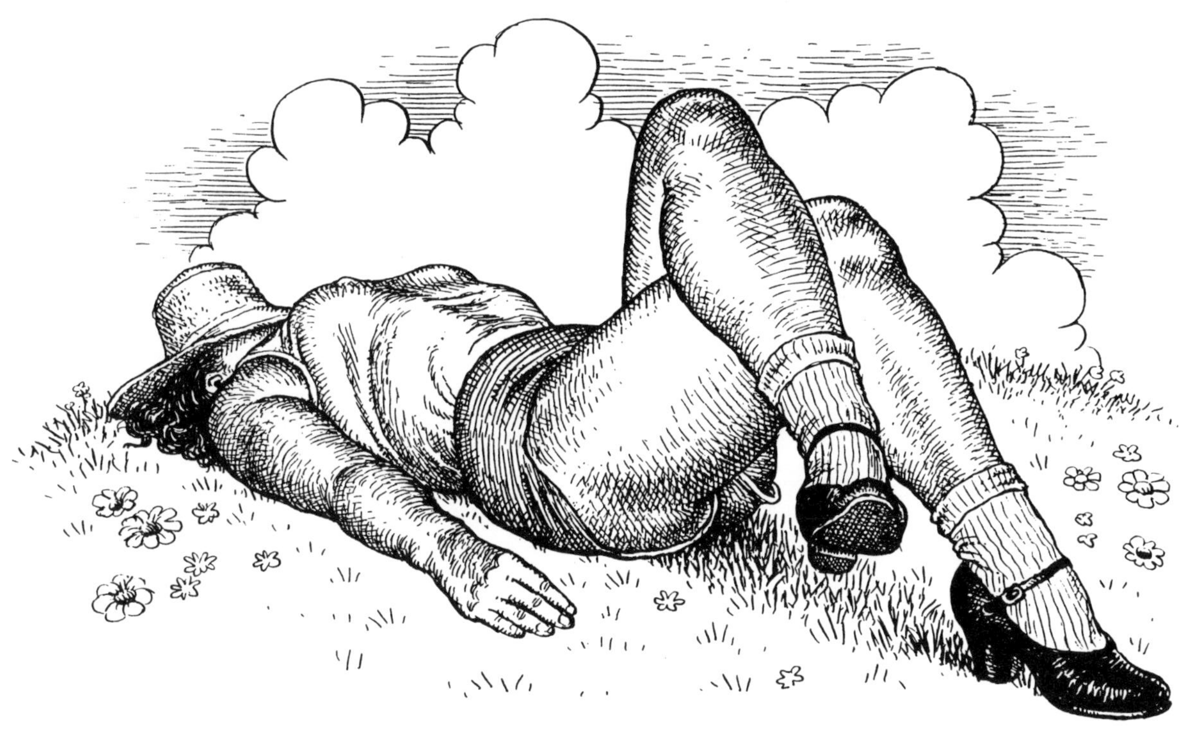

"SPLENDOR IN THE GRASS" or "CAUGHT NAPPING"

A SENSE OF SERENITY AND NATURAL SIMPLICITY PERVADES THIS SCENE. IN ADDITION, THE ARTIST HAS INFUSED WARMTH AND LIFE INTO HIS FINE PENWORK.

"**I**T'S THE DUTY OF EVERY WOMAN WHO HAS A GOOD FIGURE TO PRESERVE IT AS LONG AS THEY CAN, AND THEY SHOULD NOT WAIT UNTIL THEY GET FAT, FROWSY AND FORTY, BUT SHOULD TAKE SYSTEMATIC EXERCISES TO PRESERVE THE SINUOUSNESS OF THEIR MUSCLES ALL THEIR LIFE."

> — RUBIE STEVENS *from an article,*
> *"Why Cabaret?" in*
> ARTISTS AND MODELS MAGAZINE,
> February, 1926

I BELIEVE THAT IT MAY HAPPEN THAT ONE WILL SUCCEED, AND ONE MUST NOT BEGIN TO DESPAIR, EVEN THOUGH DEFEATED HERE AND THERE; AND EVEN THOUGH ONE SOMETIMES FEELS A KIND OF DECAY, THOUGH THINGS GO DIFFERENTLY FROM THE EXPECTED, IT IS NECESSARY TO TAKE HEART AGAIN AND NEW COURAGE. FOR THE GREAT THINGS ARE NOT DONE BY IMPULSE BUT BY A SERIES OF SMALL THINGS BROUGHT TOGETHER. AND GREAT THINGS ARE NOT SOMETHING ACCIDENTAL, BUT MUST CERTAINLY BE WILLED.

> —VINCENT VAN GOGH

"Though one should take care not to remain imprisoned in the forms we have inherited, one should neither, from love of progress, imagine that one can detach oneself completely from the past."
— CLAUDE MONET

"It is empathy with the human condition and artistic freedom that ultimately produce the highest work."
— JUSTIN GREEN

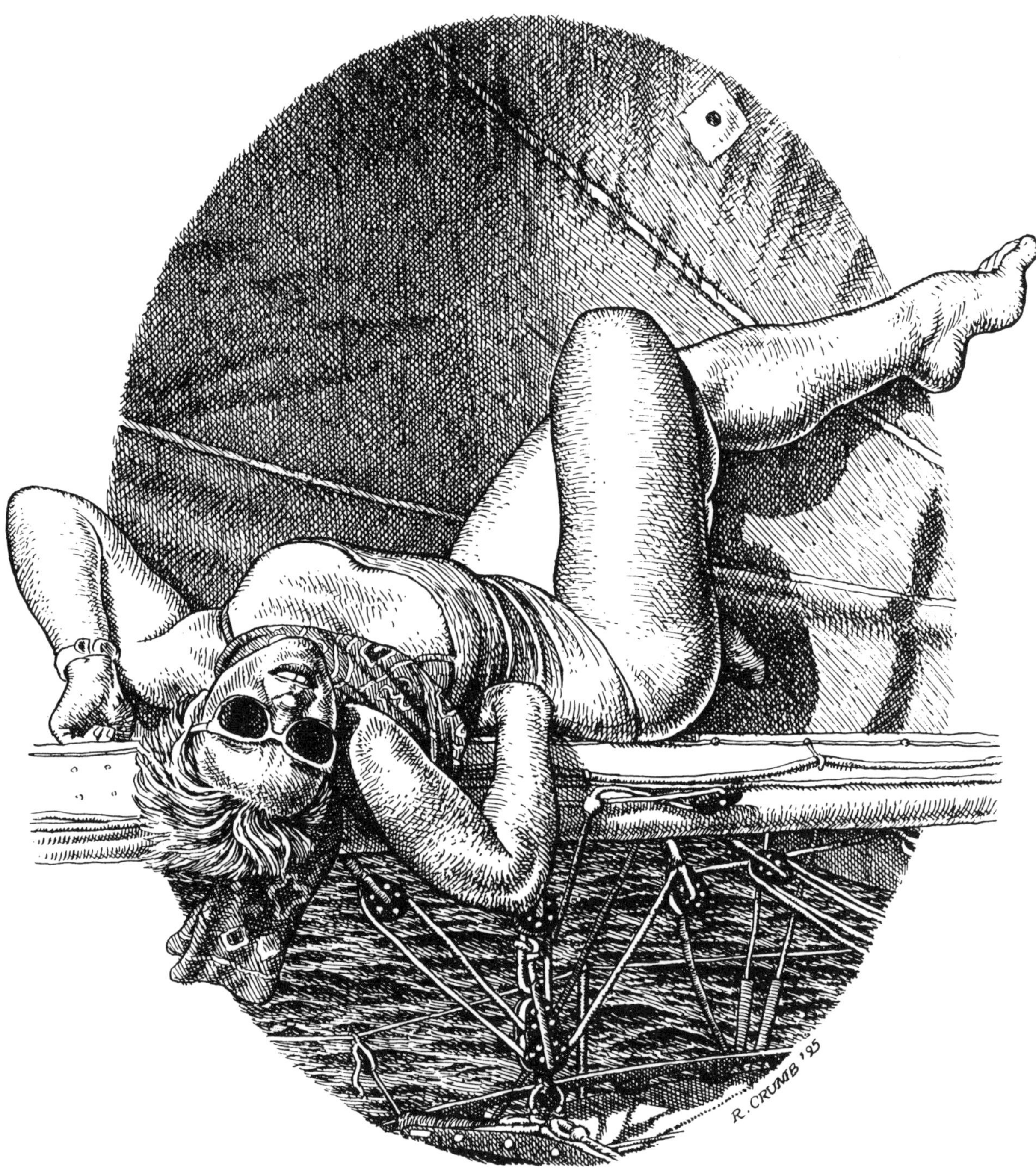

Full of lively animation, this figure suggests the activity and joy of life which is accredited in mythology to the daughters of Neptune. As a composition it is unusual, and splendidly balanced.

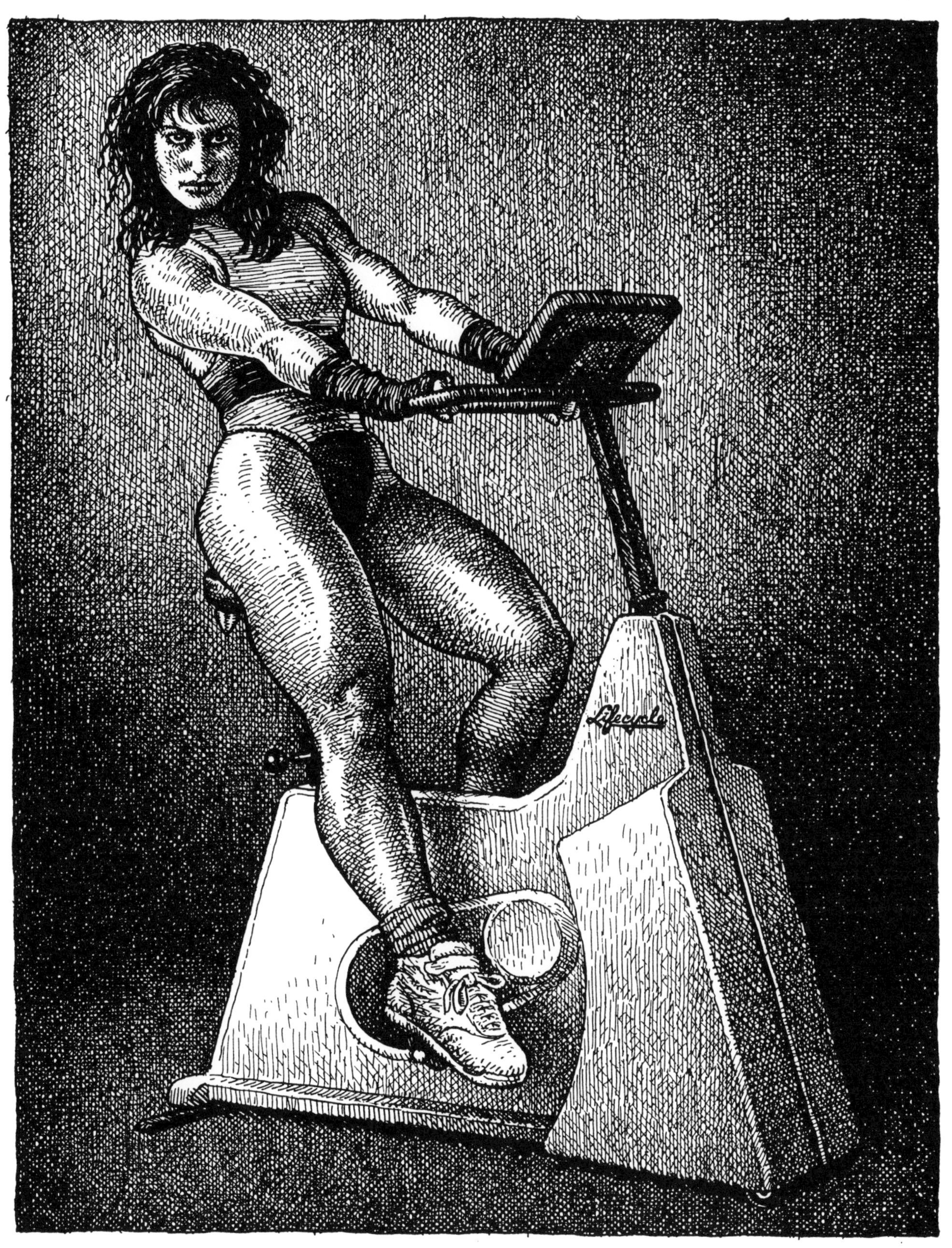

The real originality and power of this drawing accentuates the American woman's strongly developed appreciation of physical fitness.

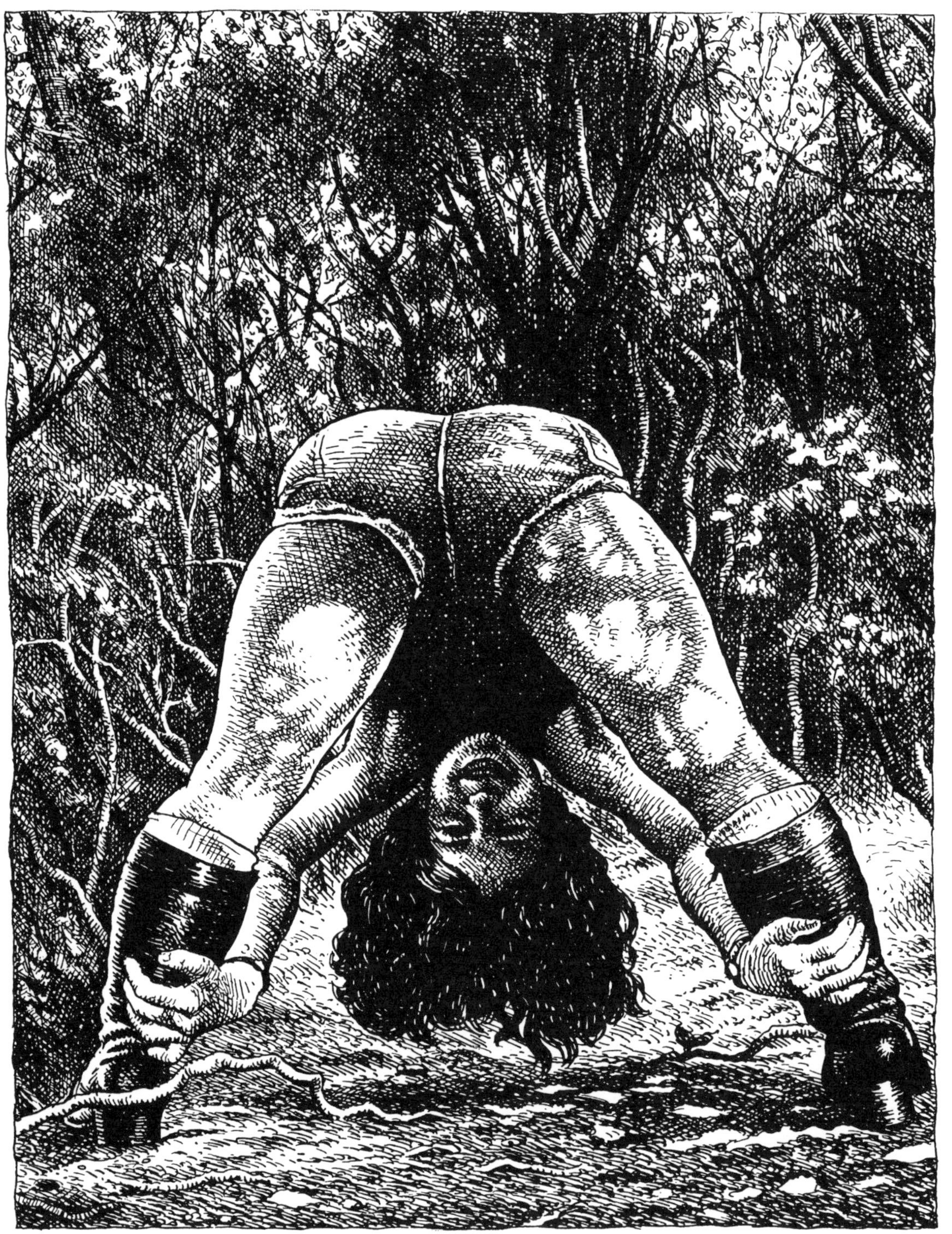

THIS STUDY SHOWS A BEAUTIFUL GIRL IN A FROLICSOME MOOD, YET IF THE ARTIST IS NOT BRILLIANTLY SKILLFUL, SUCH A POSE WILL RESULT IN NEITHER SYMMETRY NOR GRACE.

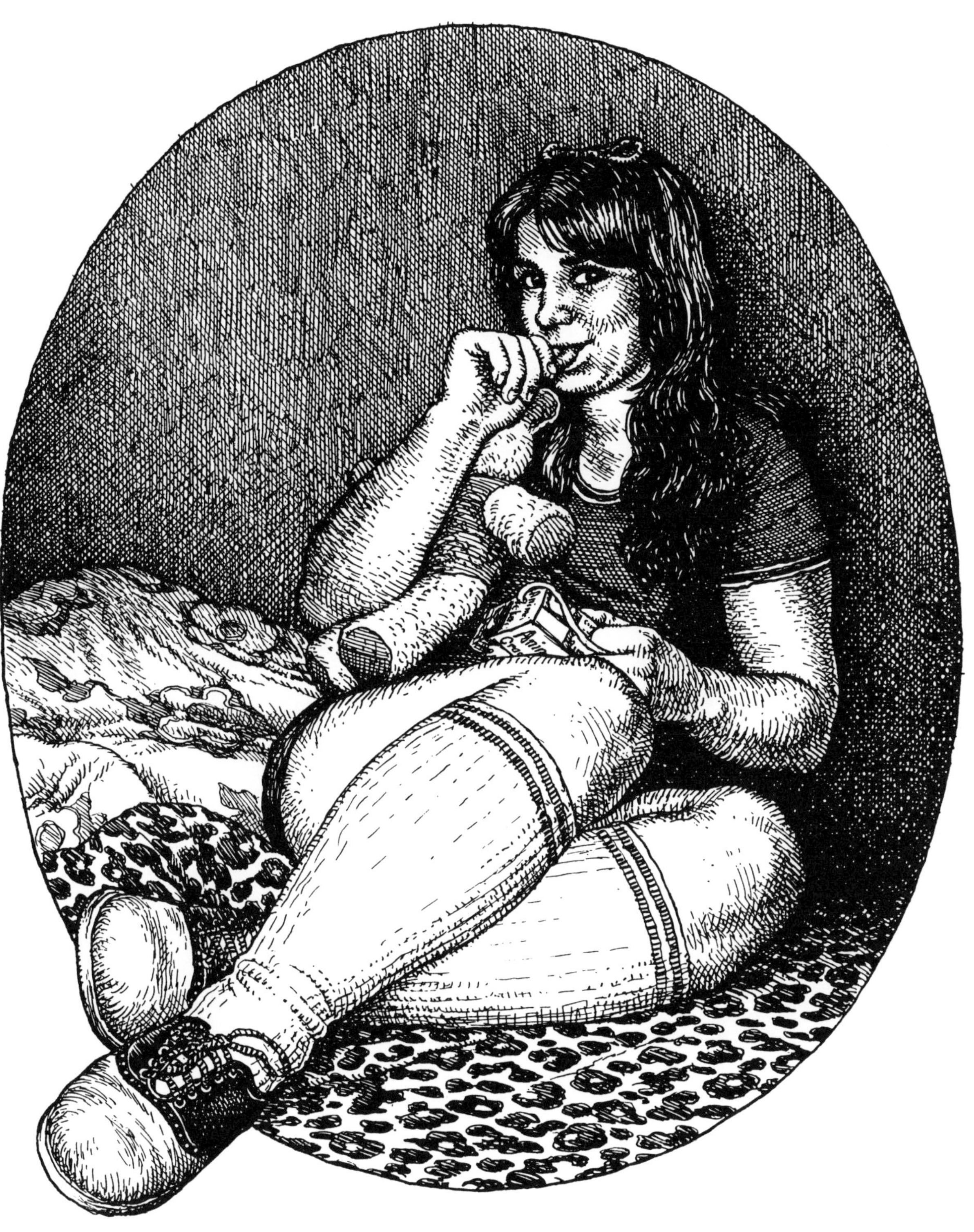

HERE IS A SECOND POSE BY THE PLAYFUL YOUNG LADY SHOWN ON THE PREVIOUS PAGE. HER WELL-ROUNDED FORM DELIGHTS THE EYE IN THIS CHILDISH COSTUME AND ATTITUDE. THE ARTIST'S IMAGINATION IS STIMULATED BY SUCH PICTURES, WHICH GIVE HIM THE HIGH LEVEL OF MOTIVATION REQUIRED FOR HIS METICULOUSLY DETAILED PEN-AND-INK RENDERING TECHNIQUE.

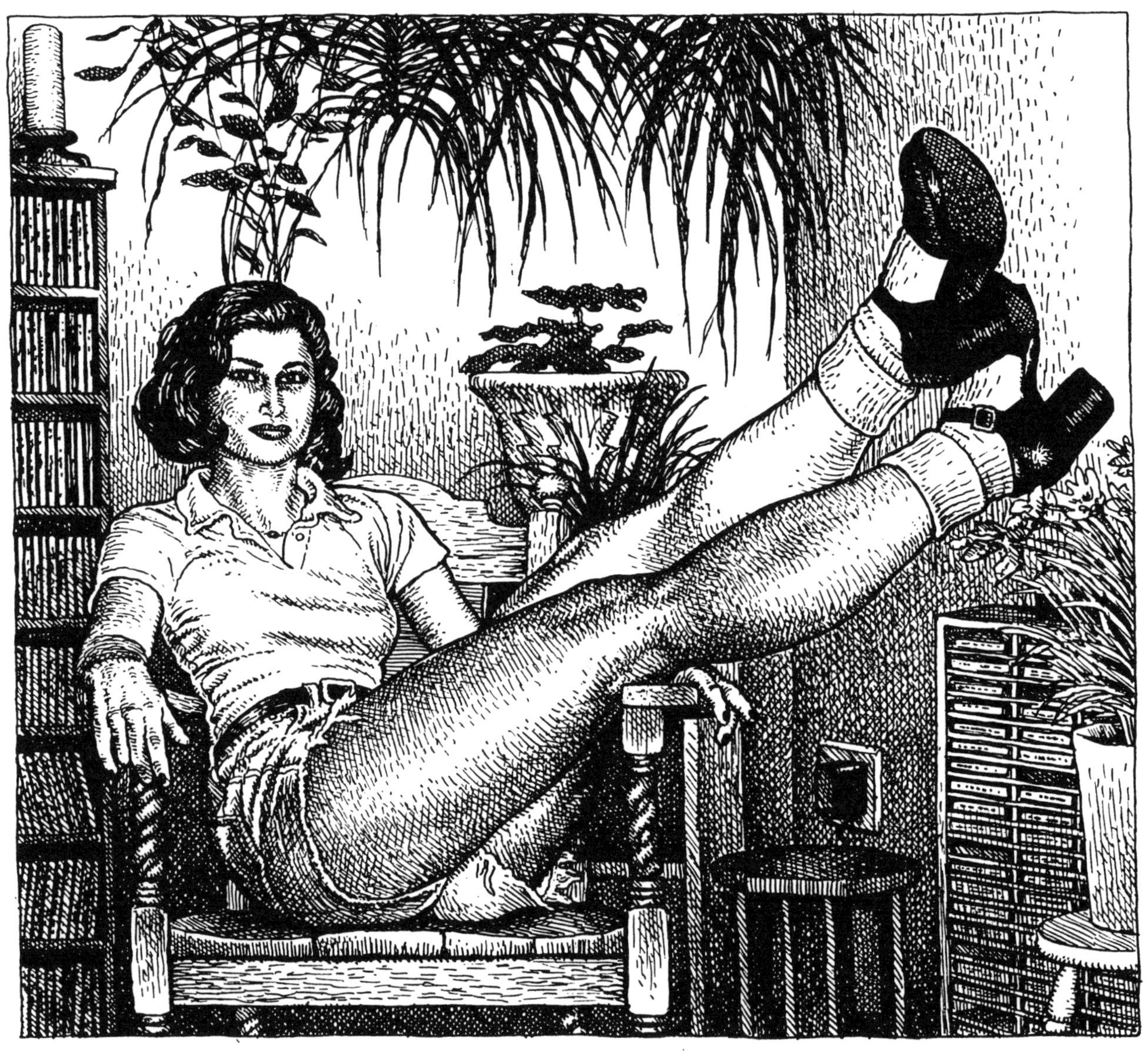

MANY HUNDREDS OF MODELS HAVE TO BE EXAMINED BY ARTISTS TO FIND ONE WHO POSSESSES AS PERFECT A FIGURE AS THE SUBJECT OF THIS SEATED STUDY. SHE EXUDES AN ELUSIVE CHARM WHICH A PRINCESS OF ROYAL BLOOD MIGHT ENVY.

"WE DON'T HAVE TO DISCUSS MY PICTURES — WE CAN SEE THEM. I BASE EVERYTHING ON THE VISIBLE. I DON'T WANT TO INVENT NEW THEMES AND DON'T WANT TO ARRANGE THEMES AS SALVADOR DALI DOES, FOR EXAMPLE...ART DEFIES ALL DEFINITION. YOU ARE AN EMPTY VESSEL FOR A LONG TIME, THEN SOMETHING GROWS THAT YOU DON'T WANT, SOMETHING CREEPS INTO IT THAT YOU AC-TUALLY CANNOT DO. THE GOD OF CHANCE CREATES IN US. I AM EMPHATICALLY OPPOSED TO DOGMA IN ART. THE FACT OF THE MATTER IS THAT ART IS NOT A SCIENCE AND IS NOT SUBJECT TO ANY TANGIBLE LAW. THE PAINTER HAS TO WORK WITH THE LIVING PHENOMENON. IT IS HIS TASK TO INFORM THE WORLD AND SHOW PEOPLE THAT THEY CANNOT LIVE ON BREAD ALONE. I AM AGAINST THE PAINTERS WITHOUT OBJECTS, WHO PAINT WITH A BROOM, SHOOT AT THE CANVAS WITH A CROSS-BOW AND LET COLORED GRAVY RUN DOWN IT..."

— OTTO DIX, 1958

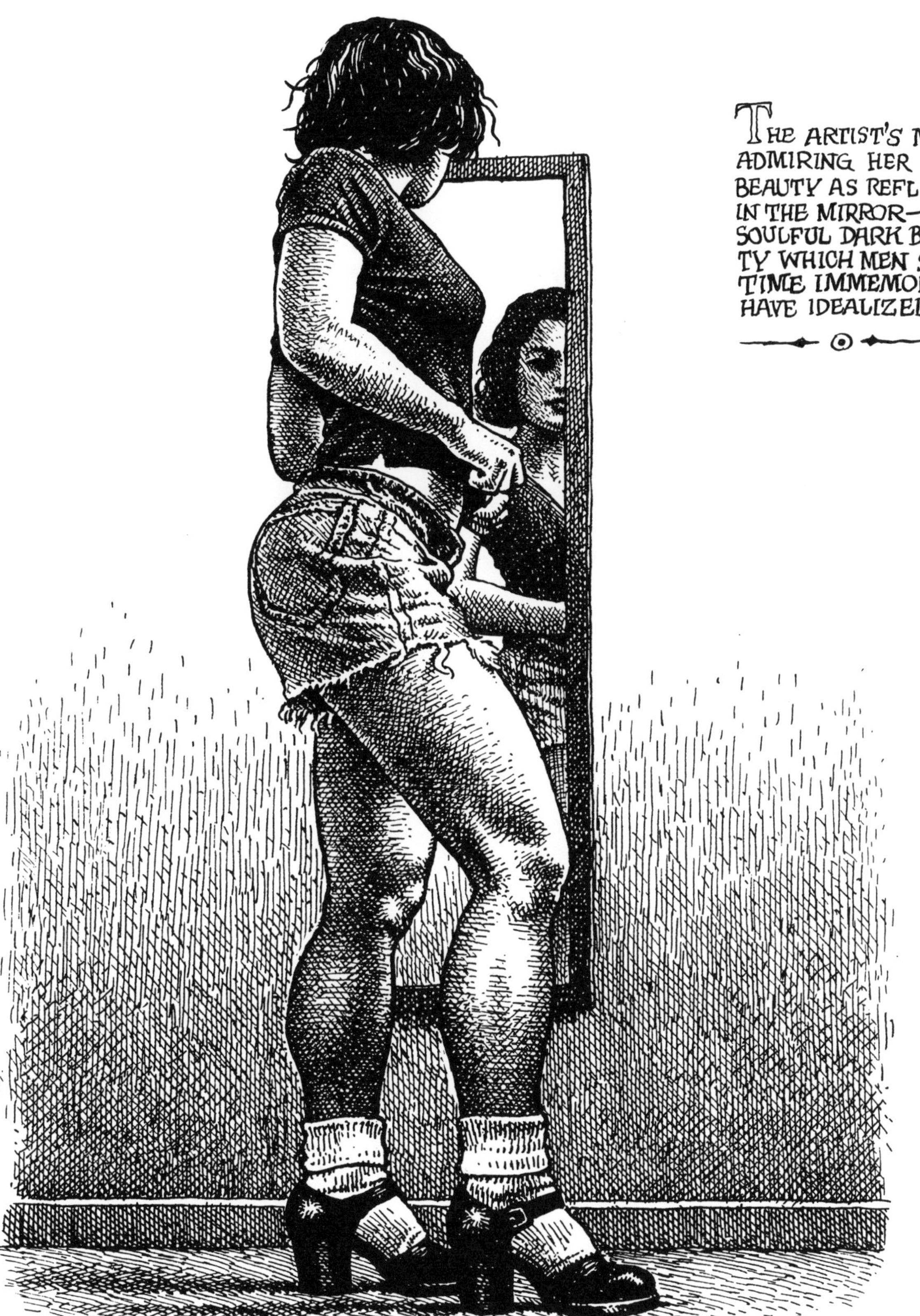

"DO NOT FAIL TO DRAW SOMETHING EVERY DAY, FOR NO MATTER HOW LITTLE IT IS IT WILL BE WELL WORTHWHILE, AND DO YOU A WORLD OF GOOD."
— CENNINI, 1300s

"ART IS A RESULT OF A CREATIVE IMPULSE DERIVED OUT OF A CONSCIOUSNESS OF LIFE"
— JOHN SLOAN

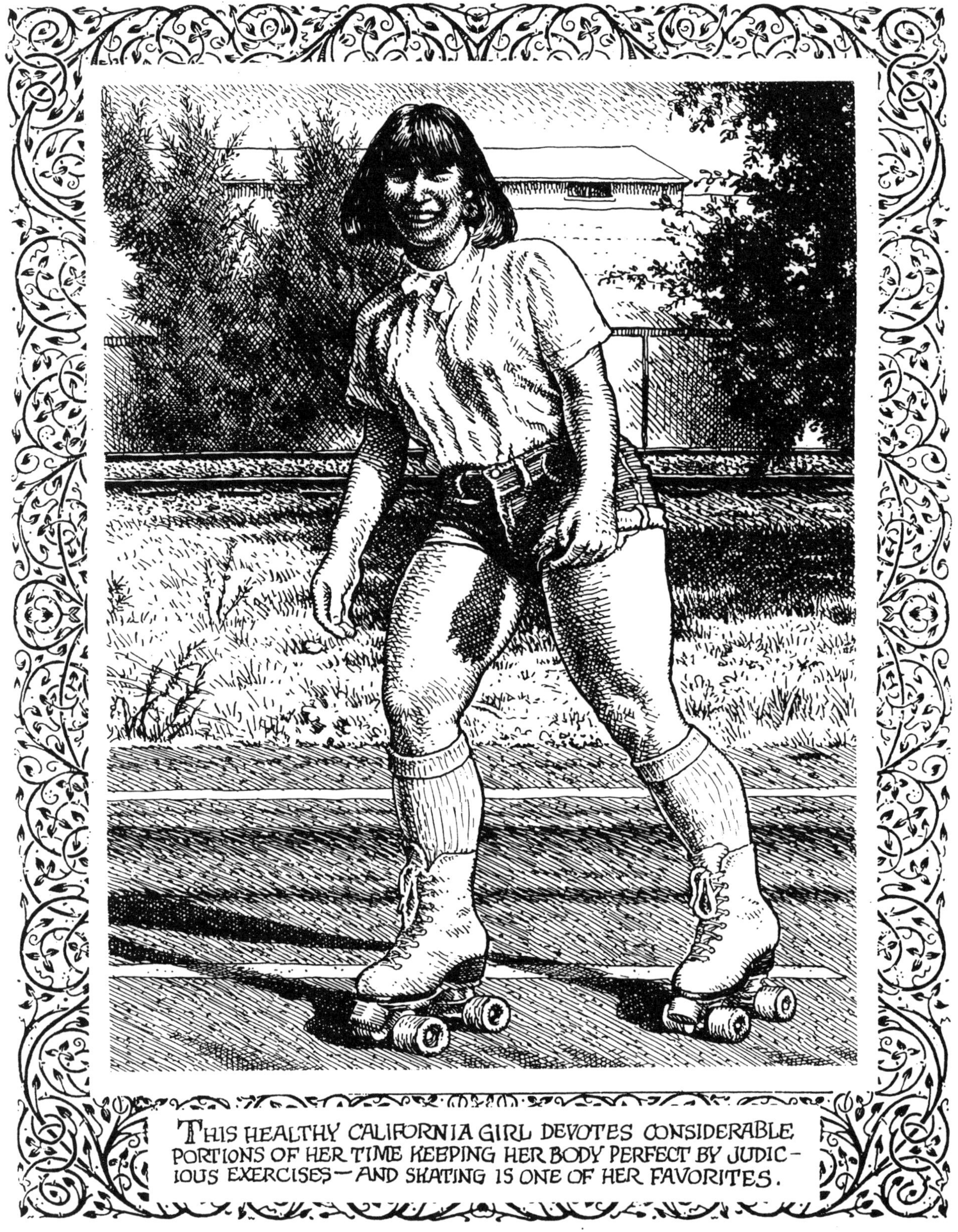

This healthy California girl devotes considerable portions of her time keeping her body perfect by judicious exercises — and skating is one of her favorites.

"Setting out to do what ultimately cannot be perfected is what makes art. The effort to do the impossible leads to creative work."
— John Sloan

"Like a child, I paint with an artless soul and the instincts of my fingertips."
— Pierre Auguste Renoir

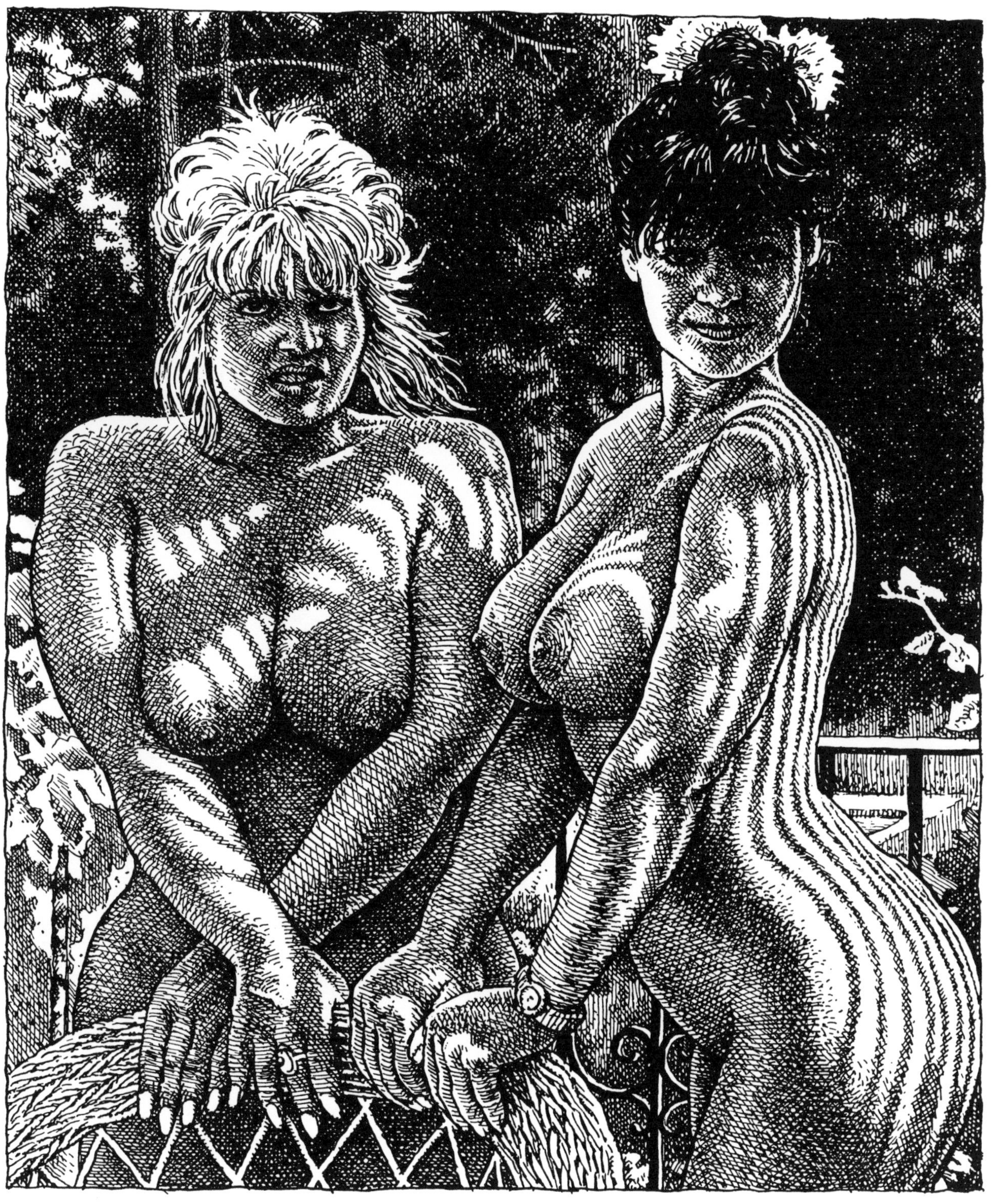

THIS DRAWING HAS THE VIVIDNESS AND DYNAMIC QUALITY FOR WHICH THE ARTIST IS NOTED. THE STRONG, ARRESTING FIGURES BASKING IN THE WARMTH OF THE SUN ARE OF CLASSICAL PROPORTIONS. THE ARTIST HAS CAUGHT UP THE EXQUISITE SHADINGS WHICH A MORNING SUNBEAM CAN CREATE, AND BEAUTIFULLY REPRODUCED THEM.

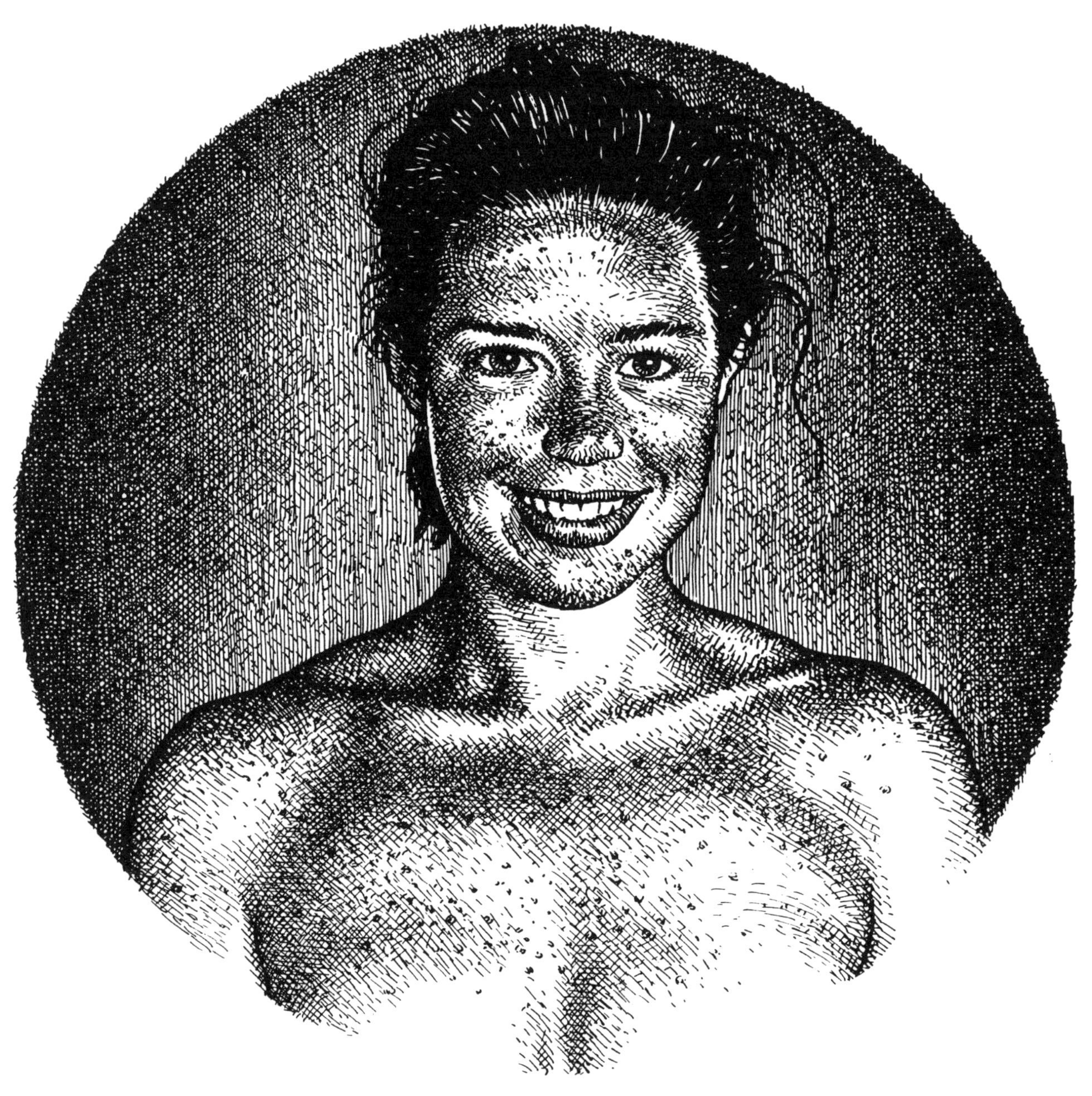

"A DAUGHTER OF THE GODS" — SO A POET MIGHT DESCRIBE THIS BEAUTIFUL, FRECKLE-FACED VISION. SHE HAS AN IRRESISTIBLE SMILE AND IS SO LOVELY THAT ALL SUCCUMB TO HER CHARMS.

"LOOKING AT PICTURES REQUIRES ACTIVE PARTICIPATION, AND, IN THE EARLY STAGES, A CERTAIN AMOUNT OF DISCIPLINE. ... BUT ON THE WHOLE I HAVE FOUND THAT MY FEELINGS FALL INTO THE SAME PATTERN OF IMPACT, SCRUTINY, RECOLLECTION AND RENEWAL."
— KENNETH CLARK

"THERE IS NO GREAT ART WITHOUT A GREAT TECHNIQUE BACK OF IT."
— WILLIAM MERRITT CHASE

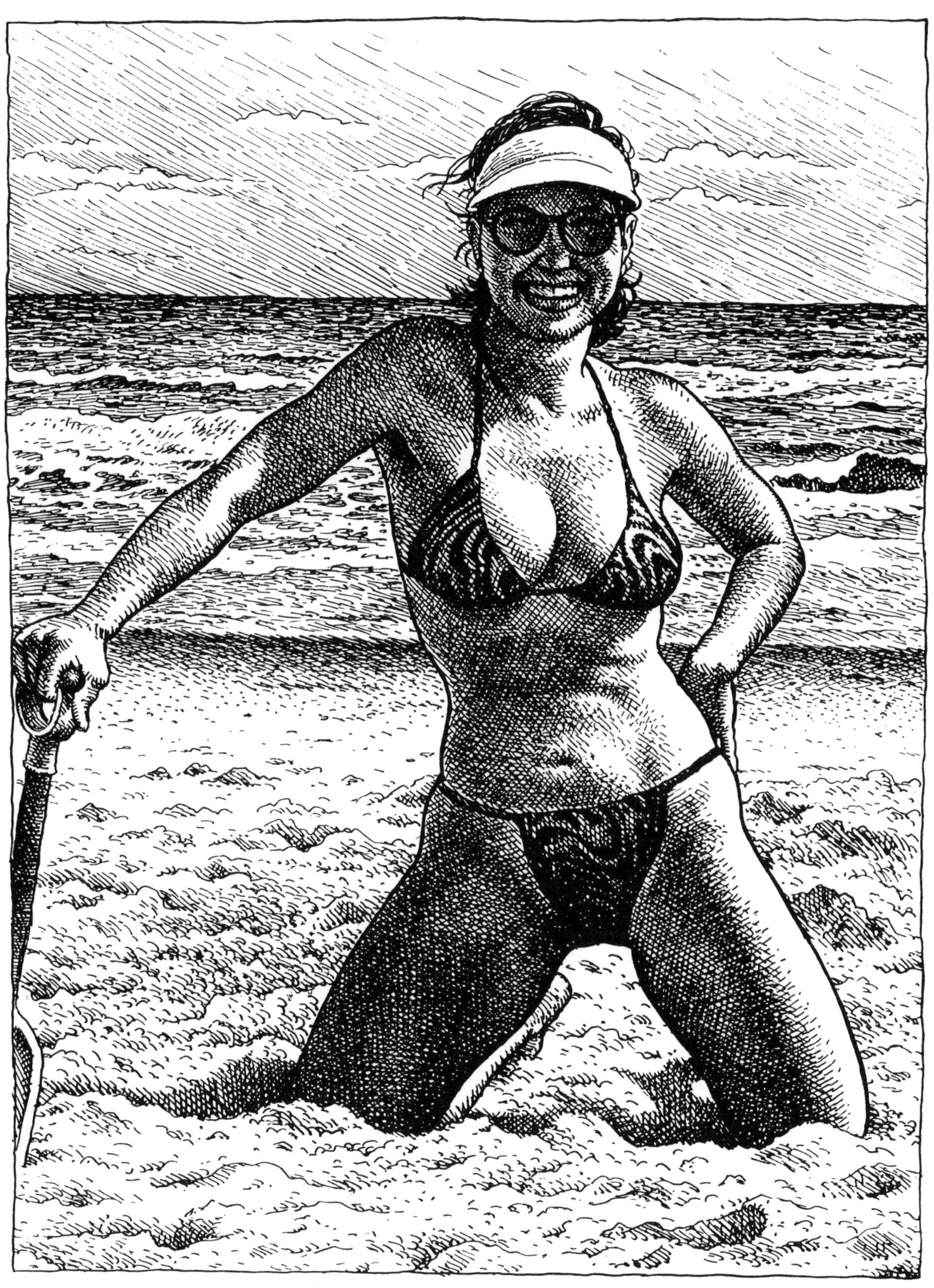

Our sweet freckle-face once again, having fun in the sun — girls possessing figures of such perfection as this cheerful model may have been found in ancient Greece, but happily are also not entirely unknown in our own time. A life of proper physical care and moderation of habits is most certainly conducive to bodily beauty and is sure to benefit the health.

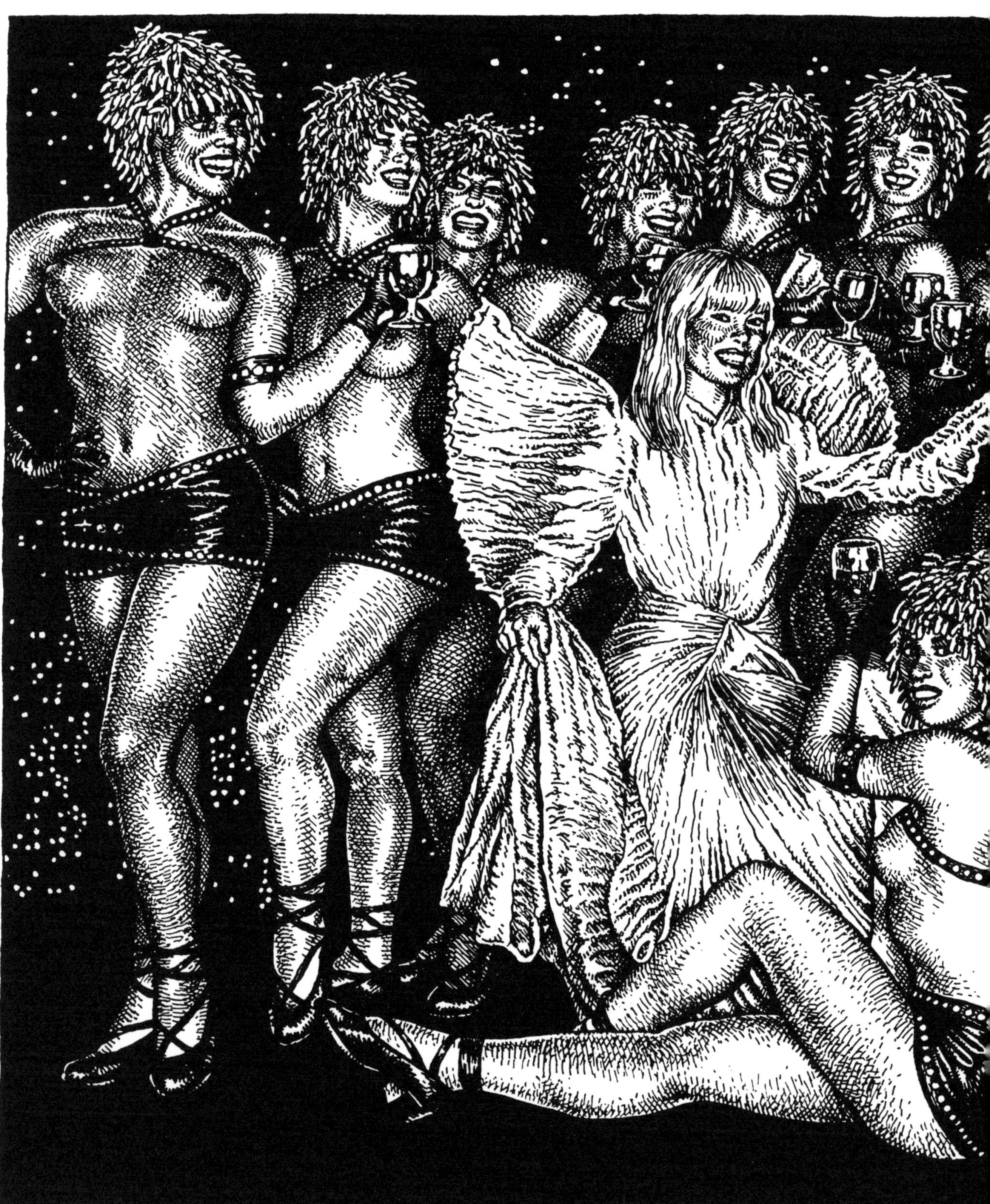

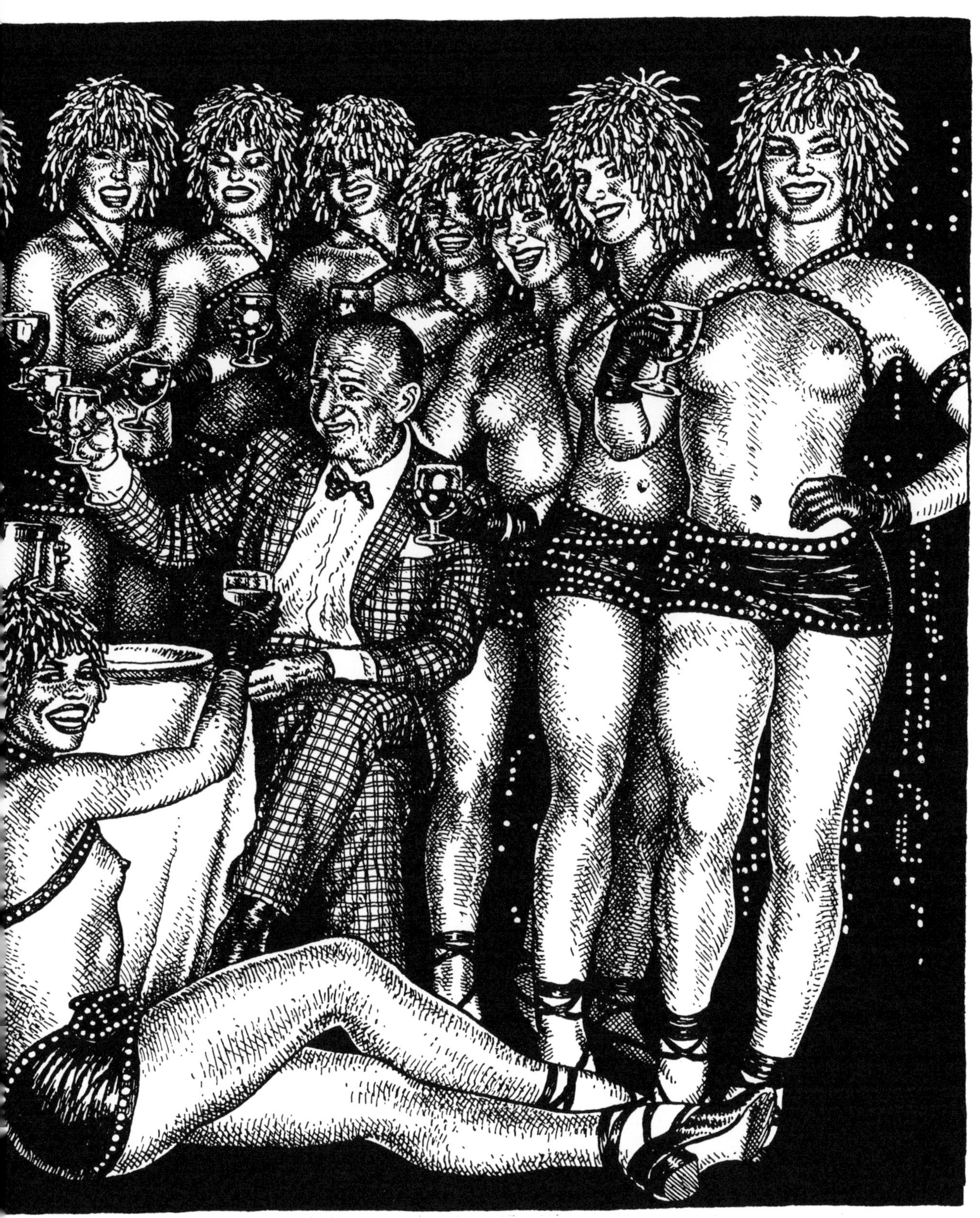

A typical bevy of bouncing beauties at the Crazy Horse Saloon in Paris surround lovely Lova Moor and her husband, Alain Bernardi, owner, in happier days before he committed suicide.

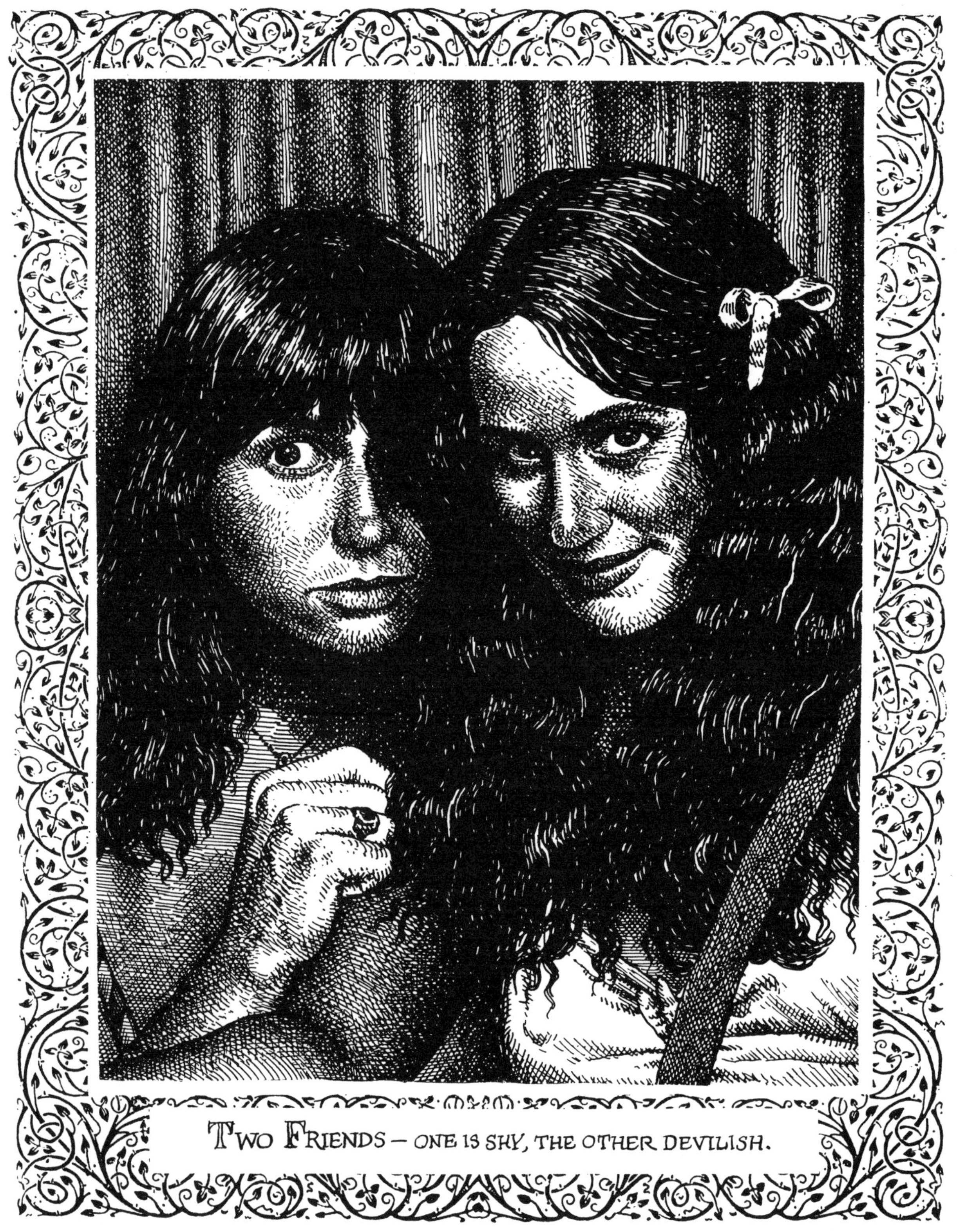

Two Friends — one is shy, the other devilish.

"Since bad art has a harmful effect on society, it should never go unchallenged; but since the bad artist (like the good one) is an artist at all only because he claims he is, and has gotten at least one other person to believe him, how is he to be challenged? The only available rules are those of the gunfighter."

— John Gardner

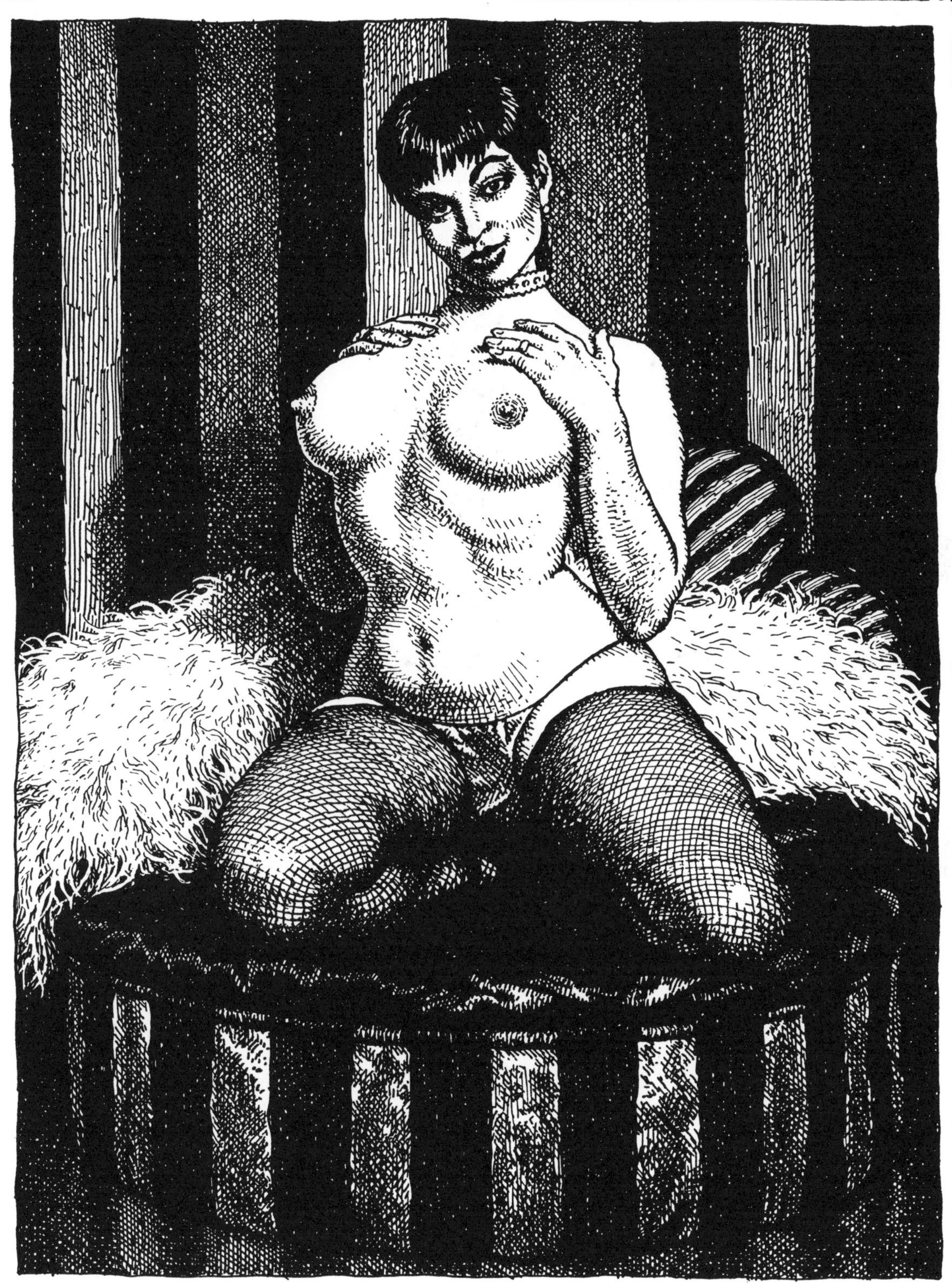

GERALDINE GARDNER, NIGHTCLUB PERFORMER OF THE 1950s, IN A POSE SHOWING THE BEAUTIFUL LINES OF HER BODY THAT MAKE HER AN IDEAL SUBJECT FOR THE ARTIST'S PEN. THE CAPTION ON THE ORIGINAL PHOTO FROM WHICH THIS DRAWING WAS TAKEN CLAIMS THAT "HER BEDROOM STRATEGY REALLY SPARKLES."

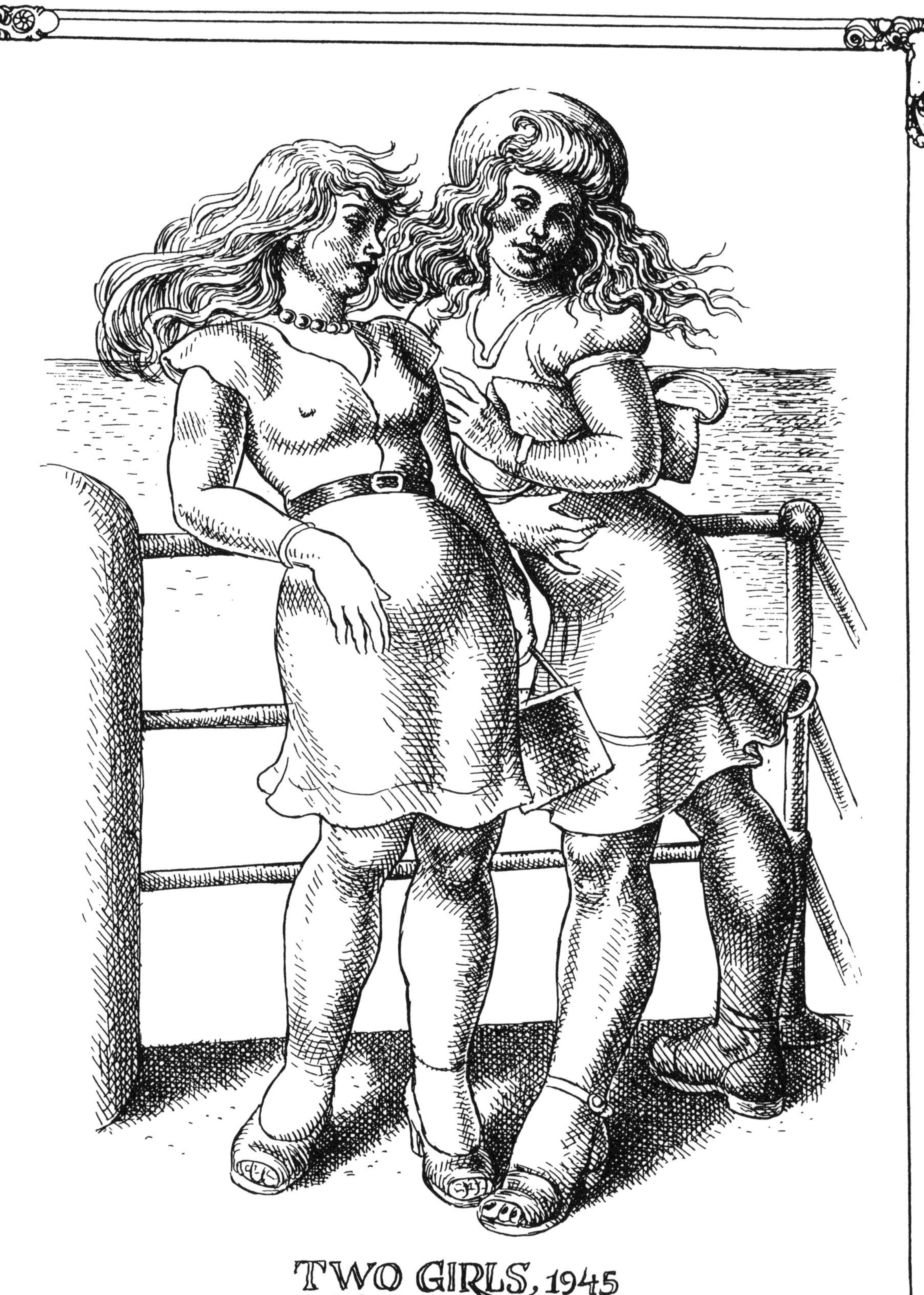

TWO GIRLS, 1945
copied from Reginald Marsh

Marsh was inspired by the sight of beautiful women in the everyday life of the city. There is a vibrant, sensual quality in this artist's work which has never been surpassed.

"THE BASIC PROJECT OF ART IS ALWAYS TO MAKE THE WORLD WHOLE AND COMPREHENSIBLE, TO RESTORE IT TO US IN ALL ITS GLORY AND ITS OCCASIONAL NASTINESS, NOT THROUGH ARGUMENT BUT THROUGH FEELING, AND THEN TO CLOSE THE GAP BETWEEN YOU AND EVERYTHING THAT IS NOT YOU, AND IN THIS WAY PASS FROM FEELING TO MEANING. IT'S NOT SOMETHING THAT COMMITTEES CAN DO. IT'S NOT A TASK ACHIEVED BY GROUPS OR BY MOVEMENTS. IT'S DONE BY INDIVIDUALS, EACH PERSON MEDIATING IN SOME WAY BETWEEN A SENSE OF HISTORY AND AN EXPERIENCE OF THE WORLD."

— ROBERT HUGHES, *"Shock of the New"*, 1980

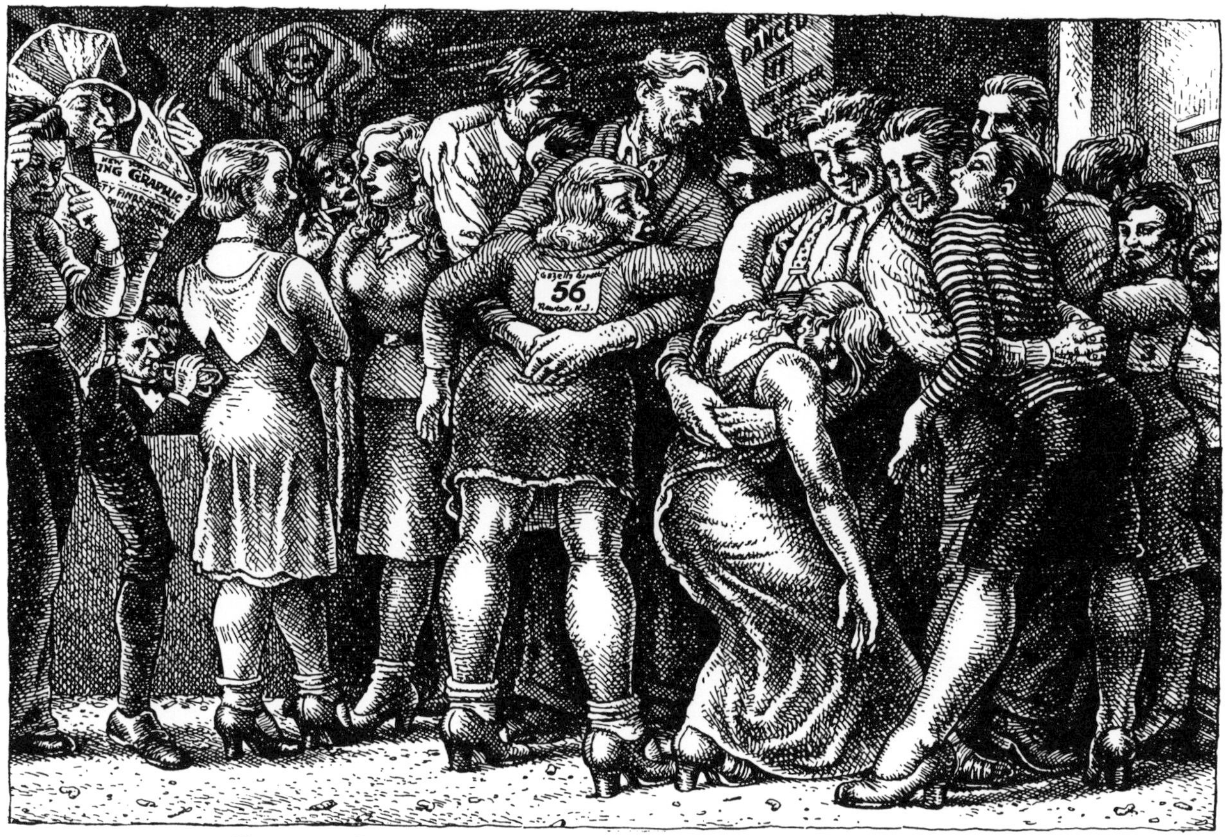

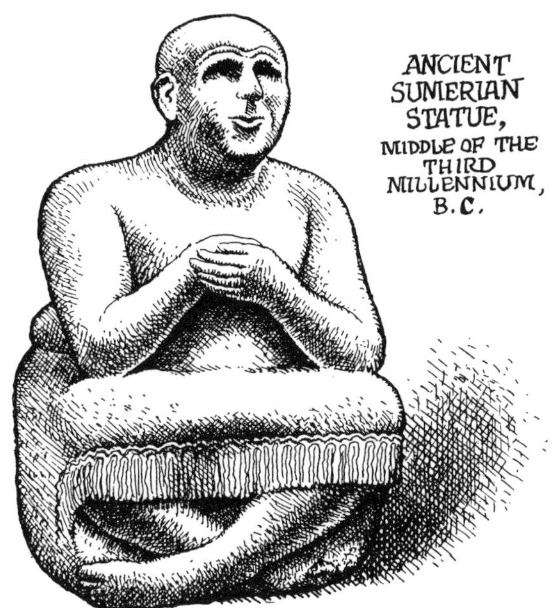

"ZEKE YOUNGBLOOD'S DANCE MARATHON, 1932
— *Copied from* REGINALD MARSH

ANCIENT
SUMERIAN
STATUE,
MIDDLE OF THE
THIRD
MILLENNIUM,
B.C.

"AN EPOCH CAN ONLY BE RECORDED BY THE ARTISTS OF THAT TIME, THAT IS TO SAY, THE ARTISTS WHO HAVE LIVED THROUGH IT. EACH AGE MUST HAVE ITS OWN ARTISTS TO EXPRESS IT AND TO RECORD IT FOR THE FUTURE."

— GUSTAVE COURBET

"CONTENT IS NOT THE SAME THING AS SUBJECT MATTER: IT IS WHAT THE ARTIST DISCOVERS *IN* HIS SUBJECT. IT IS ITS CONTENT THAT MAKES ANY WORK OF ART DYNAMIC. IT IS THE CONTENT THAT THE ARTIST DISTILLS FROM LIFE AND WHICH, THROUGH ITS INFLUENCE ON THE SPECTATOR AS HE COMPREHENDS IT, FLOWS BACK INTO LIFE....

THE CONTENT OF A WORK OF ART CAN ONLY DERIVE FROM DEFINITE, SPECIFIC, PARTICULAR EXPERIENCE. THE ARTIST CANNOT AIM AT SUCH QUALITIES DIRECTLY, THEY WILL BE ACHIEVED BY THE MOST FAITHFUL INSIGHT INTO WHAT IT MEANS TO BE A PARTICULAR PERSON IN A PARTICULAR SITUATION."

— JOHN BERGER

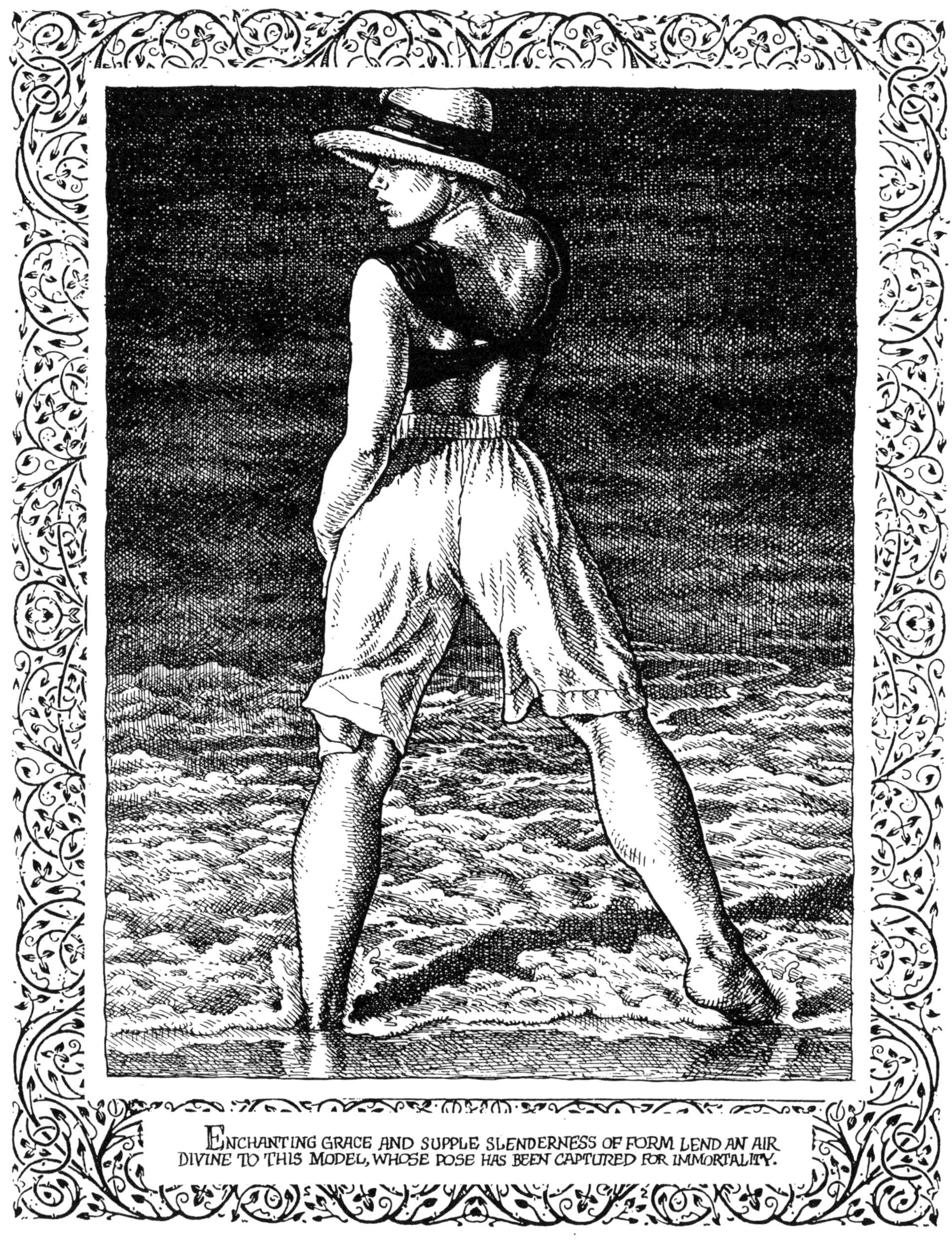

"IT'S REALLY ABSURD TO MAKE AN IMAGE, LIKE A HUMAN BEING, WITH PAINT, TODAY,
WHEN YOU THINK ABOUT IT... BUT THEN ALL OF A SUDDEN IT WAS EVEN MORE ABSURD
NOT TO DO IT."

— WILLEM DE KOONING, 1960

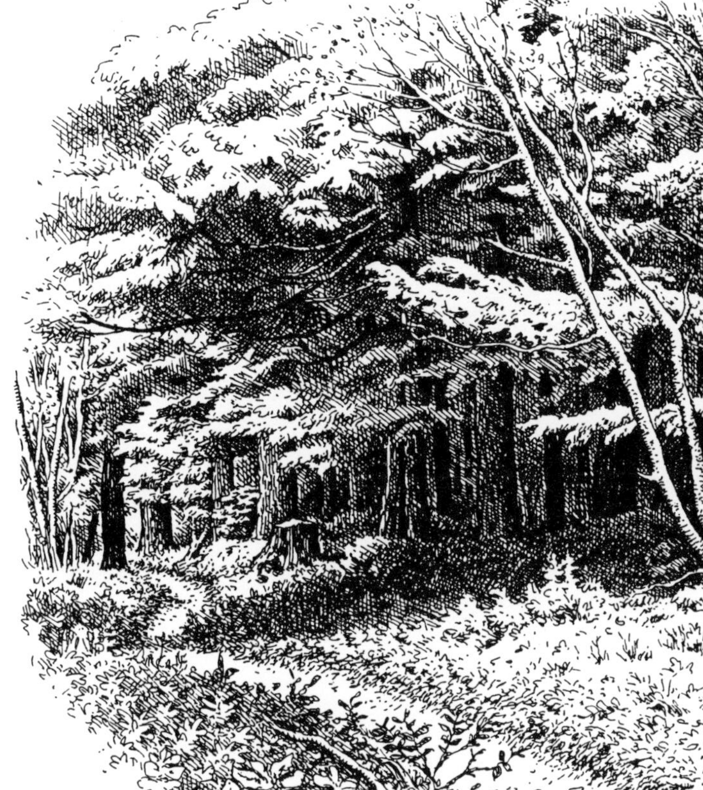

H ERE IS A POIGNANT
STUDY IN CONTRAST BE-
TWEEN AN ENCHANTING
SCENE IN NATURE AND A TYP-
ICAL MODERN URBAN LANDSCAPE,
BOTH DRAWN BY THE SAME ARTIST
FROM LIFE. IN ONE WE ARE GIVEN AN EXQUISITE SENSE OF SERENITY, SOLITUDE
AND REFLECTION AMID THE BENEVOLENT BOWERS OF OUR GOD-GIVEN HERITAGE,
WHILE IN THE OTHER WE ARE MADE WITNESS TO AN ALL-TOO COMMON-PLACE
HUMAN ENVIRON-
MENT OF OUR TIME,
WITH ITS STUCCO-
SURFACED APART-
MENT BUILDINGS,
POWER LINES, CARS
AND STREETS. AH,
HOW FAR WE'VE
FALLEN SINCE THE
DAYS OF ADAM AND
EVE!

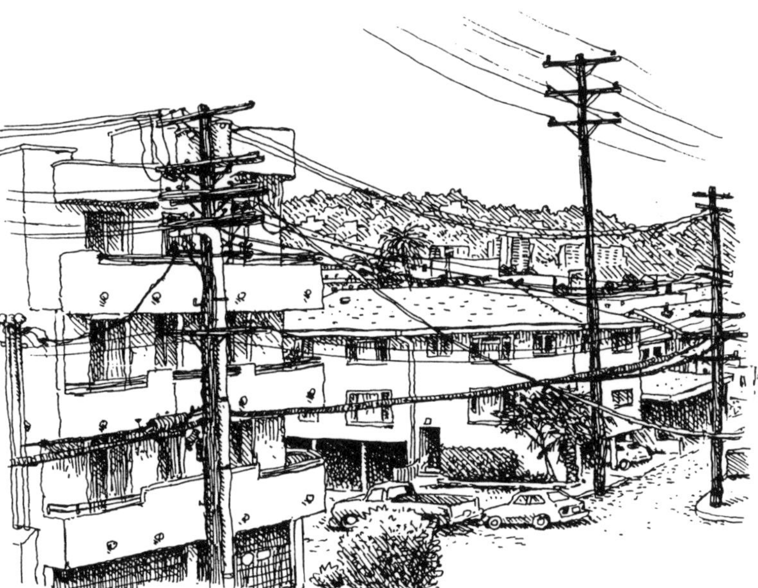

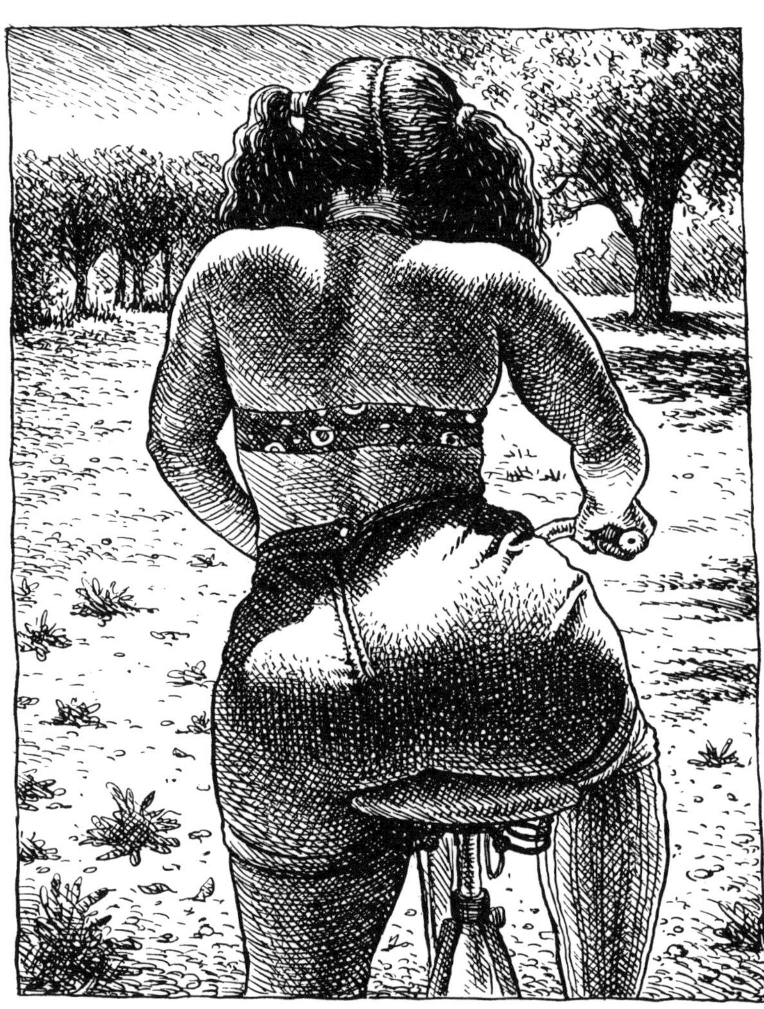

DESPITE THE RELENTLESS DRIVE TOWARD ELIMINATION OF THE OBJECT IN MODERN ART MOVEMENTS, THE FEMALE FORM CONTINUES TO DEMAND ATTENTION.

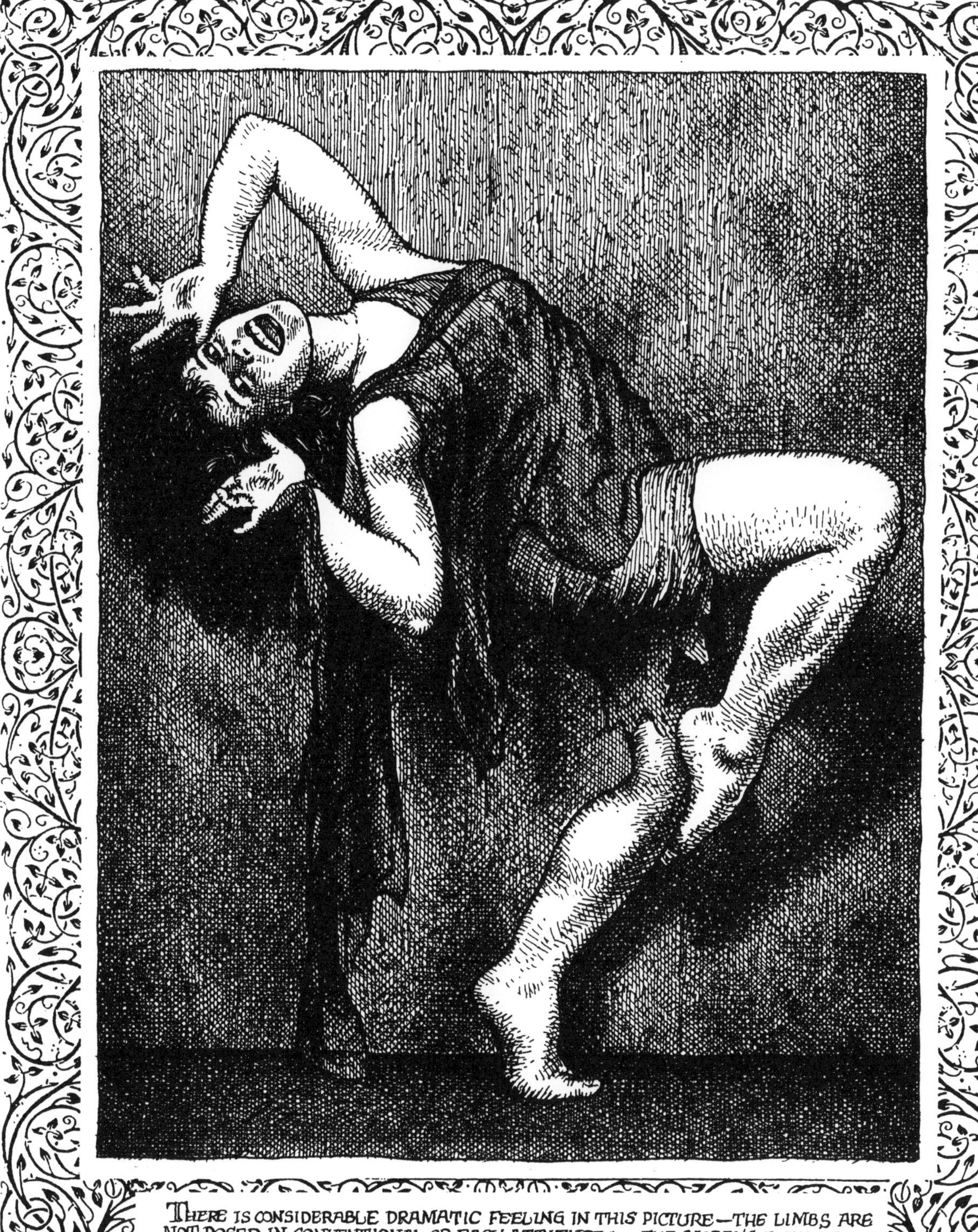

"When one follows nature, one obtains everything."
— Auguste Rodin

"Genius is only recognized in people who succeed."
— William Merritt Chase

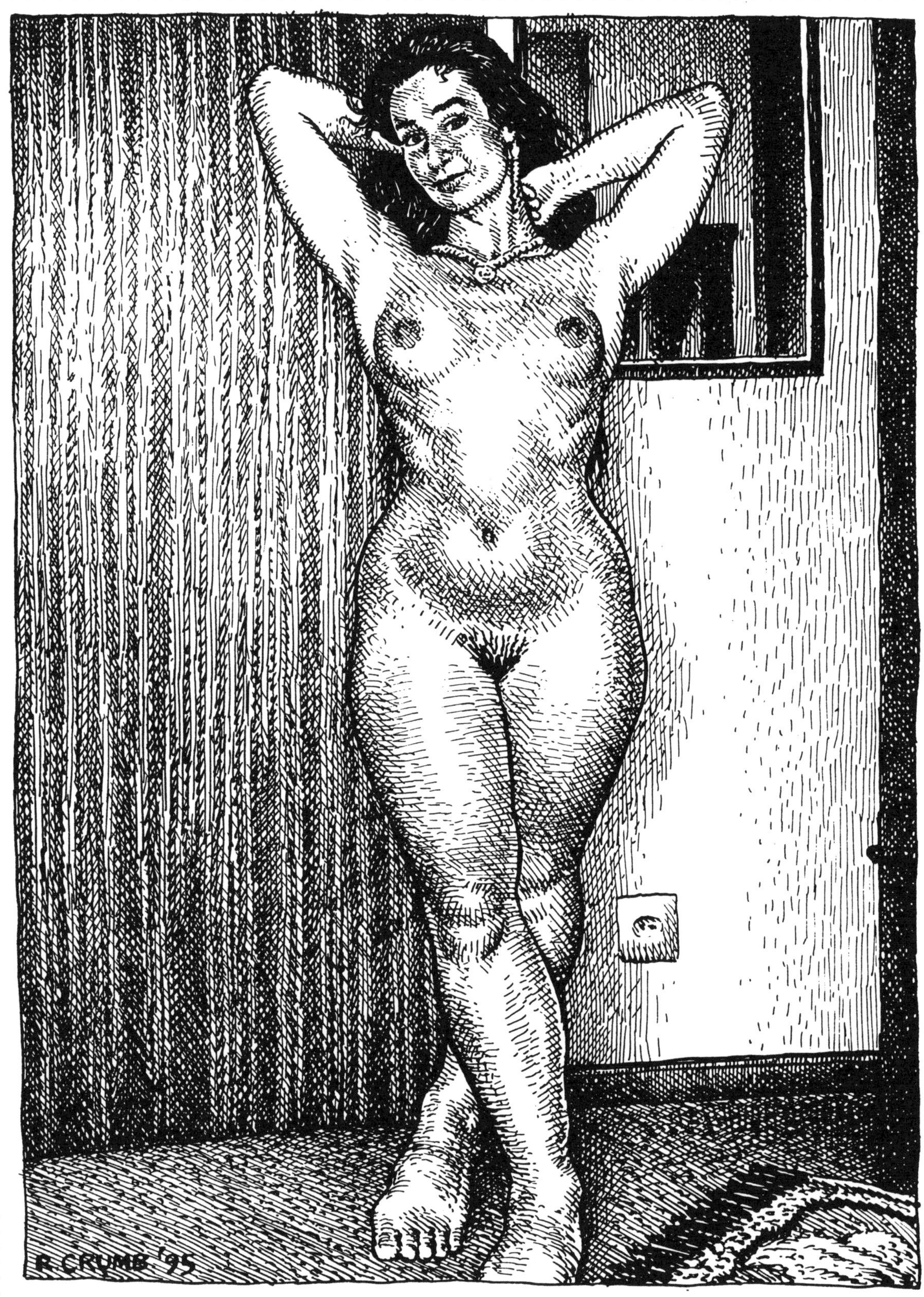

HERE IS A FACE AND FIGURE DISTINCTLY EUROPEAN IN ITS TYPE — SHE WOULD HAVE BEEN ADORED AS A MODEL BY THE EARLY ITALIANS. IT IS INDEED A PRIVILEGE TO BEHOLD SUCH PERFECTION OF THE FEMALE FORM.

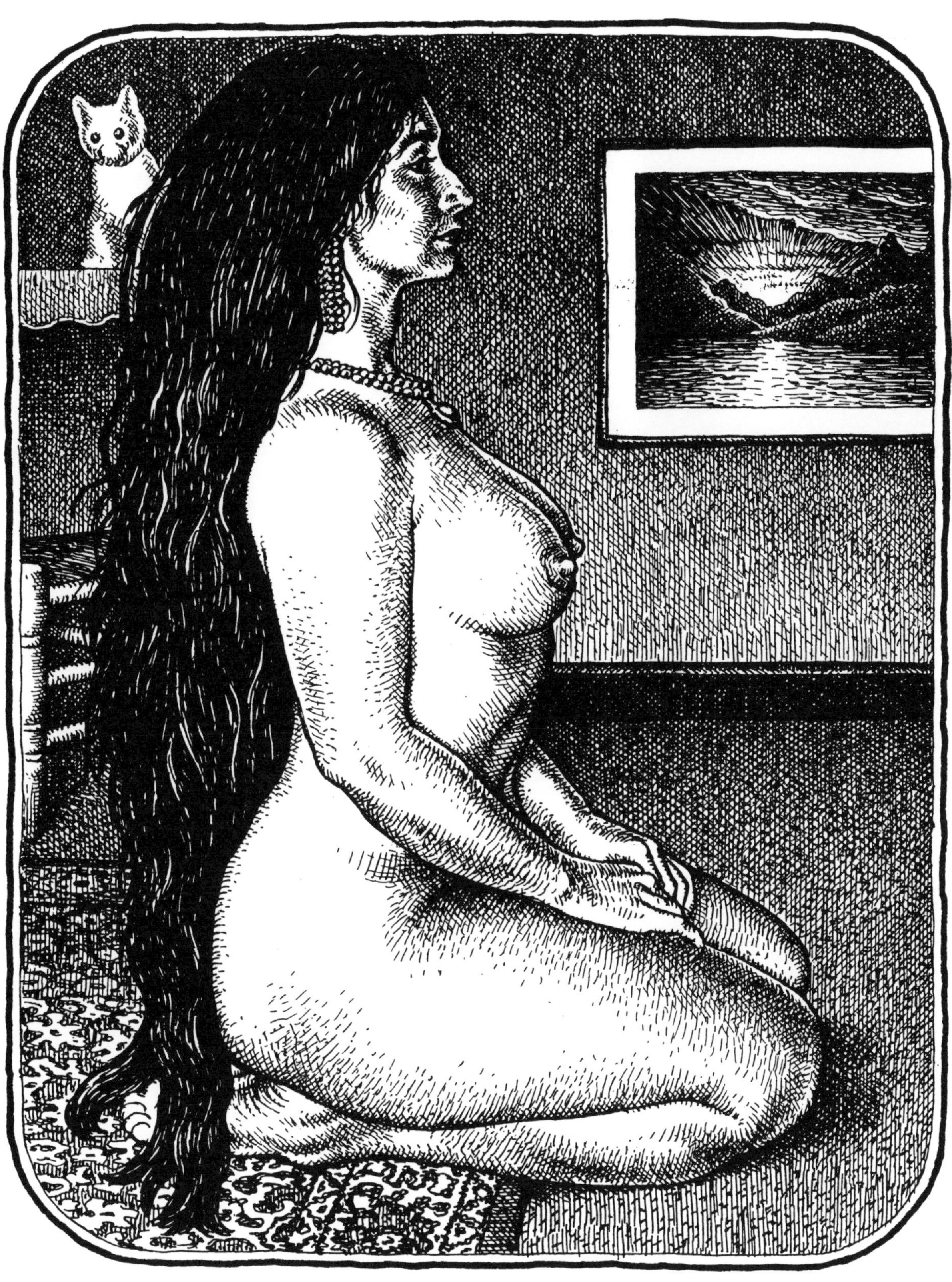

THE SAME SUPERB MODEL AS SHOWN ON THE OPPOSITE PAGE IS HERE SHOWN IN ANOTHER POSE, WHICH DISPLAYS HER MAGNIFICENT LONG BLACK HAIR IN ADDITION TO HER UNUSUALLY FINE ANATOMICAL CHARACTERISTICS.

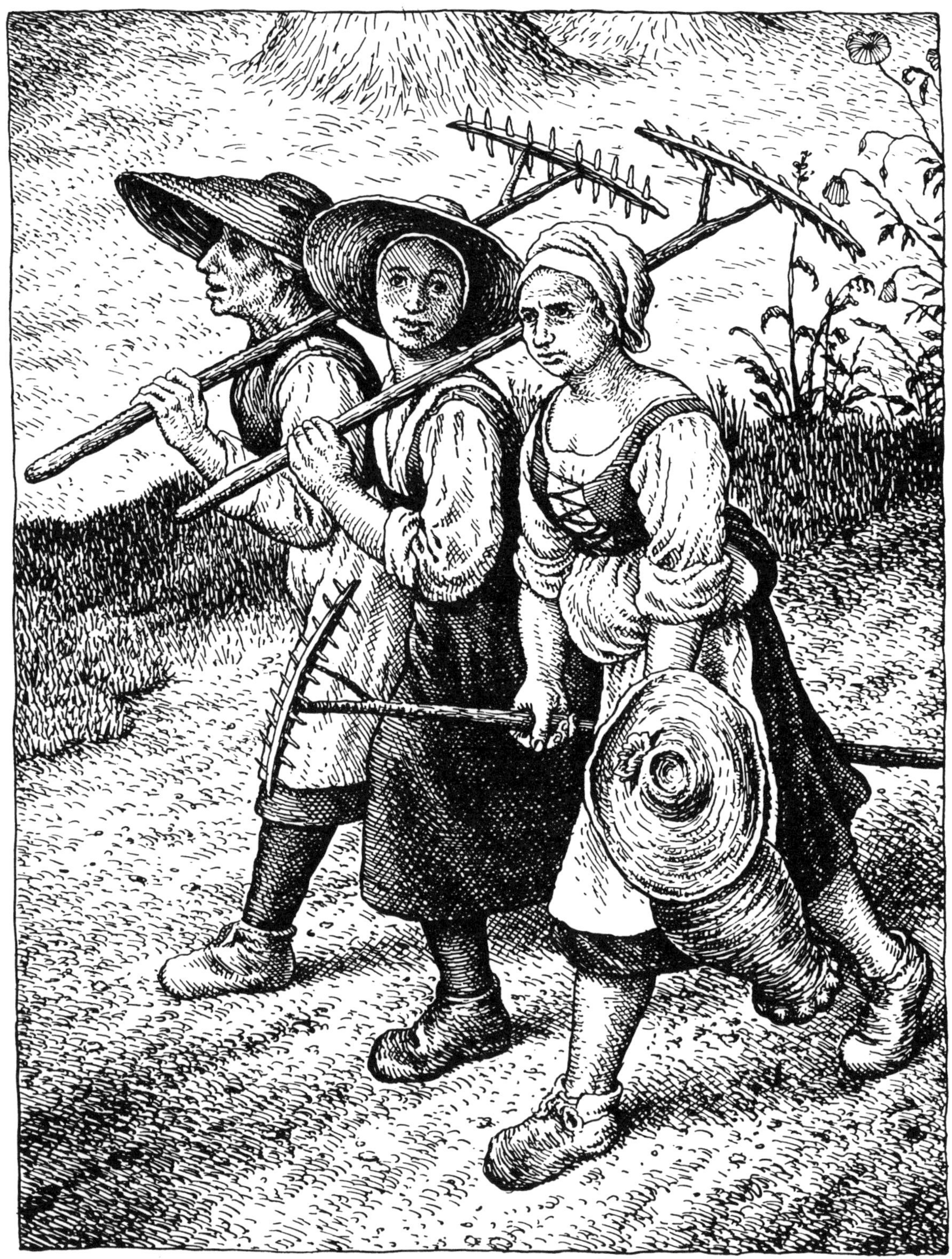

Detail from HAY MAKING (JULY) after BRUEGEL

Prolonged contemplation of any picture by the great 16th century Flemish master proves to be an enriching experience. For instance, a close study of this detail reveals to us much more than just a picture of three peasant women on their way to work in the fields. It is a deep character study of three ages of life. On the left is old age, detached, perhaps resigned, at peace with the world, possibly. In the middle walks youth, bright-eyed, hopeful and innocent, and on the right strides middle age, who stares grimly straight ahead, with her mind full of cares and responsibilities, the "prime of life."

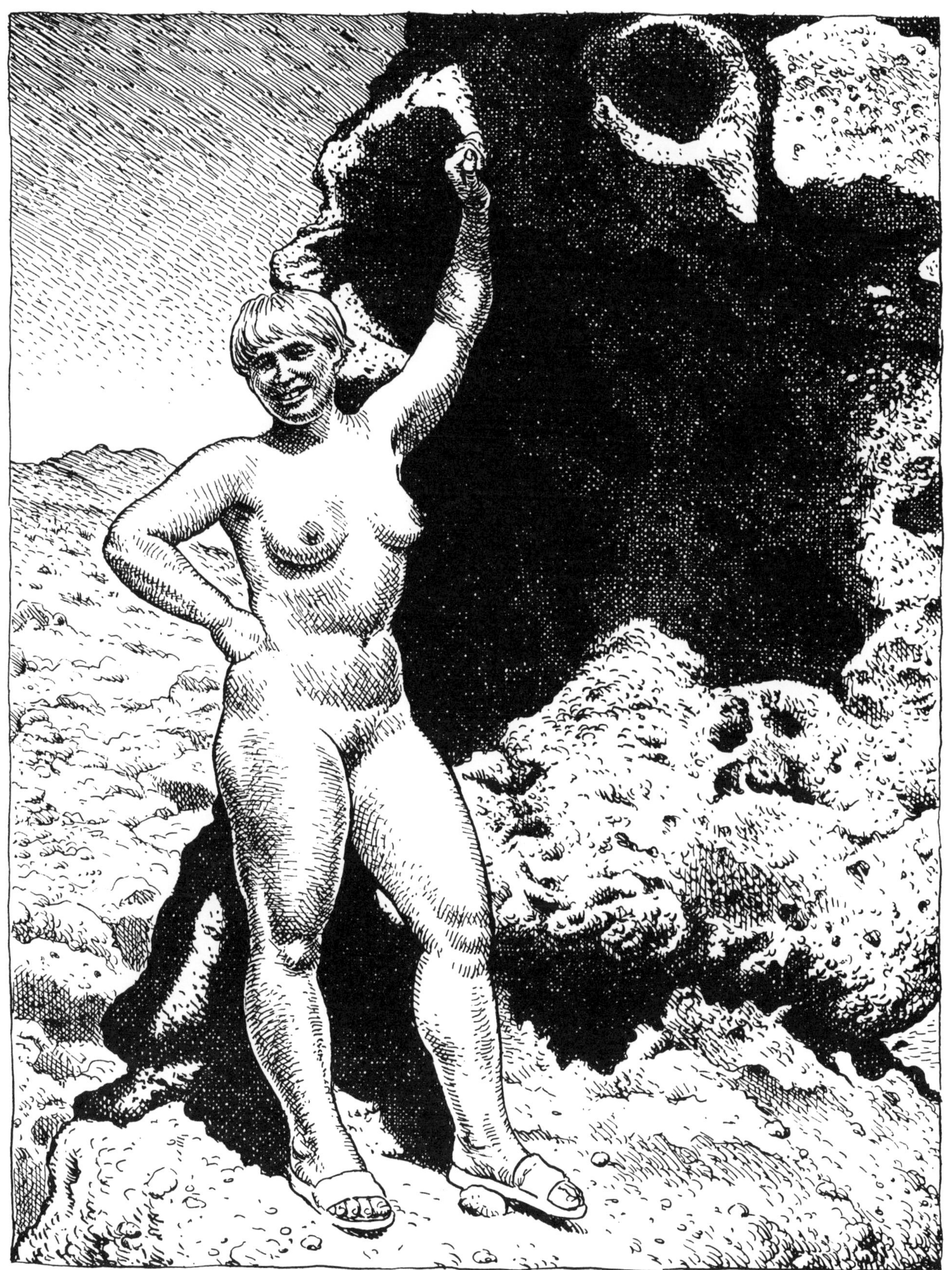

An amazing study of a finely formed woman in her sixties — she seems to carry with her the very spirit of nature — and her strong, healthy body certainly represents the height of classic feminine beauty. The art student will be particularly interested in the play of light and shadow created by this powerful female form standing against a background of textured rocks.

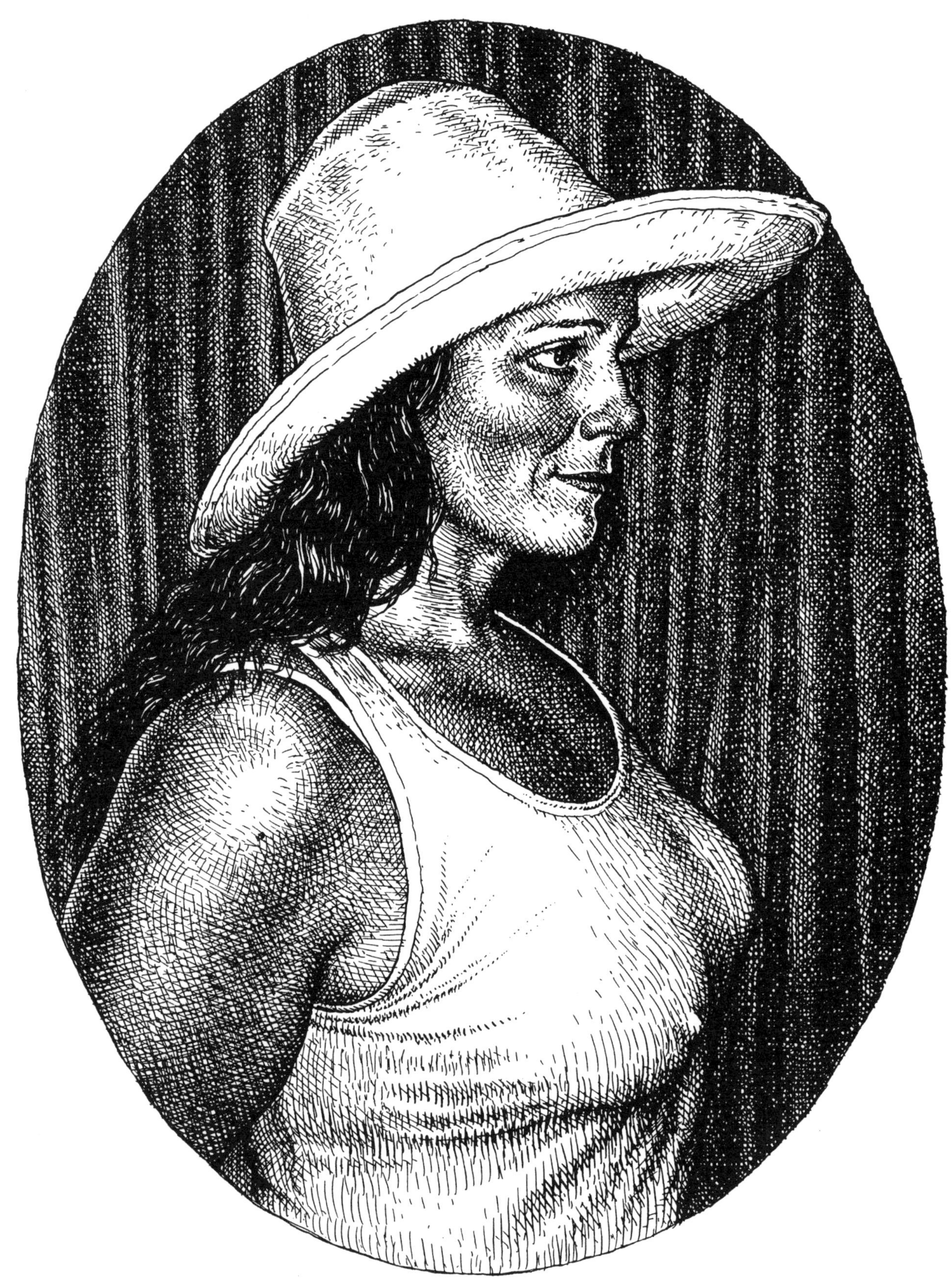

The sweetly bashful expression combined with the wholesome strength and solidity of the physique make this beautiful rural American woman, to our way of thinking, a treat for the art student. The picture is drawn with true passion and very real depth of feeling.

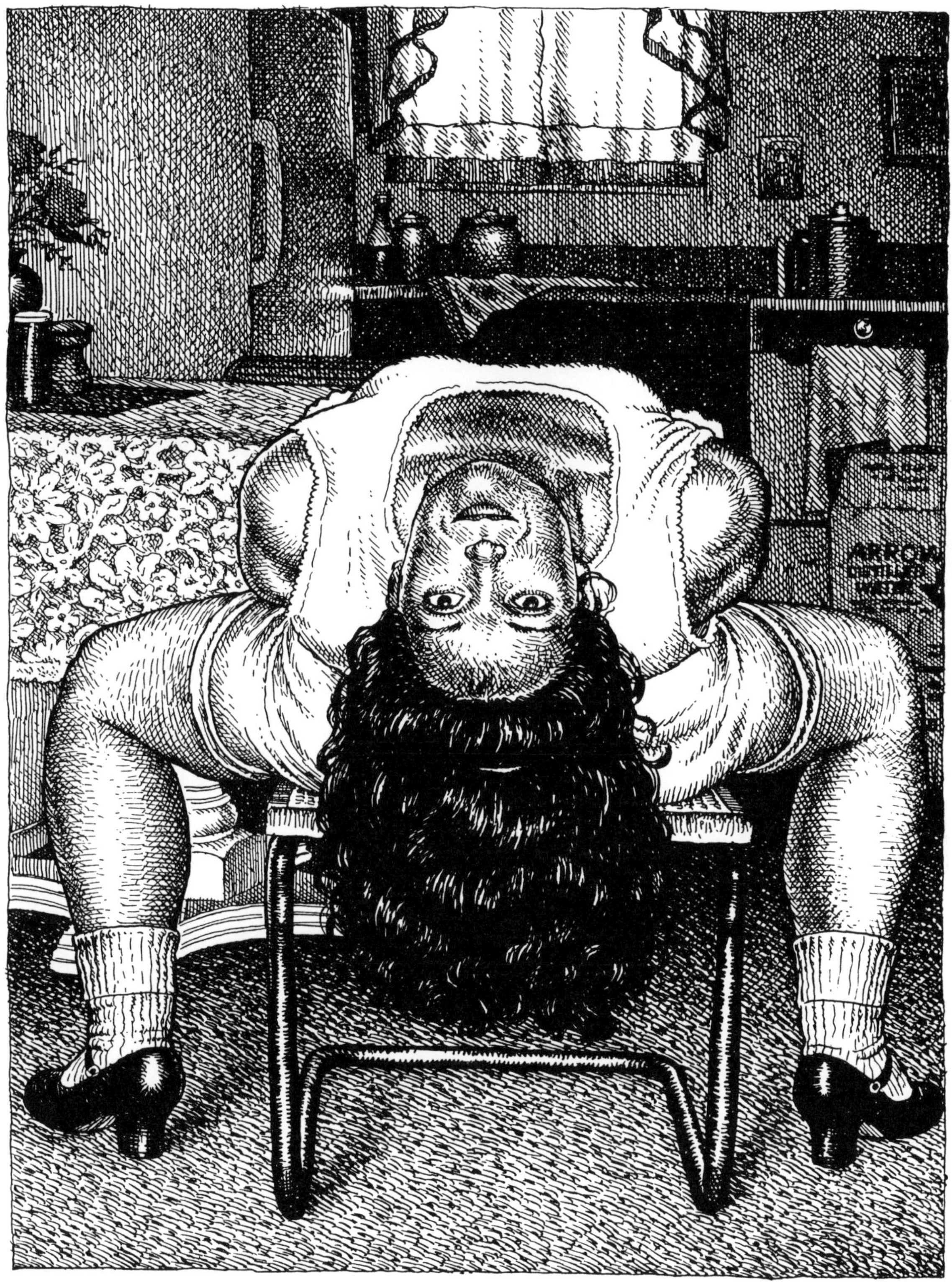

There is infinite, never ending variety to the human body and the poses in which it may be placed by the skilled artist. It is in these unusual angles of the body that the true artist finds inspiration for the creation of innovative and exciting compositions.

"You should often amuse yourself, when you take a walk for recreation, in watching and taking note of the attitudes and actions of men as they talk and dispute, or come to blows with each other... noting these down in a little pocket-book which you ought always to carry with you."
— Leonardo da Vinci

"Art springs from humanity as it is, from history, from time, and it is always more complex in statement, if not method, than science. It is for other human beings; it is consolatory or menacing, but always more or less therapeutic in intention, and its therapy has to apply to a thing far too complex (and indeed ritualistic) for science to control or cure — the human mind."
— John Fowles, "The Aristos"

"To be at odds with his times — there lies the raison d'être of the artist!"
— André Gide

This giant female bodybuilder proves those unthinking people wrong who believe feminine beauty can never be harmonious with well-developed musculature.

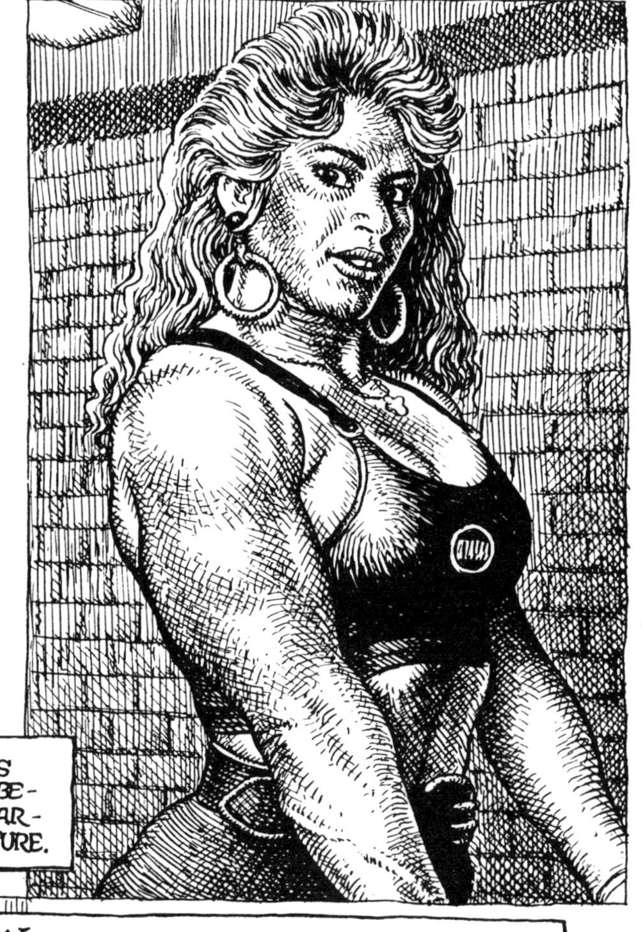

With her lovely golden hair and tremendous physical presence she seems the very incarnation of liberated female exuberance and brash self-confidence.

"Money, the measure of [the art] market, has become the fourth dimension of art. Once ancillary to the appreciation of art, price now lodges itself like a reflex at the center of our aesthetic faculty. We can no longer think about art without glancing down the long perspectival price tunnel whose brightly lit foreground features all $82.5 million worth of Vincent Van Gogh's 'Dr. Gachet', with the rest of human artifice receding by degrees into less remunerative twilight."
— James Gardner, "Culture or Trash", 1993

"Imagination is more important than knowledge."
— Albert Einstein

"WITHOUT UNCEASING PRACTICE NOTHING CAN BE DONE. PRACTICE IS ART. IF YOU LEAVE OFF YOU ARE LOST. THE WHOLE BUSINESS OF MAN IS THE ARTS, AND ALL THINGS COMMON. NO SECRECY IN ART."

— WILLIAM BLAKE

ANONYMOUS MAN WITH BANJO

IN THIS PICTURE THE QUAINT CHARACTER IN HIS RUSTIC SETTING FORMS A MOST INTRIGUING STUDY.

"IT IS HARDER TO SEE THAN IT IS TO EXPRESS. THE WHOLE OF ART RESTS IN THE ARTIST'S ABILITY TO SEE WELL INTO WHAT IS BEFORE HIM. NOTHING WILL DO BUT THE MOST PRECISE STATEMENT. HE MUST NOT ONLY BEND TECHNIQUE TO HIS WILL, BUT HE MUST INVENT TECHNIQUE THAT WILL FIT HIS NEED."

"IT WOULD BE EASY TO DIVIDE ARTISTS INTO TWO CLASSES: THOSE WHO GROW SO MUCH WITHIN THEMSELVES AS TO MASTER TECHNIQUE BY THE FORCE OF THEIR NEED, AND THOSE WHO ARE MASTERED BY TECHNIQUE AND BECOME STYLISTS."

— ROBERT HENRI
"Art Spirit"

"A WORK OF ART MUST BE BORN OF CONSCIOUS INTENTION AND DELIBERATE STRIVING: AND THE SPECTATOR, ALTHOUGH HE MAY NOT IMMEDIATELY AND FULLY UNDERSTAND THE WORK, MUST BE ABLE TO INFER THIS."

"WHEN A PAINTER IS UNFAITHFUL TO HIS EXPERIENCE IN ORDER TO MEET A CONVENTIONAL DEMAND OF THE PERIOD'S TASTE, HIS TALENTS ARE BETRAYED."

"THE FUNCTION OF THE ORIGINAL ARTIST IS TO RENEW THE TRADITION TO WHICH HE BELONGS."

—JOHN BERGER

"A "MAINSTREAM," FOR BETTER OR WORSE, UNDENIABLY EXISTS: BETTER, BECAUSE MUTUALITY AND RECIPROCITY, WHICH FORM THE FOUNDATION OF ALL CIVILIZED INTERACTION, REQUIRE AGREED-UPON NORMS, AND WORSE, BECAUSE A MAINSTREAM CAN BECOME A TYRANNY OF MAJORITY VALUES. ALTERNATIVE NARRATIVES CONTINUALLY TAKE ON NEW IMPORTANCE BY REDEFINING THE MAINSTREAM TO INCLUDE THEMSELVES (AS COURBET DID). ARTISTS' CREATIVE STRUGGLE TO RECONCILE THEIR INDIVIDUAL IMAGINATIVE LIFE WITH THEIR SOCIAL EXISTENCE CAN — THROUGH THE EMPATHETIC READING OF VIEWERS — AFFECT THE LEVEL ON WHICH OTHERS EXPERIENCE EVENTS."

— JONATHAN FINEBERG, "Art Since 1940" (1995)

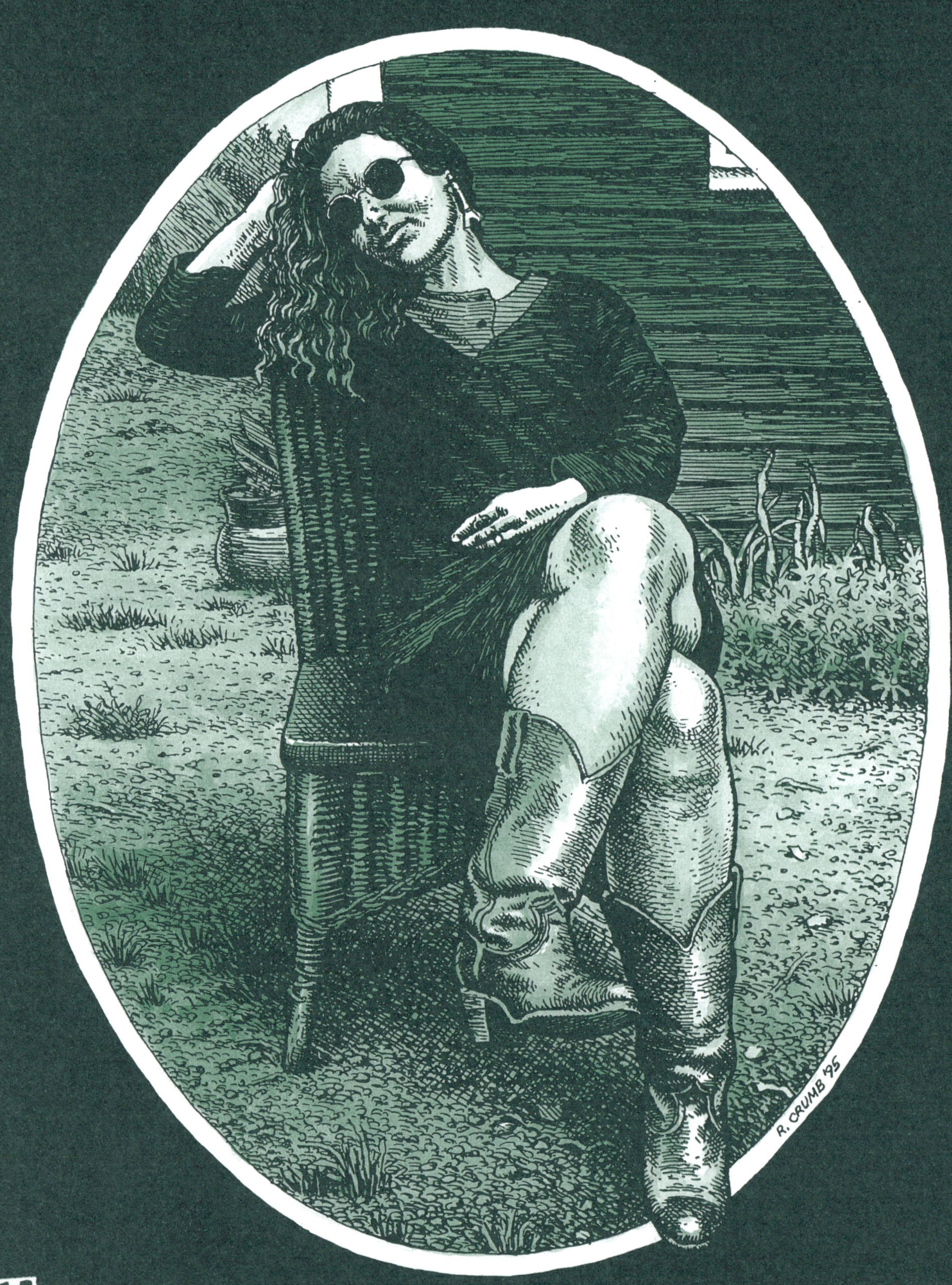

R. CRUMB '95

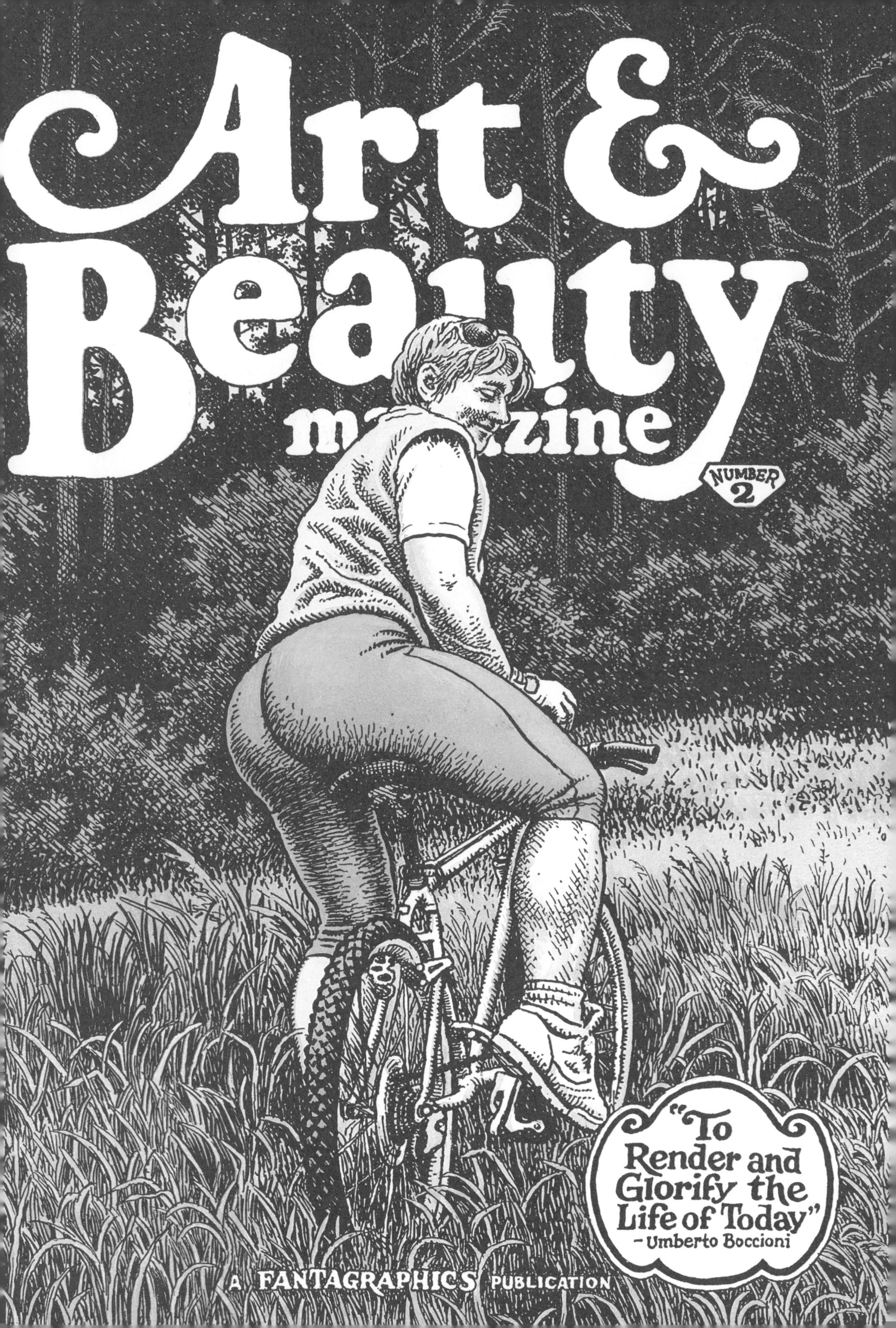

Art &
Beauty
magazine
NUMBER 2
"To Render and Glorify the Life of Today"
— Umberto Boccioni
A FANTAGRAPHICS PUBLICATION

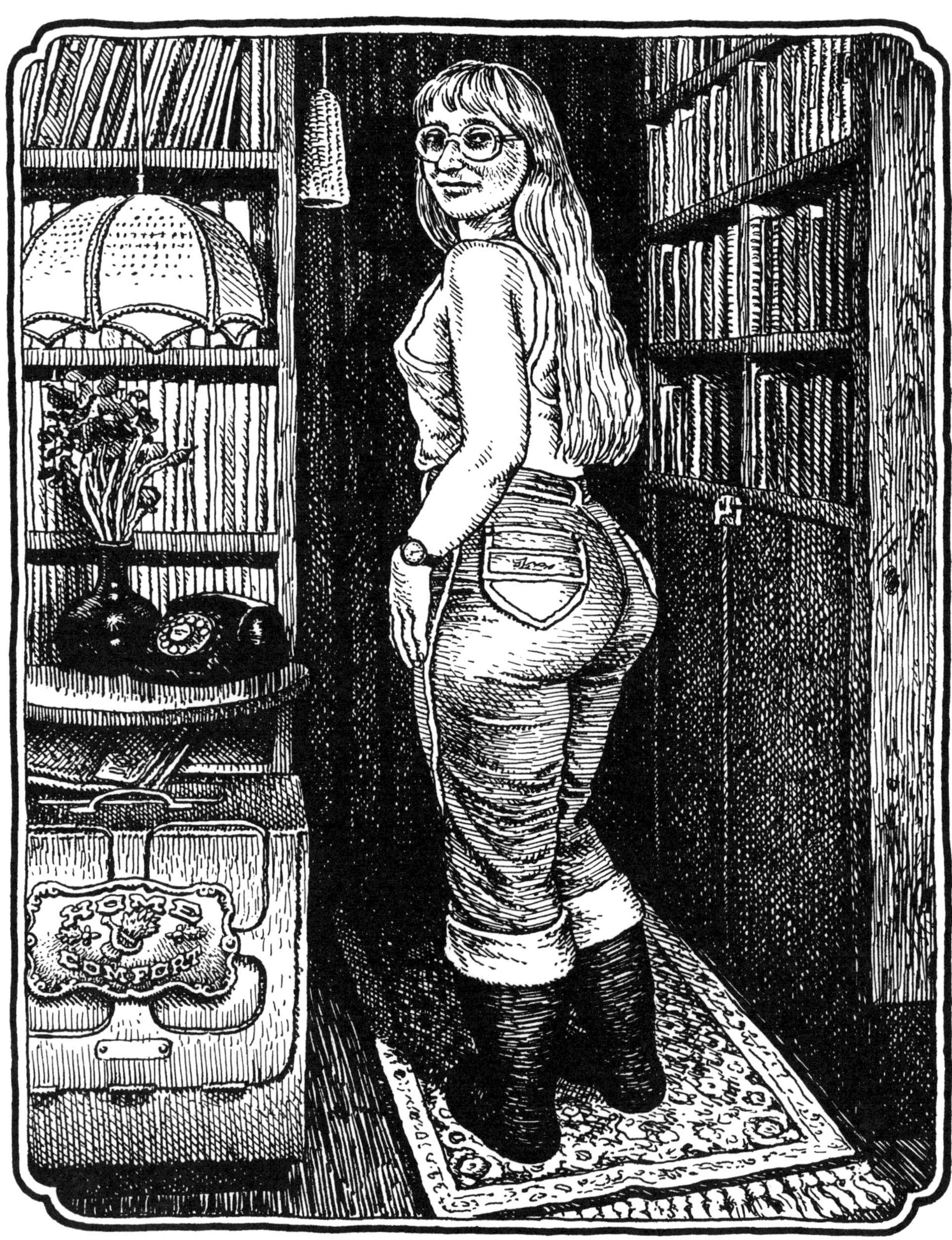

THERE IS AN INELUCTABLE CHARM ABOUT THIS "GIRL NEXT DOOR", WHOSE DEMURE, SENSITIVE AND INTELLECTUAL VISAGE AND PETITE, DELICATE FORM FROM THE WAIST UP STAND IN EXCITING AND INTRIGUING JUXTAPOSITION TO THE LUXURIANT, SENSUOUS PULCHRITUDE OF THE LOWER PORTION OF HER PHYSIQUE.

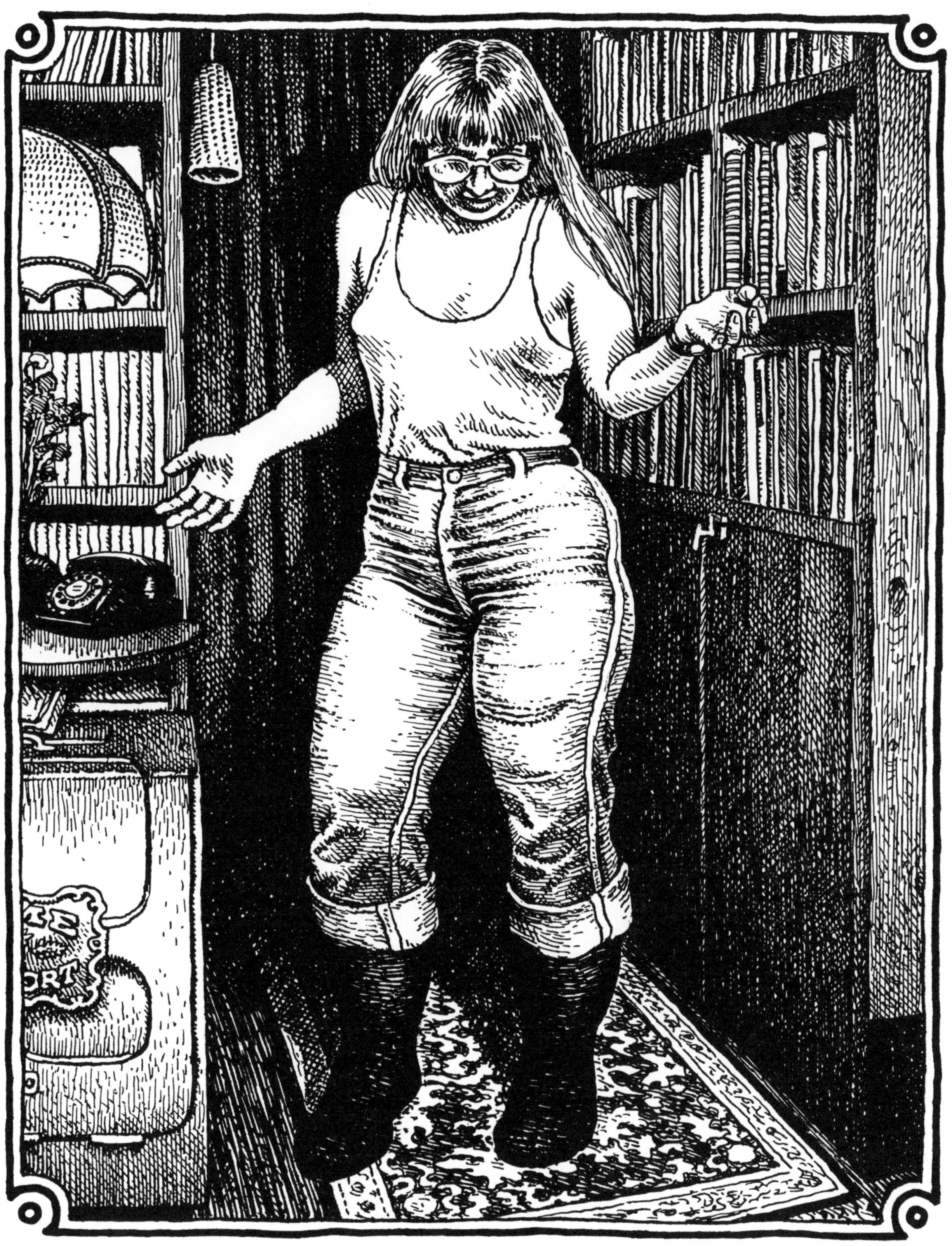

THE ARTIST CAPTURES AN AMUSING AND TOUCHING MOMENT WHEN OUR "GIRL NEXT DOOR" SURVEYS HER OWN BODY WITH EVIDENT WONDER AND, PERHAPS, BEWILDERMENT, AS IF SHE FEELS THAT THE DAINTY, ALMOST ETHEREAL UPPER PART, AND THE EARTHY, ROBUST CREATURE BELOW THE WAIST ARE VERILY TWO DIFFERENT PERSONS!

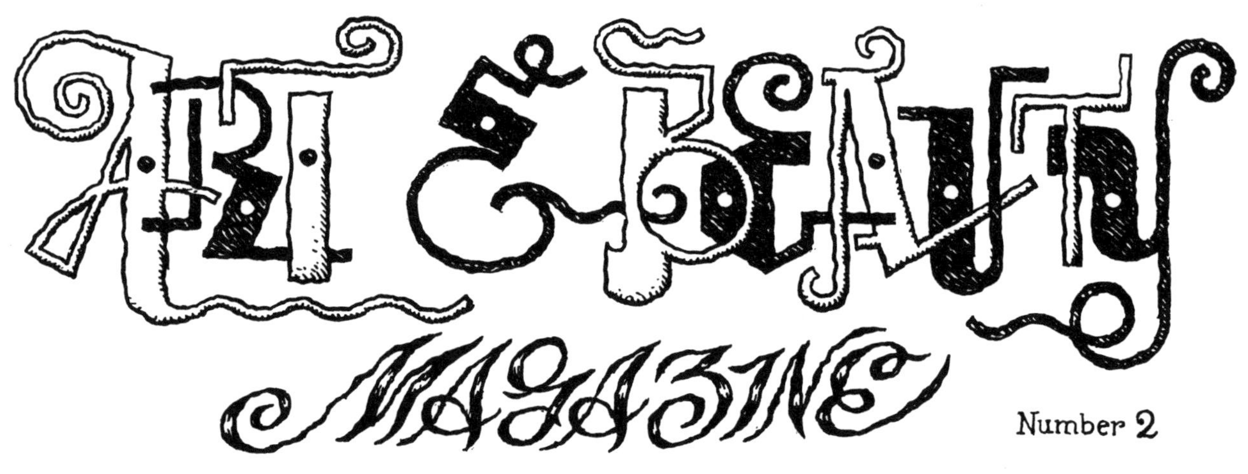

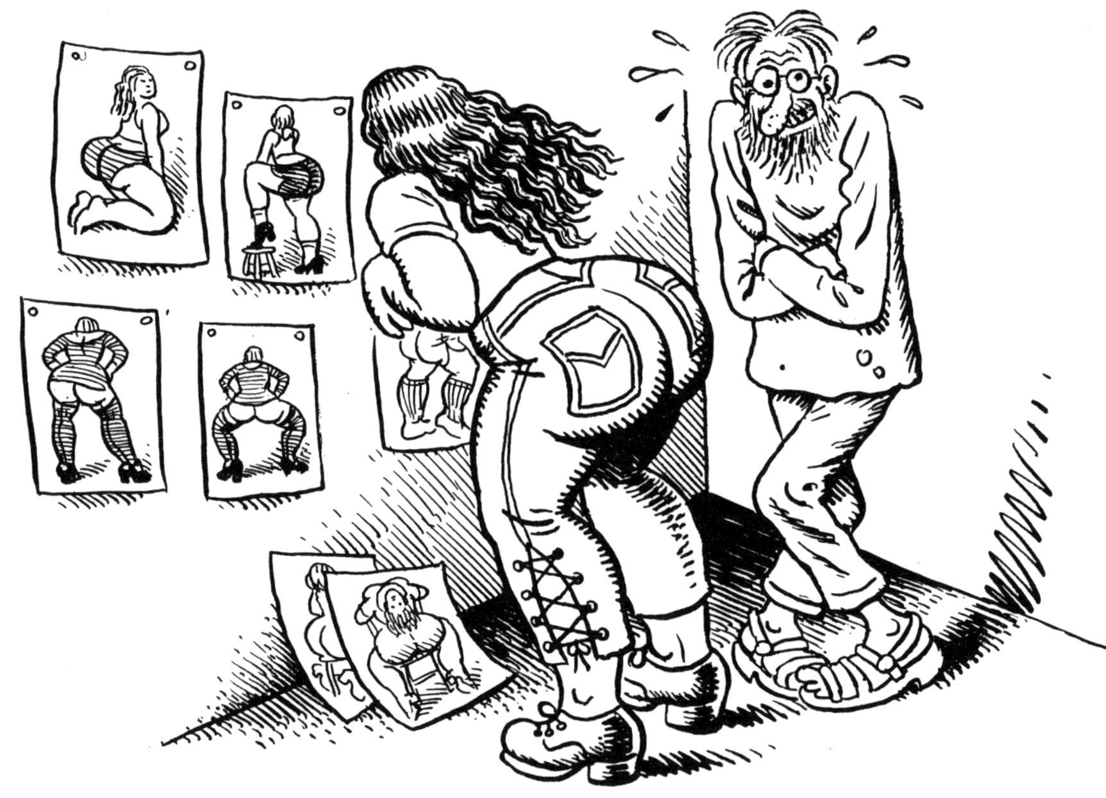

He brought her up to his studio to show her his etchings.
She: *"My God! You're obsessed!"*
He: *"A thing of beauty is a joy forever."*

"IF THE PAINTER WISHES TO SEE ENCHANTING BEAUTIES, HE HAS THE POWER TO PRODUCE THEM. IF HE WISHES TO SEE MONSTROSITIES, WHETHER TERRIFYING, OR LUDICROUS AND LAUGHABLE, OR PITIFUL, HE HAS THE POWER AND AUTHORITY TO CREATE THEM... INDEED, WHATEVER EXISTS IN THE UNIVERSE, WHETHER IN ESSENCE, IN ACT, OR IN THE IMAGINATION, THE PAINTER HAS FIRST IN HIS MIND AND THEN IN HIS HANDS."

—— LEONARDO DA VINCI

"MIND YOU, THE MOST PERFECT STEERSMAN THAT YOU CAN HAVE, AND THE BEST HELM, LIE IN THE TRIUMPHAL GATEWAY OF COPYING FROM NATURE... AND ALWAYS RELY ON THIS WITH A STOUT HEART, ESPECIALLY AS YOU BEGIN TO GAIN SOME UNDERSTANDING OF DRAFTSMANSHIP. DO NOT FAIL, AS YOU GO ON, TO DRAW SOMETHING EVERY DAY, FOR NO MATTER HOW LITTLE IT IS IT WILL BE WELL WORTH WHILE, AND IT WILL DO YOU A WORLD OF GOOD."

—— CENNINO CENNINI, A TUSCAN PAINTER
CIRCA 1372—?

ART & BEAUTY MAGAZINE, Number 2, ©2003 by R. Crumb. Published by Fantagraphics Books, 7563 Lake City Way, N.E., Seattle, Washington, 98115, U.S.A. Visit our website: http://www.fantagraphics.com/
Printed in Canada

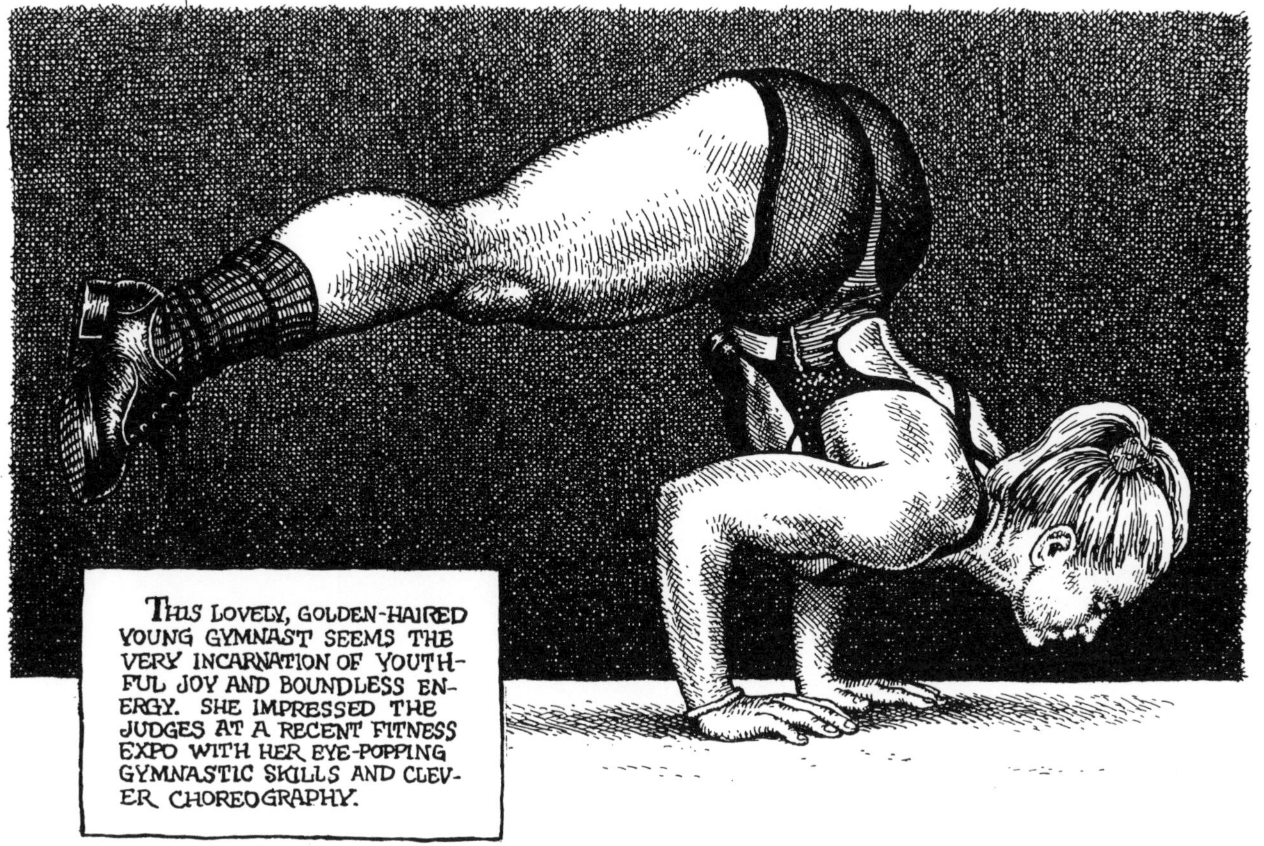

CALLING ALL CONNOISSEURS
EDITORIAL by R. CRUMB

IN OLDEN DAYS ARTISTS WERE INSPIRED BY LEGENDS OF THE HEROISM OF THE GODS AND GREAT WARRIORS TO RENDER THE HUMAN FIGURE (USUALLY THE MALE) IN DRAMATIC AND VALIANT POSES OF BATTLE AND FEATS OF COMBAT. WHILE THIS TRADITION OF GLORIFYING THE ARTS OF WAR AND VIOLENT CONFRONTATION HAS CONTINUED TO THRIVE EVEN DOWN TO OUR OWN TIME, WE NOW ALSO SEE IN OUR MEDIA, TELEVISION, NEWSPAPERS AND MAGAZINES, HEROIC VISUAL IMAGES OF PROFESSIONAL AS WELL AS AMATEUR ATHLETES IN THE THROES OF THE MOST ARDUOUS PHYSICAL ORDEALS. THE HEROISM EMBODIED IN THESE IMAGES IS IN THE MEETING AND STRUGGLING TO CONQUER THE MOST EXTREME CHALLENGES TO PHYSICAL PROW-ESS, AGILITY, DETERMINATION AND ENDURANCE.

WHAT IS MOST REMARKABLE IN THE PRESENT PERIOD IS THE EXTRAORDINARY FORWARD ADVANCE OF WHAT USED TO BE TERMED "THE WEAKER SEX" INTO THE MOST STRENUOUS, DARING, AND FIERCELY COMPETITIVE OF THE VARIOUS SPORTS AND ATHLETIC CONTESTS. THESE BRAVE GIRLS AND WOMEN HAVE ASTOUNDED ALL THE WORLD, SHOWING THAT THEY ARE CAPABLE OF ACHIEVEMENT EQUAL TO THAT OF THE MALE IN NEARLY ALL CATAGORIES. THIS TYPE OF WOMAN POSSESSES A NEW KIND OF SELF-CONFIDENCE, FEARLESSNESS, AND SENSE OF INDEPENDENCE. SHE HAS ARRIVED AT A POINT WHERE SHE NO LONGER NEED FEAR BEING OSTRACIZED OR DISDAINED AS "UNFEMININE", "DYKISH", "OVERLY MASCULINE", OR "UNLADYLIKE". SHE STRIDES BOLDLY ALONG THE PUBLIC THOROUGHFARES, PROUD OF HER MUSCULAR DEVELOPMENT AND BEING PHYSICALLY ON A PAR WITH MEN WHERE STRENGTH IS CON-CERNED. THERE NOW ARISES A NEW STANDARD OF BEAUTY WHICH INCLUDES A FINE ATHLETIC LEVEL OF MUSCULATURE AS PART OF THE IDEAL FEMININE FIGURE. THIS IS SURELY REVOLUTIONARY, FOR NOW IT BECOMES ACCEPTABLE, IN THE MORE ADVANCED AREAS OF CIVILIZATION AT LEAST, FOR GIRLS AND WO-MEN TO BE BOTH STRONG, FEARLESS, INDEPENDENT *AND* ATTRACTIVE OBJECTS OF EROTIC DESIRE AT THE SAME TIME. THE NEW FEMALE FIGURE WHICH DISPLAYS OBVIOUS PHYSICAL POWER IS NOW BE-COMING WIDELY ADMIRED, SEEN AS *ENHANCING* THE WONDERFUL PROVOCATIVE CURVES OF THE CLASSIC EROTIC IDEAL. THE OLDER AESTHETIC NOW APPEARS TO THE MODERN, DISCERNING MALE EYE AS TOO SOFT, FLACCID, LACKING IN *DEFINITION*. THE CONTEMPORARY MALE NOW *EXPECTS* WOMEN TO BE "BUFF", TO "WORK OUT," OR BE INVOLVED IN SOME SORT OF STRENUOUS PHYSICAL ACTIVITY, IN SHORT, TO SHOW SOME DEGREE OF MUSCLE DEVELOPMENT, THOUGH HE MAY BE UTTERLY UNAWARE OF HOW MANY HOURS OF SWEAT SHE HAS PUT IN TO ACHIEVE THAT FINELY HONED SHAPELINESS.

THE BEAUTIFUL FEMININE CHAMPIONS OF SPORT AS SEEN EVERY DAY IN MAGNIFICENT ACT-ION IN THE MASS MEDIA ARE INEVITABLY A SOURCE OF INSPIRATION TO THE ARTIST IN SEARCH OF VISUAL IMAGES THAT ARE HEROIC AND AT THE SAME TIME EROTIC IN THEIR WHOLESOMENESS, AND THAT ARE ALSO, IT MUST BE SAID, ONE OF THE MORE POSITIVE PHENOMENA OF THIS "POST-MODERN" AGE. AND SO, HAPPILY, WE DEDICATE A SPECIAL SECTION OF THIS ISSUE OF ART & BEAUTY TO POR-TRAITS OF THE ATHLETIC FEMALE FIGURE IN ACTION, GLEANED FROM A MISCELLANEOUS VARIETY OF MAGAZINES AND DAILY NEWSPAPERS, AND INTERPRETED WITH PEN AND INK.

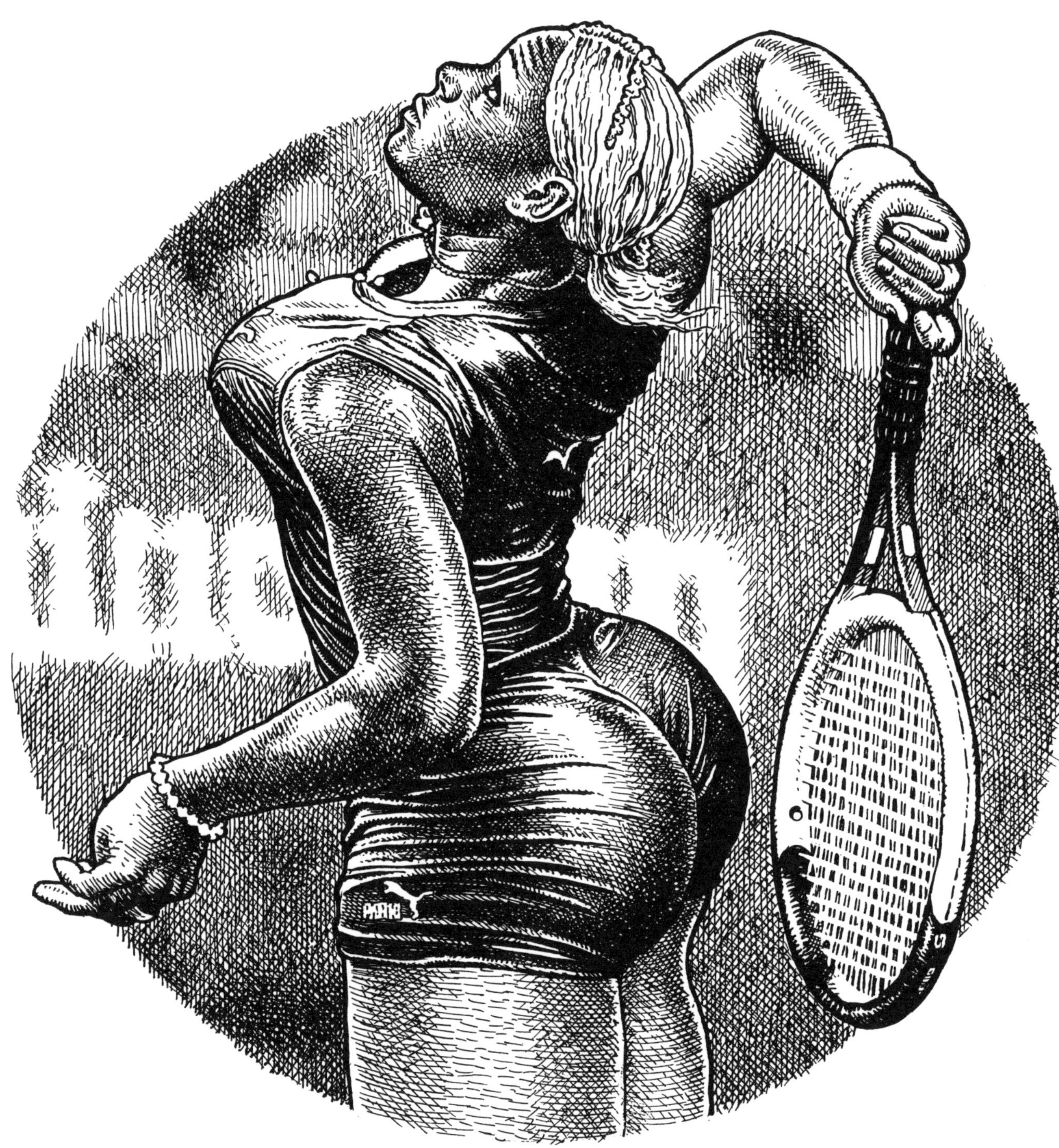

A HIGHLY SATISFYING CHALLENGE FOR THE ARTIST'S SKILLS ARE THE GLEAM-
ING HIGHLIGHTS ON THE RESPLENDENT CONTOURS OF TENNIS CHAMPION SERENA WIL-
LIAMS AS SHE APPEARED ON THE FIRST NIGHT OF THE U.S. OPEN, AND WHERE, NEED-
LESS TO SAY, SHE DEFEATED HER OPPONENT. "THIS IS MY NEW DESIGN, IT'S MY LITTLE
CATSUIT," SERENA SAID OF THE SHIMMERING, BODY-CLINGING BLACK LYCRA UNI-
TARD SHE COURAGEOUSLY CLAD HERSELF IN FOR THE MATCH. "IT MAKES ME RUN
FASTER AND JUMP HIGHER", SHE SAID, "AND IT'S REALLY SEXY. I LOVE IT." SERENA
AND HER SISTER VENUS ARE NOT ONLY SETTING THE PACE ON THE COURT THESE DAYS,
BUT ARE ALSO DRIVING ON-COURT FASHION IN THE EVER-MORE STYLISH WORLD
OF WOMEN'S CHAMPIONSHIP TENNIS.

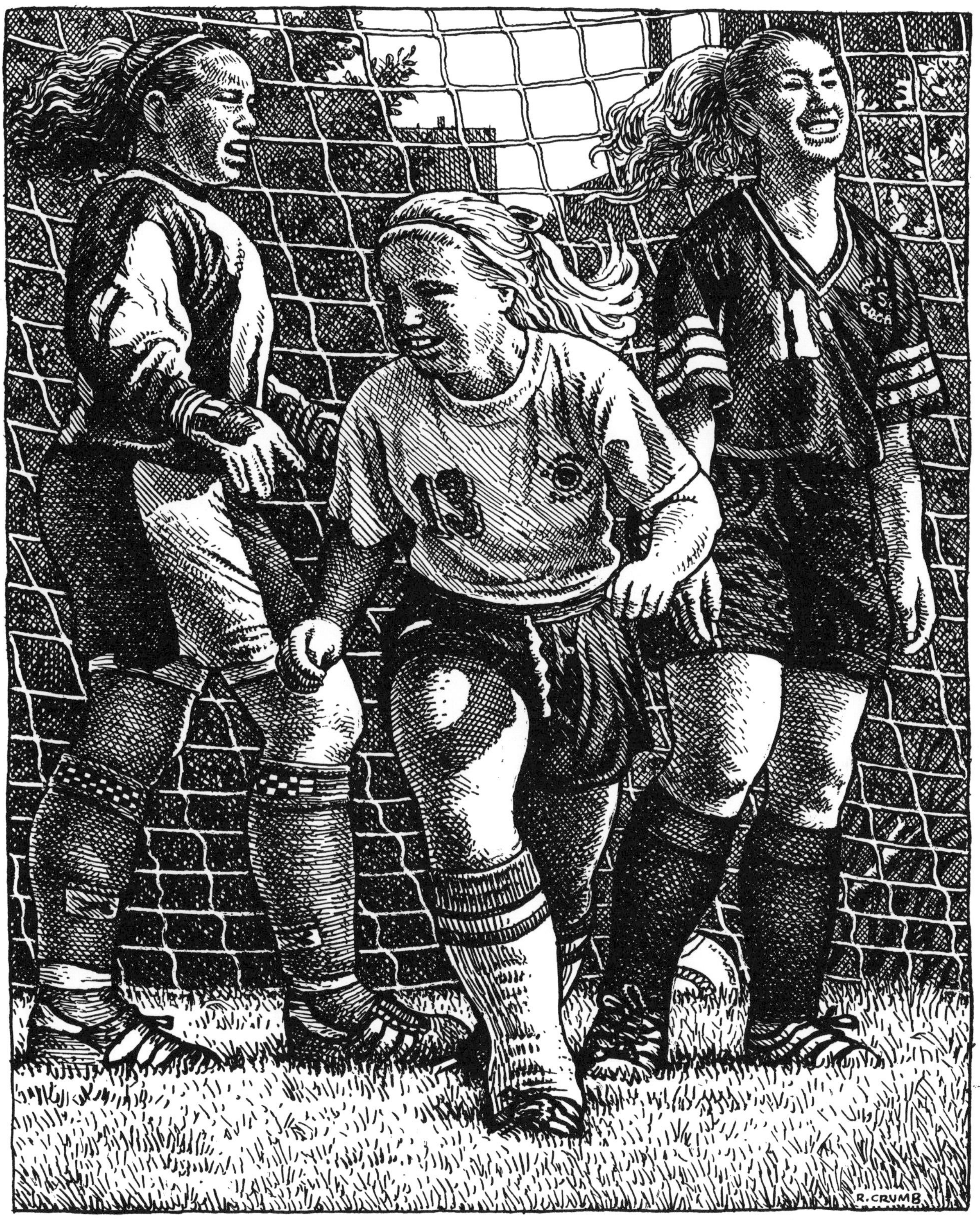

THE THREE GRACES, AMERICAN STYLE

AS THE GREAT SHOWMAN FLORENCE ZIGFELD ONCE SAID, "THERE IS NOTHING WHICH THE AMERICAN GIRL IS NOT CAPABLE OF ACCOMPLISHING." ALL THE TRADITIONAL LIMITS IMPOSED ON THE FEMALE OF THE SPECIES FROM TIME IMMEMORIAL HAVE BEEN, ONE BY ONE, BOLDLY BRUSHED ASIDE BY THE ASSERTIVE, FORCEFUL DAUGHTERS OF THE NEW RACE WHICH INHABITS THE AMERICAN CONTINENT. THE WORLD HAS NEVER BEFORE SEEN THEIR LIKE. THE THREE HIGH-SCHOOL SOCCER PLAYERS CAPTURED IN ACTION IN THIS FINE RENDITION ARE THE NORM TODAY RATHER THAN THE EXCEPTION. THESE HEALTHY, VIGOROUS YOUNG MAIDENS ARE ENTIRELY FREE TO TEST THE LIMITS OF THEIR GREAT ENERGY, STAMINA AND INTELLIGENCE. ONLY TIME WILL REVEAL THE PROMISE OF THIS NEW "BALL GAME," THIS NEW STAGE OF HUMAN EVOLUTION!

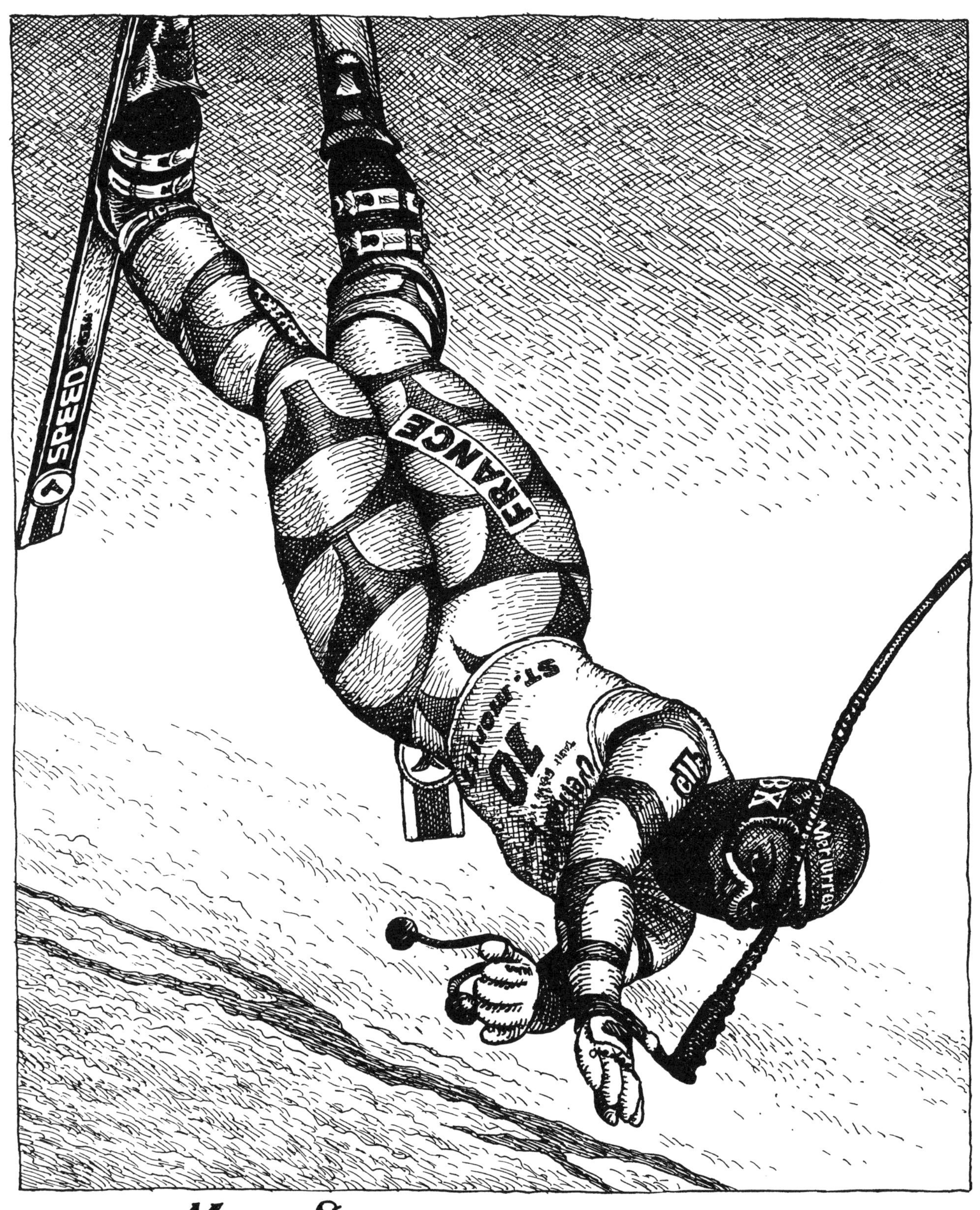

Melanie Suchet, DOWNHILL SKIER, IS CAUGHT SUS-PENDED IN MID-AIR, A MOMENT BEFORE HER FINE, STRONG FORM CAME CRASHING TO THE EARTH, IN A RECENT COMPETITION AT ST. MORITZ. THE VIEWER IS AFFORDED A DYNAMIC PORTRAYAL OF THE LITHE BEAUTY AND GRACE OF THIS FRENCH FEMALE CHAMPION, HER FIGURE IN SPECTACULAR MOTION. TRAGEDY WAS AVERTED AS THE YOUNG ATHLETE SUFFERED ONLY TORN KNEE LIGAMENTS AS A RESULT OF THE ACCIDENT.

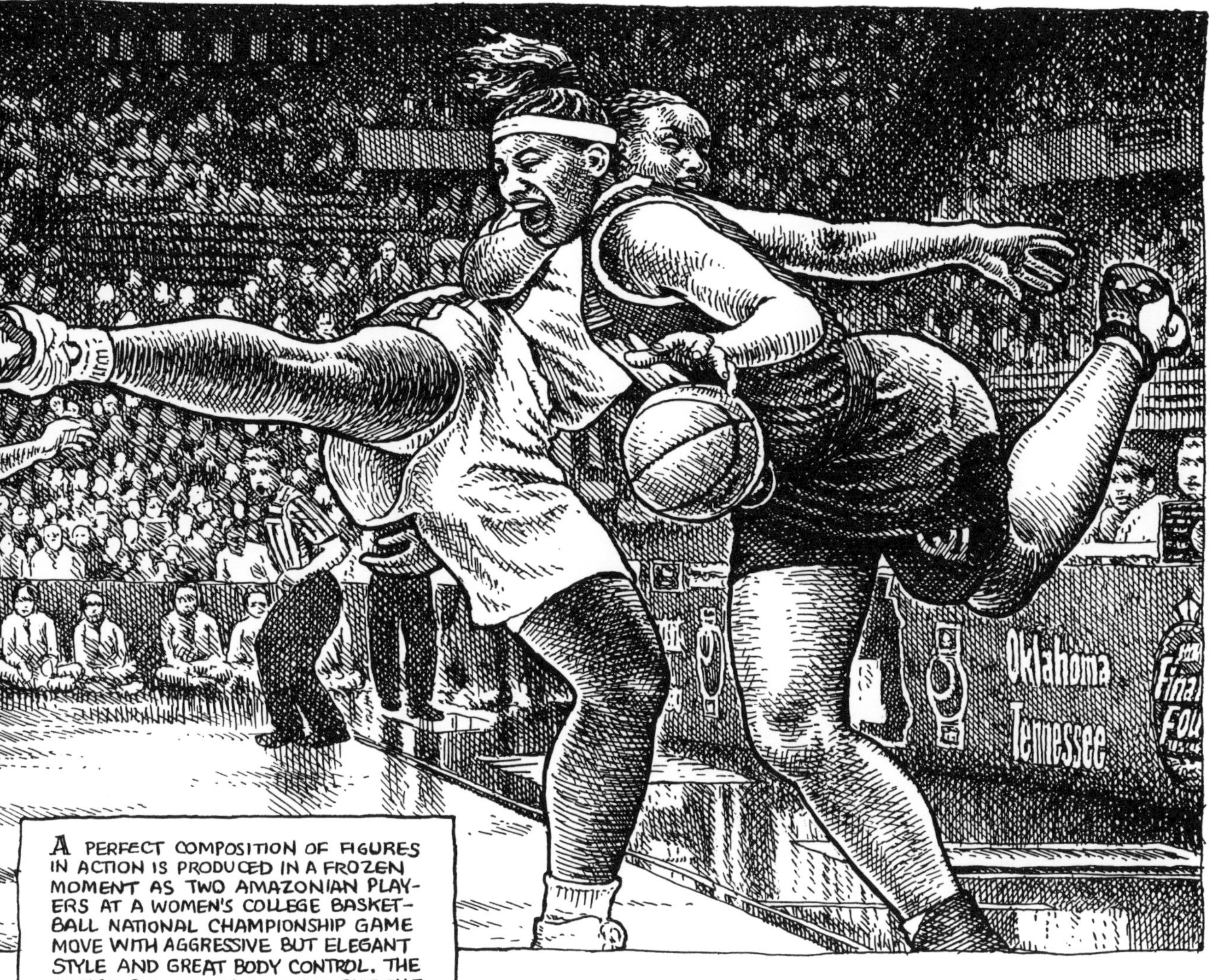

A PERFECT COMPOSITION OF FIGURES IN ACTION IS PRODUCED IN A FROZEN MOMENT AS TWO AMAZONIAN PLAYERS AT A WOMEN'S COLLEGE BASKETBALL NATIONAL CHAMPIONSHIP GAME MOVE WITH AGGRESSIVE BUT ELEGANT STYLE AND GREAT BODY CONTROL. THE ARTIST SKILLFULLY CAPTURES BUT ONE OF A THOUSAND SUCH MOMENTS OF SYMMETRY AND GRACE SHOWN BY THE YOUNG WOMEN IN THESE GAMES AS THEY FIGHT TO BRING THEIR TEAMS TO GLORIOUS VICTORY!

"WHY DOES NOT ONE HOLD TO WHAT ONE HAS, LIKE THE DOCTORS AND THE ENGINEERS? ONCE A THING IS DISCOVERED AND INVENTED, THEY RETAIN THE KNOWLEDGE; IN THESE WRETCHED FINE ARTS EVERYTHING IS FORGOTTEN, NOTHING IS KEPT.

MILLET GAVE THE SYNTHESIS OF THE PEASANT... THEN HAVE WE IN GENERAL LEARNED HOW TO SEE THE PEASANT? NO, HARDLY ANYONE KNOWS HOW TO KNOCK ONE OFF.

IS THE FAULT REALLY NOT A LITTLE WITH PARIS AND THE PARISIANS, CHANGEABLE AND FAITHLESS AS THE SEA?

WELL, YOU HAVE DAMN GOOD REASON TO SAY, LET US GO QUIETLY ON OUR WAY, WORKING FOR OURSELVES. YOU KNOW, WHATEVER THIS SACROSANCT IMPRESSIONISM MAY BE, ALL THE SAME I WISH I COULD PAINT THINGS THAT THE GENERATION BEFORE; DELACROIX, MILLET, ROUSSEAU, DIAZ, MONTICELLI, ISABEY, DÉCAMPS, DUPRÉ, JONGKIND, ZIEM, ISRAELS, MEUNIER, A HEAP OF OTHERS; COROT, JACQUE, ETC., COULD UNDERSTAND."

~~~ VINCENT VAN GOGH, ARLES, 1888
— LETTER TO HIS BROTHER THEO

"THE ARTIST SHOULD NOT SACRIFICE HIS IDEALS TO A LANDLORD AND A COSTLY STUDIO. A RAIN-TIGHT ROOF, FRUGAL LIVING, A BOX OF COLORS, AND GOD'S SUNLIGHT THROUGH CLEAR WINDOWS KEEP THE SOUL ATTUNED AND THE BODY VIGOROUS FOR ONE'S DAILY WORK. THE ARTIST SHOULD ONCE AND FOREVER EMANCIPATE HIMSELF FROM THE BONDAGE OF APPEARANCE AND THE UNPARDONABLE SIN OF EXPENDING ON IGNOBLE AIMS THE PRECIOUS OINTMENT THAT SHOULD SERVE ONLY TO NOURISH THE LAMP BURNING BEFORE THE TABERNACLE OF HIS MUSE."

~~~ ALBERT PINKHAM RYDER

"A PAINTING SHOULD FIRST AND FOREMOST BE A FEAST FOR THE EYE."

~~~ EUGÈNE DELACROIX
~~~

"My aim in painting has always been the most exact transcription possible of my most intimate impressions of nature. If this end is unattainable, so, it can be said, is perfection in any other ideal of painting, or in any other of man's activities....
    I have tried to present my sensations in what is the most congenial and impressive form possible for me. The technical obstacles of painting perhaps dictate this form. It derives also from the limitations of personality. Of such may be the simplifications that I have attempted."

~~~ Edward Hopper, 1933

"People ask me why I draw. My answer is always pretty much the same. I do it because my stomach keeps getting hungry and I need to make a living."

~~~ Harvey Kurtzman

"Pamela Lee has written that to say 'drawing is process' is almost tautological, for 'nothing could seem more obvious than the way in which drawing registers the process of the artist's making'. Perhaps, however, this notion of drawing as process should be seen as developing from specific moments in time and taste, rather than as a given."

~~~ Laura Hoptman, *Drawing Now*, 2002

"The artist must scorn all judgment that is not based on an intelligent observation of character. He must beware of the literary spirit which so often causes painting to deviate from its true path—the concrete study of nature—to lose itself all too long in intangible speculations."

~~~ Paul Cézanne, 1904

"Never a day without a line."

~~~ Vincent van Gogh

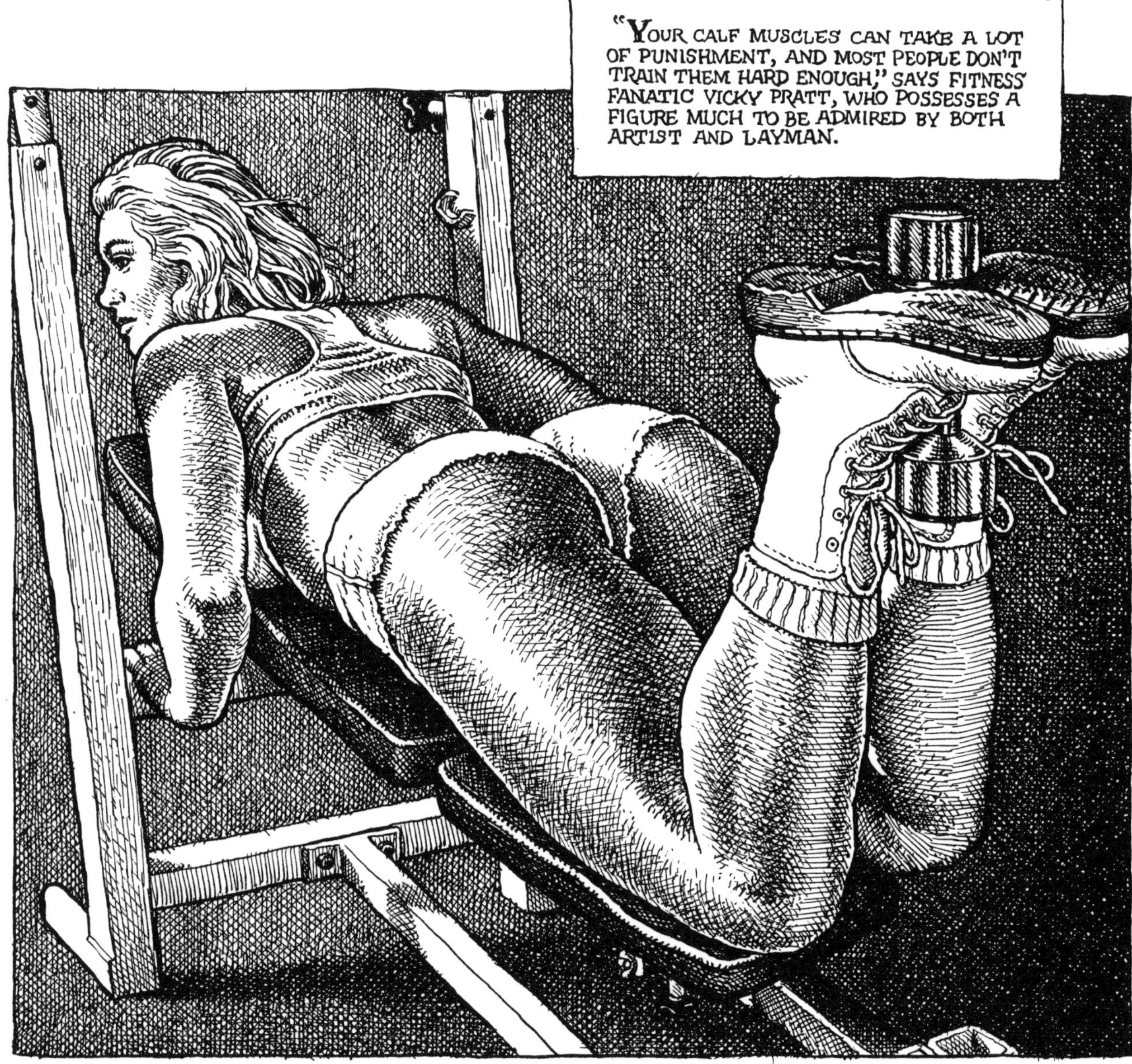
~~~

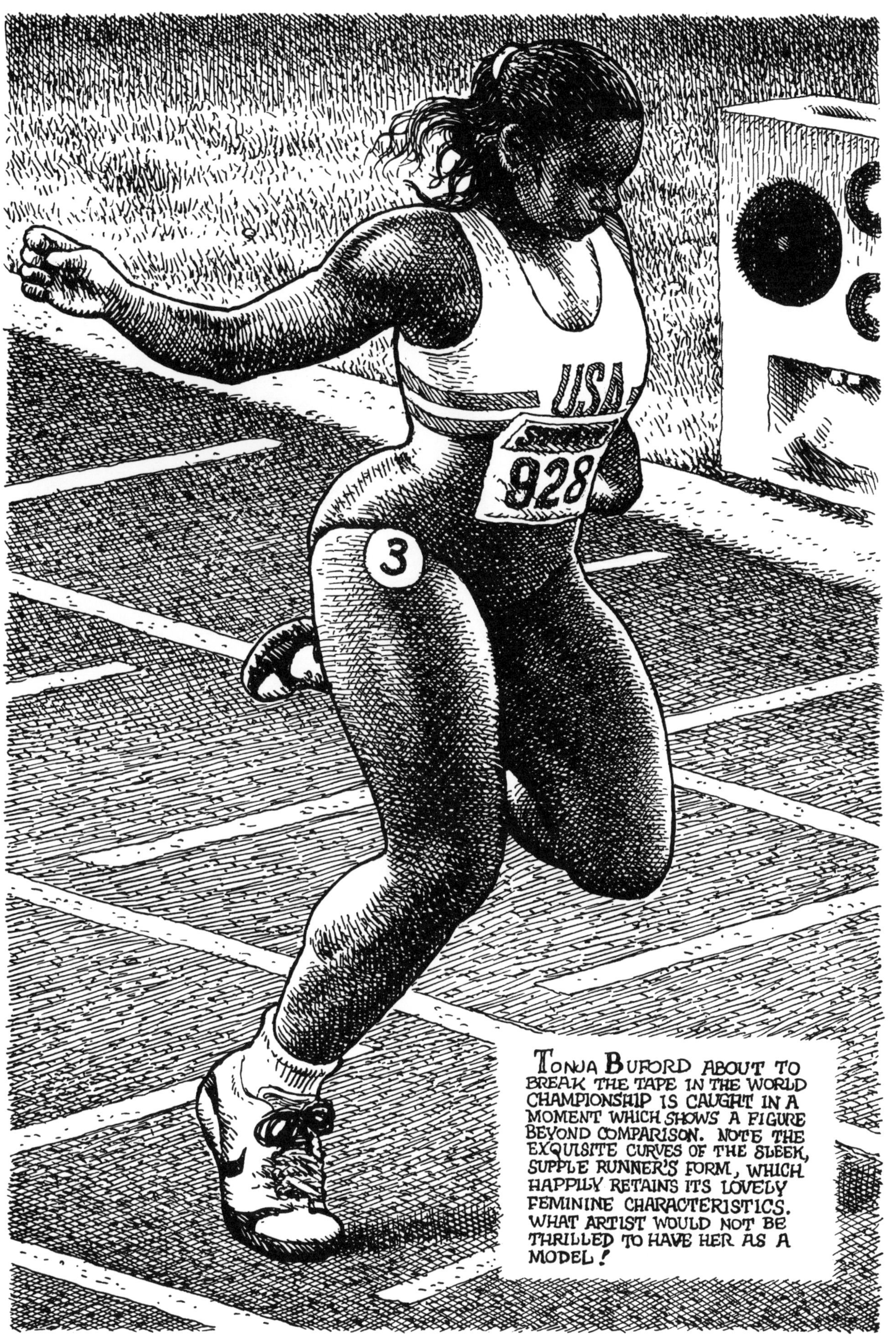

TONJA BUFORD ABOUT TO BREAK THE TAPE IN THE WORLD CHAMPIONSHIP IS CAUGHT IN A MOMENT WHICH SHOWS A FIGURE BEYOND COMPARISON. NOTE THE EXQUISITE CURVES OF THE SLEEK, SUPPLE RUNNER'S FORM, WHICH HAPPILY RETAINS ITS LOVELY FEMININE CHARACTERISTICS. WHAT ARTIST WOULD NOT BE THRILLED TO HAVE HER AS A MODEL!

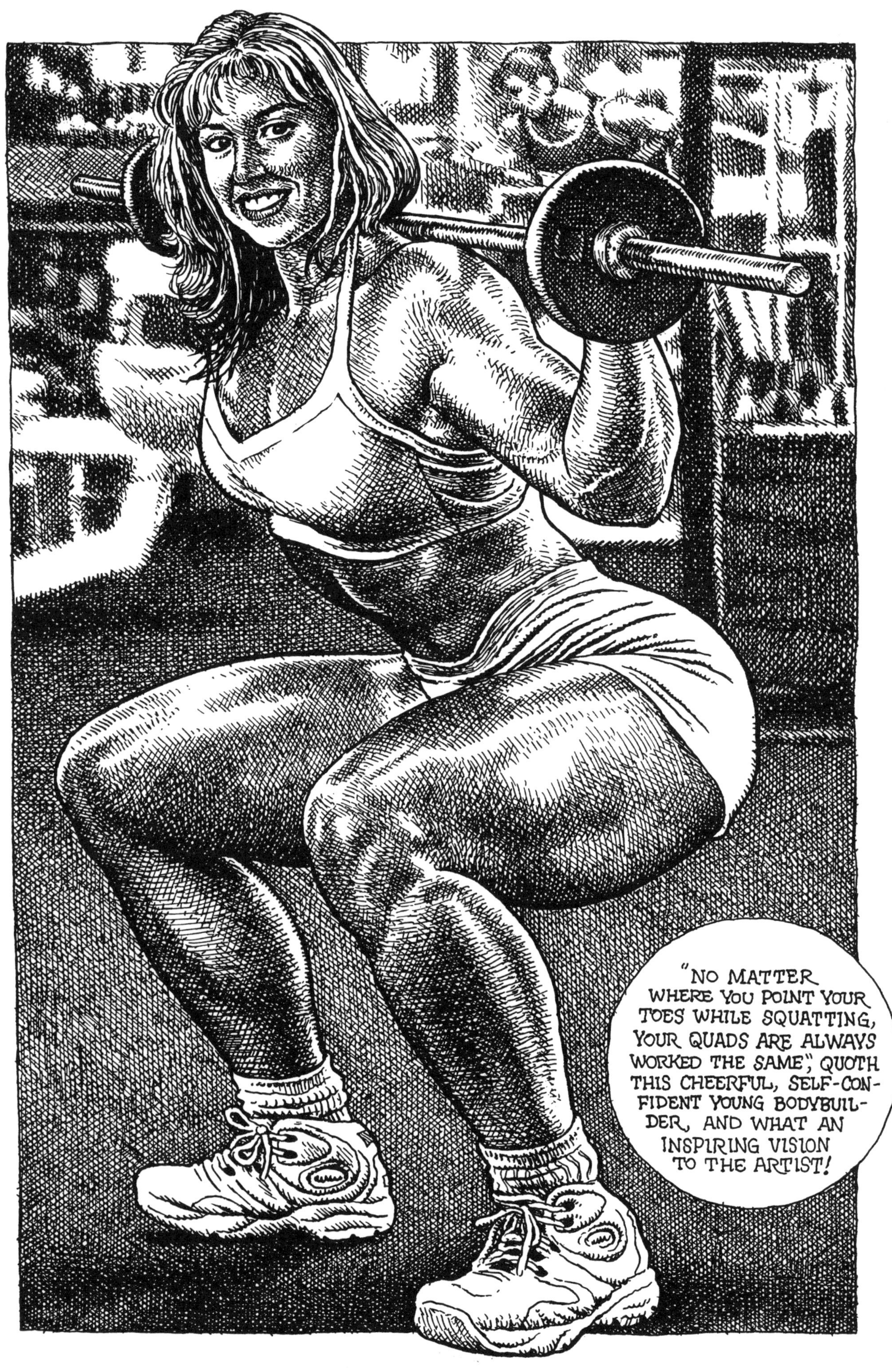

"NO MATTER WHERE YOU POINT YOUR TOES WHILE SQUATTING, YOUR QUADS ARE ALWAYS WORKED THE SAME," QUOTH THIS CHEERFUL, SELF-CONFIDENT YOUNG BODYBUILDER, AND WHAT AN INSPIRING VISION TO THE ARTIST!

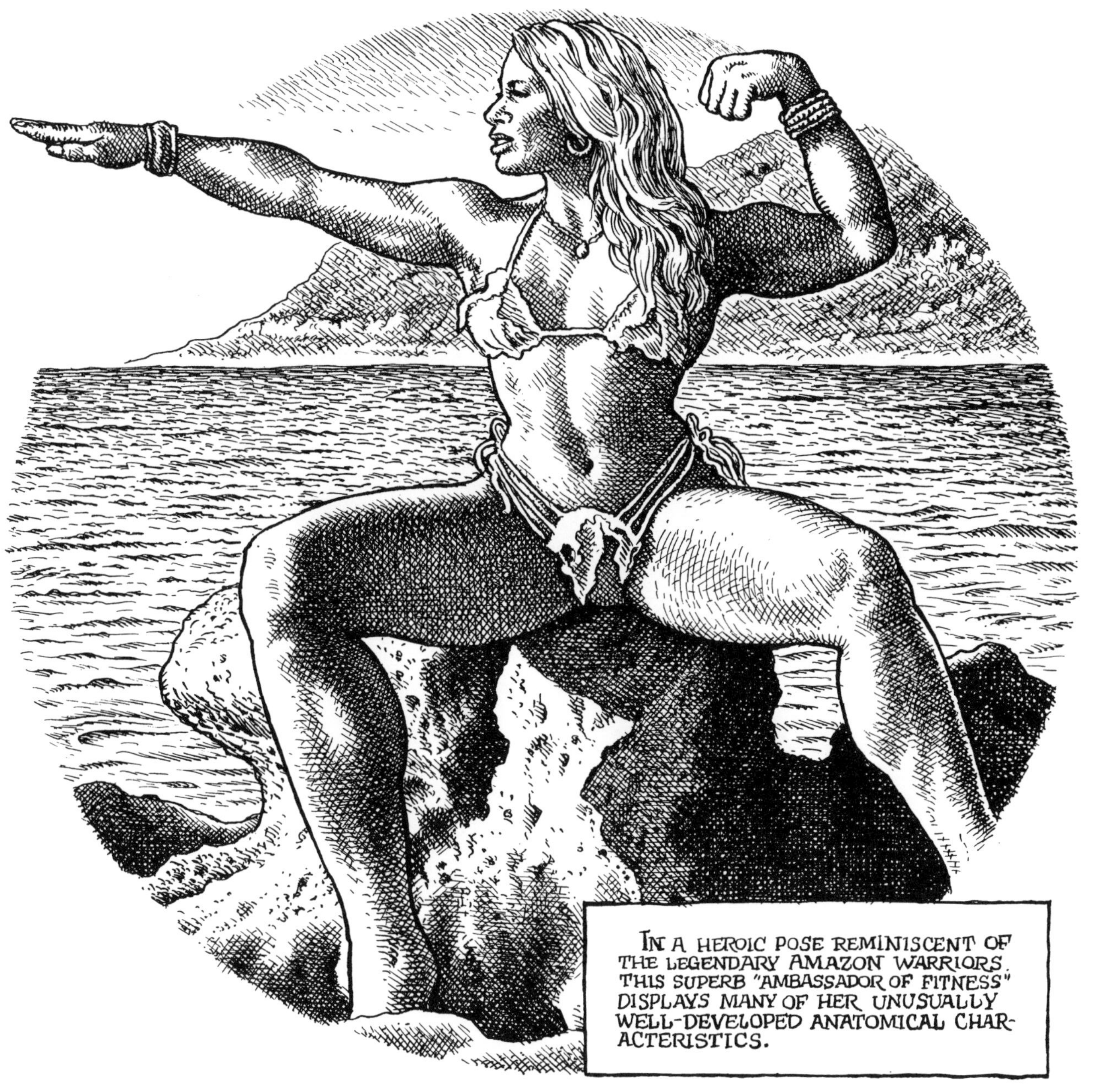

In a heroic pose reminiscent of the legendary Amazon warriors, this superb "Ambassador of Fitness" displays many of her unusually well-developed anatomical characteristics.

"It is my misfortune — and probably my delight — to use things as my passion tells me. What a miserable fate for a painter who adores blondes to have to stop himself putting them into a picture because they don't go with the basket of fruit! ...I put all the things I like into my pictures. The things—so much the worse for them; they just have to put up with it."

~~~ Picasso

"Art should give pleasure."

~~~ Aristide Maillol, 1861-1944

"A work of art must carry in itself its complete significance and impose it upon the beholder even before he can identify the subject matter."

~~~ Henri Matisse

"All the sentiment of a work of art comes unconsciously, or nearly so, from the state of the artist's soul. 'He who wishes to paint Christ's story must live with Christ,' said Fra Angelico."

~~~ Maurice Denis, 1870-1943

"...I say that the artist must lift himself above all external circumstance, even above himself, for, last but not least, he must in his works achieve a bold and unhampered resolution that denies all pain and trouble, or at least hides them from the eyes of the world"

~~~ Hans von Marées, 1837-1887
~~~

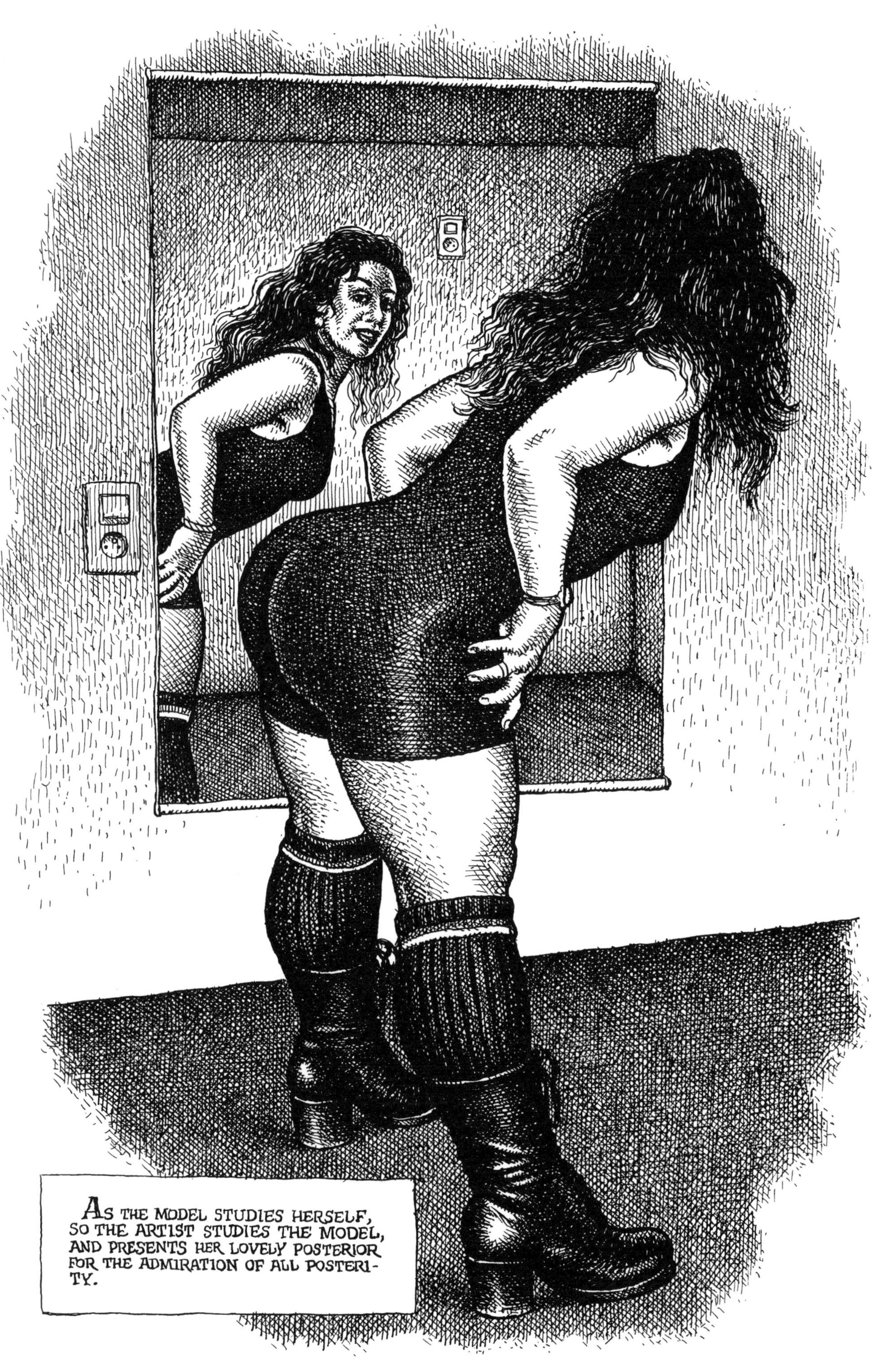

As the model studies herself,
so the artist studies the model,
and presents her lovely posterior
for the admiration of all posteri-
ty.

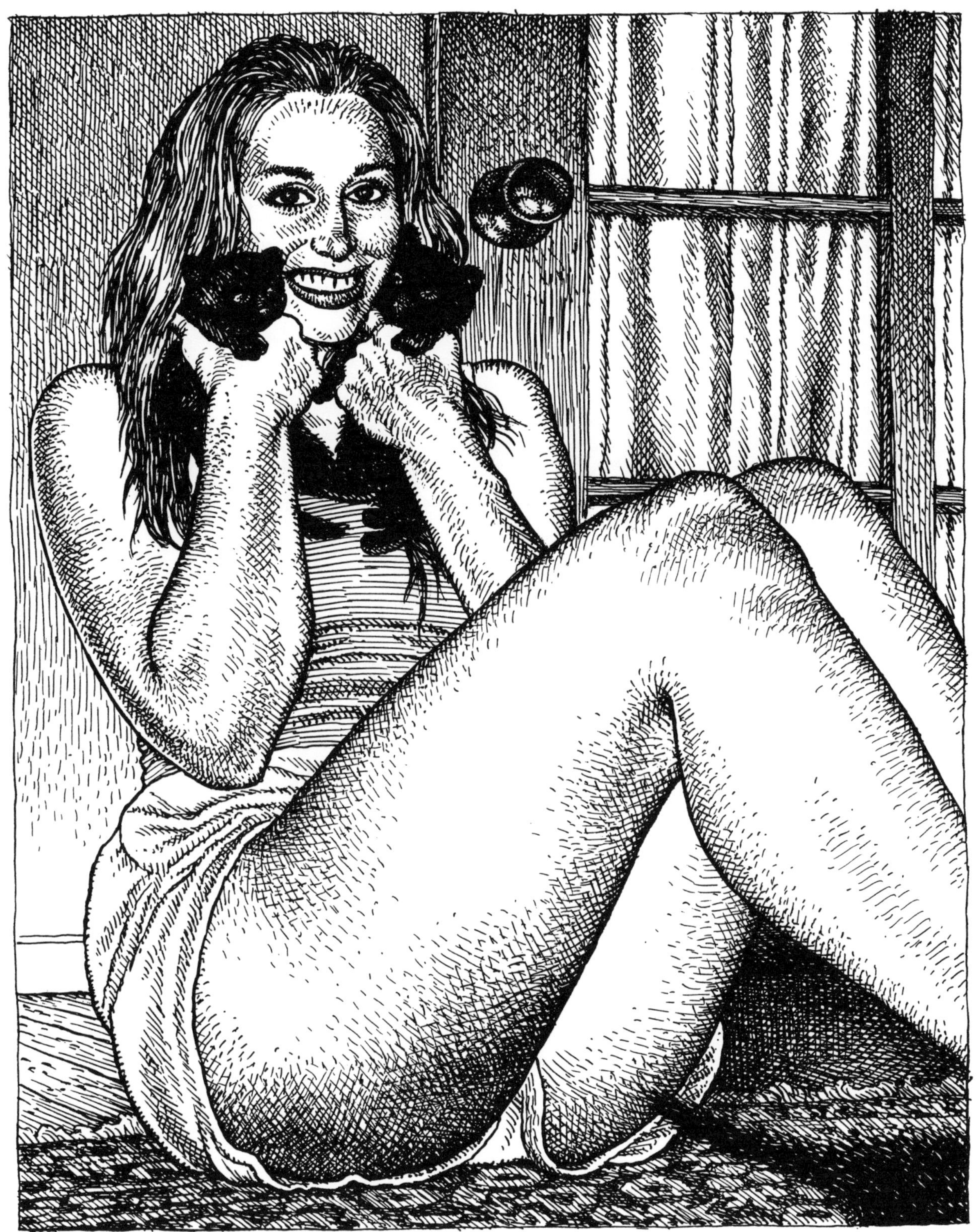

THE MAGNIFICENTLY MOLDED CURVES AND
SUPERIOR BONE STRUCTURE OF THIS BEAUTIFUL
LOVER OF ANIMALS, AND HER PROVOCATIVE SMILE,
ARE RENDERED WITH THE TRUE SENSE OF PULS-
ATING, VIBRANT LIFE WHICH SERVED TO BRING
FAME AND FORTUNE TO THE ARTIST.

"IT WAS THE PRESUMPTIVE, STERILE 'CRITICS', THE ABOMINABLE PESTS, THAT INFECTED THE WORLD WITH THE PLAGUE OF MODERNISM... NO WRITER ON ART DESERVES TO BE LISTENED TO, SINCE ALL THEIR THEORIZING COMES OUT OF THE DREGS OF AN EMPTY BOTTOM. THERE WAS NO EPOCH IN THE HISTORY OF THE WORLD AS IMPOVERISHED, AS TOTALLY STERILE, AS SUICIDALLY THRASHING AS A FISH OUT OF WATER, AS OURS. WE ARE THE VICTIMS OF 'MODERNISM' THAT WAS ENCRUSTED ON THIS POOPED-OUT ANCIENT VOLCANO BY TOTAL ABSENCE OF TALENTS, THE CHIEF CARRIERS OF THIS PLAGUE BEING THE 'CRITICS OF ART.' THEY DESTROY OUR CULTURE, WHAT REMAINS OF IT."

~~~ STANISLAV SZUKALSKI, LOS ANGELES, 1980

"AFTER A HIATUS IN THE 1980S, THE 1990S USHERED IN AN EFFLORESCENCE OF CONTEMPORARY DRAWING NOT SEEN SINCE THE HEYDAY OF 'POST-MINIMALISM.'"

~~~ LAURA HOPTMAN, *DRAWING NOW*, 2002

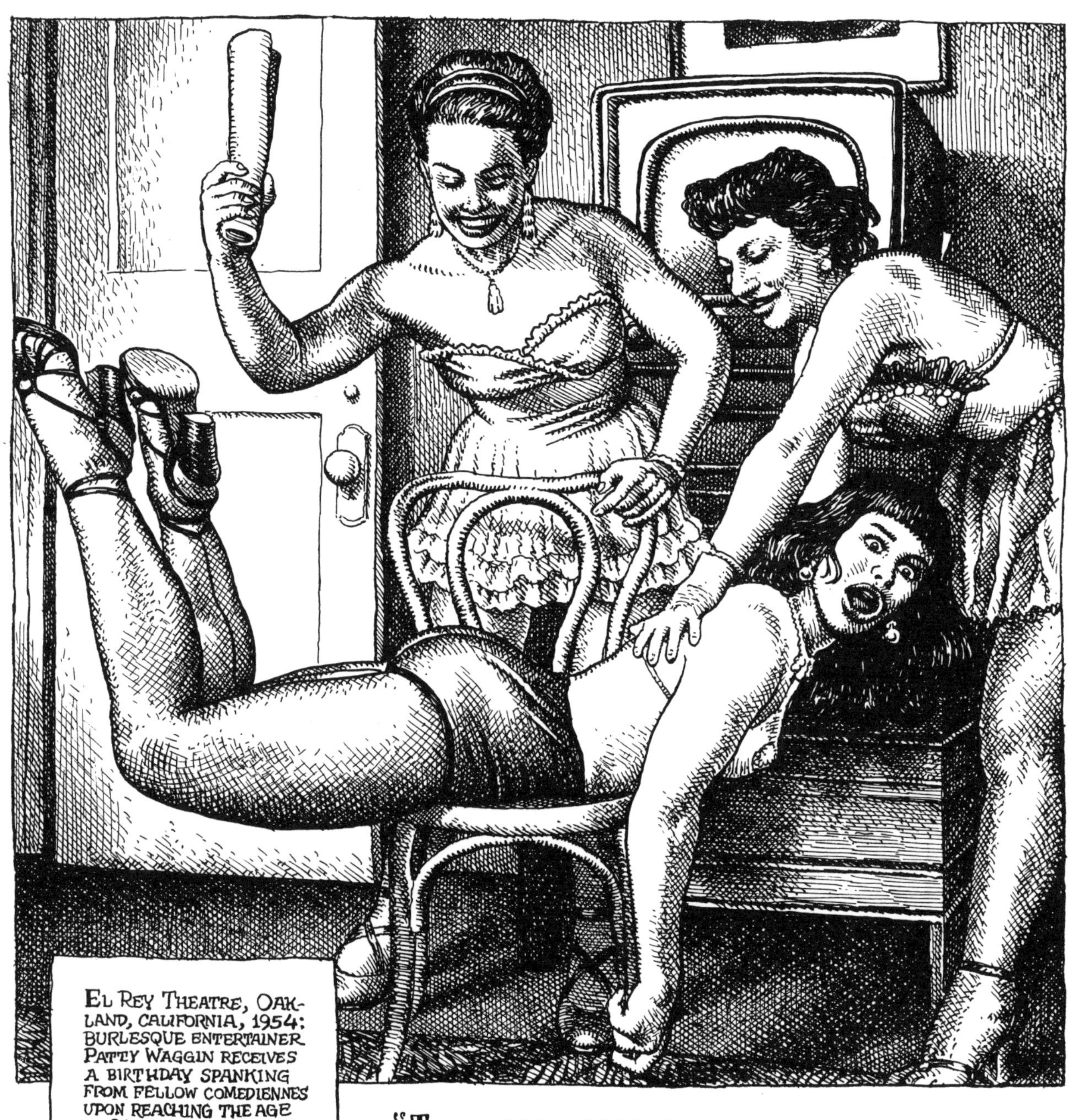

EL REY THEATRE, OAKLAND, CALIFORNIA, 1954: BURLESQUE ENTERTAINER PATTY WAGGIN RECEIVES A BIRTHDAY SPANKING FROM FELLOW COMEDIENNES UPON REACHING THE AGE OF 21. FOR THE ARTIST THE PICTURE PRESENTS A LIVELY COMPOSITION OF THREE WELL-FORMED FEMALE FIGURES IN A RABELAISIAN ACTION POSE.

"THE ARTIST HAS ONLY TO REMAIN TRUE TO HIS DREAM AND IT WILL POSSESS HIS WORK IN SUCH A MANNER THAT IT WILL RESEMBLE THE WORK OF NO OTHER MAN—FOR NO TWO VISIONS ARE ALIKE, AND THOSE WHO REACH THE HEIGHTS HAVE ALL TOILED UP THE STEEP MOUNTAINS BY A DIFFERENT ROUTE. TO EACH HAS BEEN REVEALED A DIFFERENT PANORAMA."

~~~ ALFRED PINKHAM RYDER
~~~

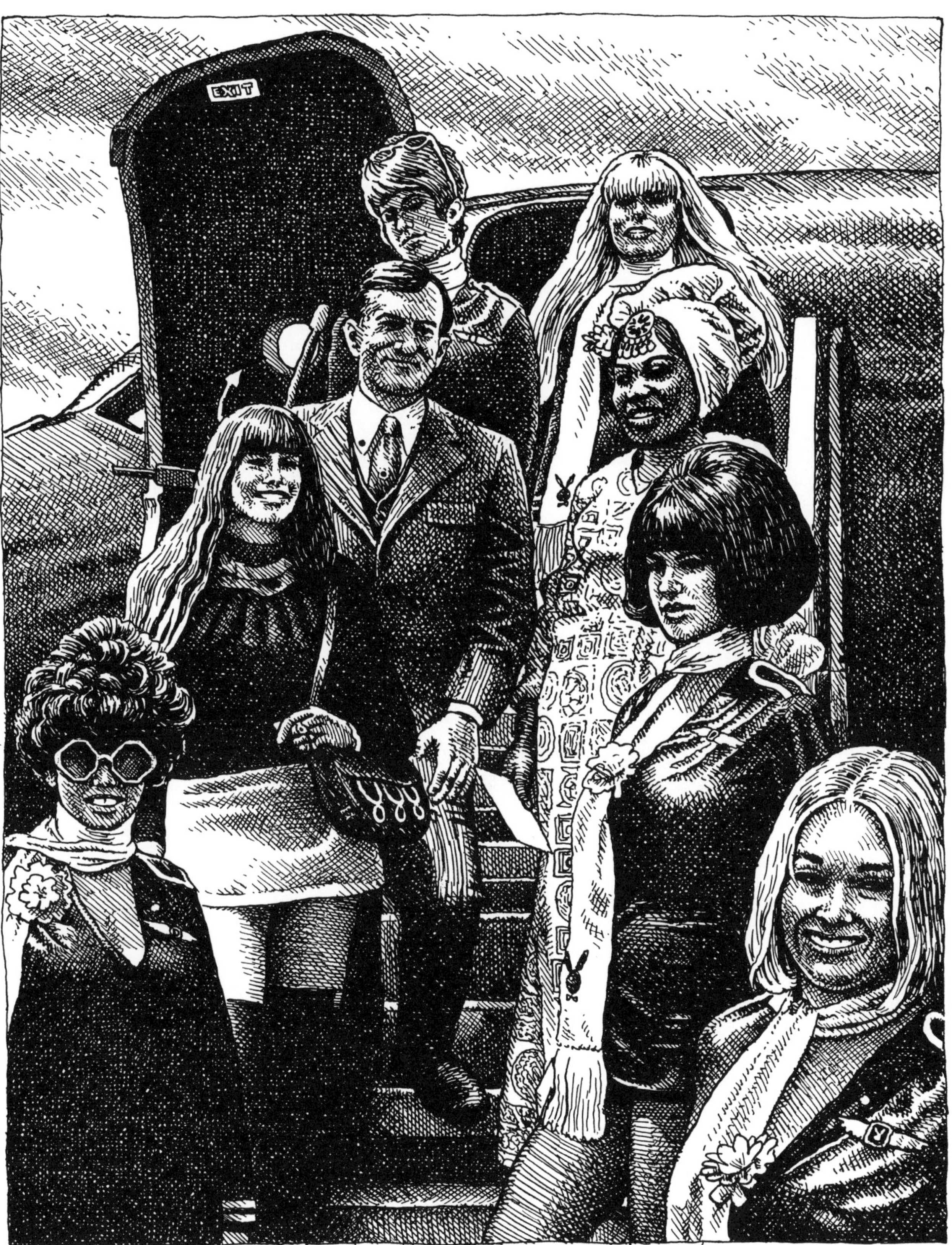

HERE IS A MAN WHO IS ALWAYS SURROUNDED BY BEAUTIFUL WOMEN. THIS FINELY DETAILED PEN-AND-INK DRAWING DEPICTS HUGH M. HEFNER IN 1970, WHEN HIS "PLAYBOY" EMPIRE WAS AT ITS PEAK. MR. HEFNER IS SEEN ALIGHTING FROM THE "BIG BUNNY", HIS PRIVATE JET PLANE, AT EMBAKOSI AIRPORT IN NAIROBI, AFRICA, ACCOMPANIED BY HIS SWEETHEART, BARBI BENTON, AND MEMBERS OF THE FLIGHT CREW. HE IS BEING GREETED BY JOSEPHINE MIKUBU, MISS KENYA. "HEF" AND BARBI WERE ABOUT TO EMBARK ON AN AFRICAN SAFARI.

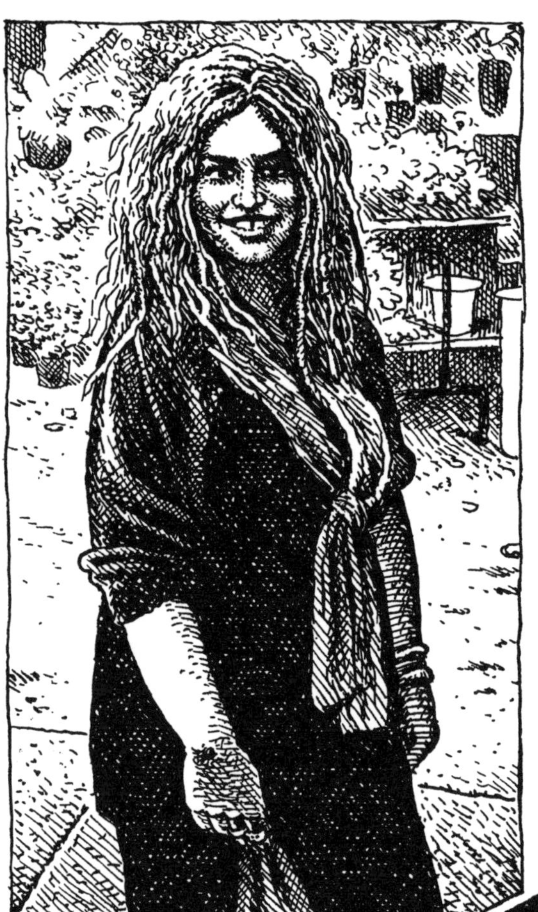

Girls

BEAUTY

THREE PORTRAITS WHICH PROVE BEYOND ALL DOUBT THAT THE OLD MASTER OF ALL-THAT-IS SURE-LY IS UTTERLY INDIFFERENT TO CLASS DISTINCTIONS IN THE GRANTING OF THE GIFT OF PHYSICAL BEAUTY TO HIS CREATURES HERE BELOW. THE STRIKING YOUNG FEMALE VAGABONDS IN THESE DRAWINGS COMPARE FAVORABLY WITH THE MOST RAVISHING INGENUES OF THE SCREEN, OR THE MOST HIGHLY ESTEEMED MODELS IN THE WORLD OF FASHION, PERHAPS EVEN MORE SO, IN THEIR VIBRANT NATURALNESS AND IN THE ABSENCE OF ARTIFICIAL AIDS TO THEIR YOUTHFUL PERFECTION. ONE ONLY HOPES AND PRAYS THAT THE HARSHNESS OF LIFE ON THE STREETS DOES NOT RAVAGE TOO SEVERELY THE INNER AND OUTER QUALITIES WHICH GIVE THESE ADVENTUROUS STREET-FEMMES THEIR POWERFUL ATTRAC-TIVENESS, AND THAT SOON THEY WILL END THIS DANG-EROUS HAND-TO-MOUTH EXISTENCE, AND WILL FIND A PLACE TO CALL HOME.

TWO VIEWS OF THE WILD AND VIVA-CIOUS ONE THEY CALL "GYPSY" ON THE STREETS OF BERKELEY, WHO IMPRESSES ONE AS BOTH BEAUTIFUL AND STRONG.

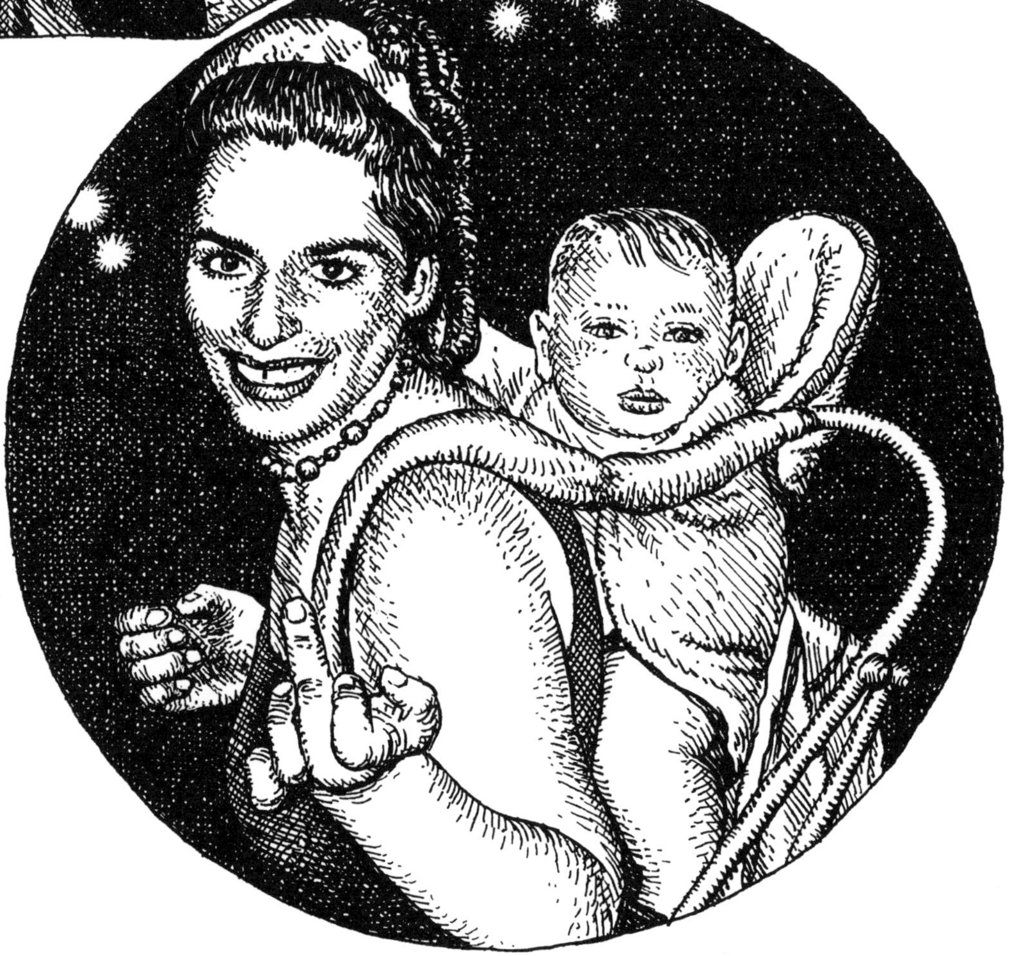

Of the Street

.....IS WHERE YOU FIND IT!

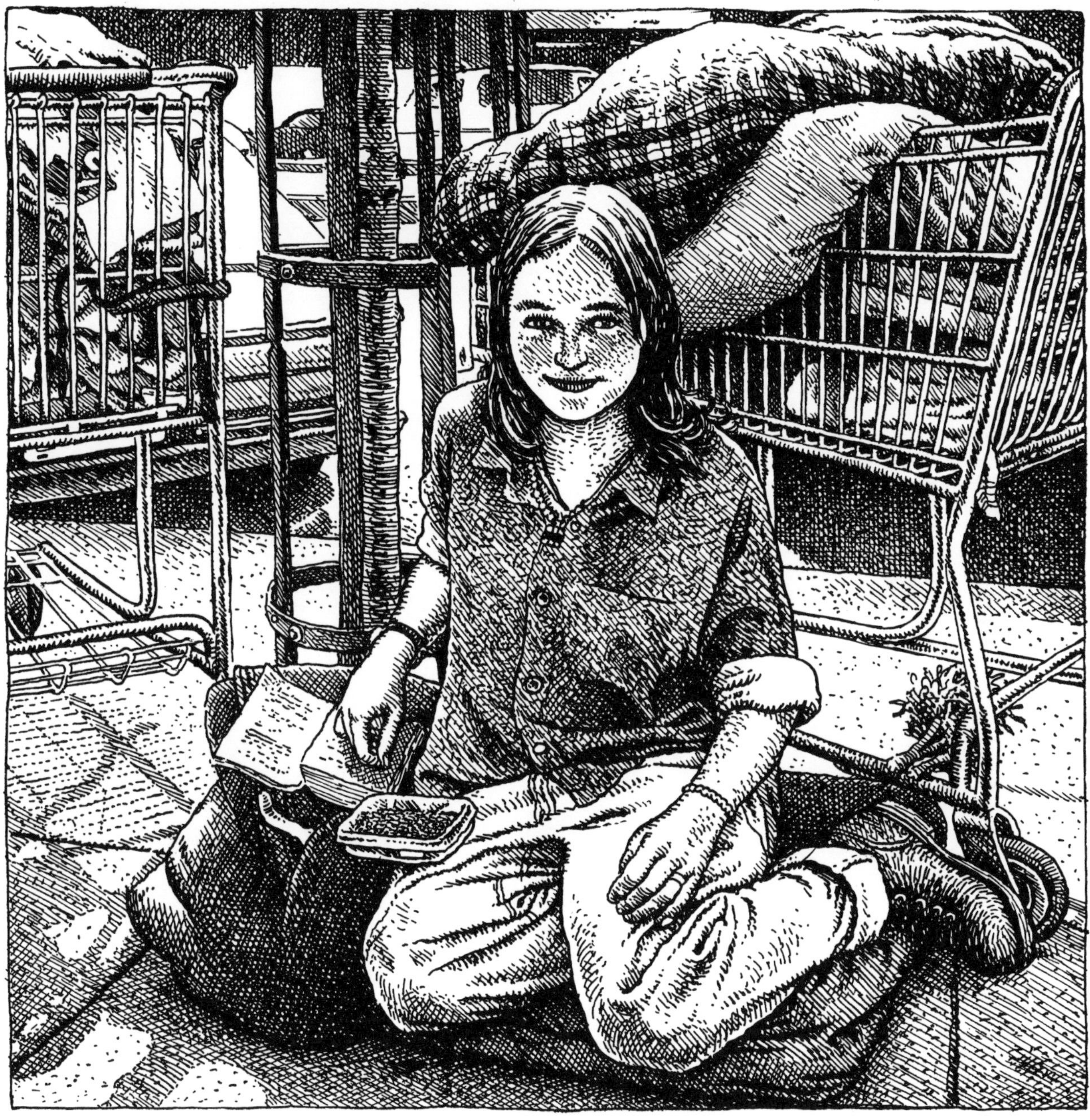

AN IMAGE THAT WILL TUG AT THE HEART-STRINGS OF ANYONE WHO HAS EVER HAD A SISTER OR A DAUGHTER THAT THEY LOVED. THE INNOCENCE AND OPENNESS ON THE FACE OF THIS YOUNG HOMELESS GIRL, WITH ALL HER WORLDLY POSSESSIONS IN TWO SUPERMARKET SHOPPING CARTS, COMPELS ONE TO WONDER HOW THINGS COULD HAVE COME TO SUCH A PASS IN THESE UNITED STATES. WHAT'S TO BECOME OF THIS SWEET-FACED STREET URCHIN, LIVING IN THE ANARCHIC AND OFTEN VIOLENT WORLD OF THE DISPOSSESSED ?? ALL THAT'S LEFT TO SAY IS, WHAT A WORLD!

THESE DRAWINGS WERE RENDERED FROM PHOTOGRAPHS REPRODUCED IN THE *TELEGRAPH STREET* CALENDAR FOR THE YEARS 1998, '99 & 2000, PUBLISHED BY ACE BACKWORDS AND B.N. DUNCAN, BERKELEY, CALIFORNIA.

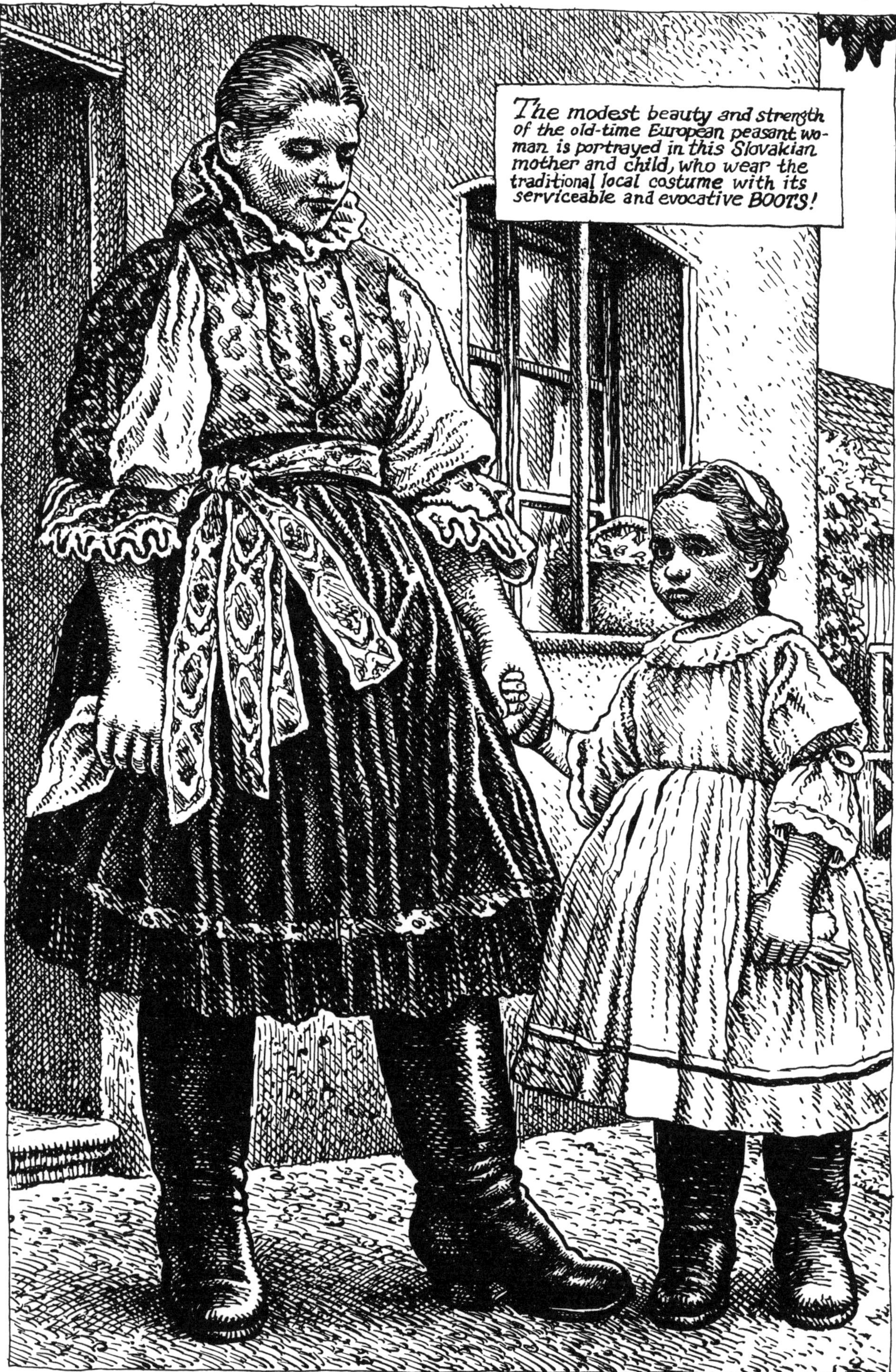
The modest beauty and strength of the old-time European peasant woman is portrayed in this Slovakian mother and child, who wear the traditional local costume with its serviceable and evocative BOOTS!

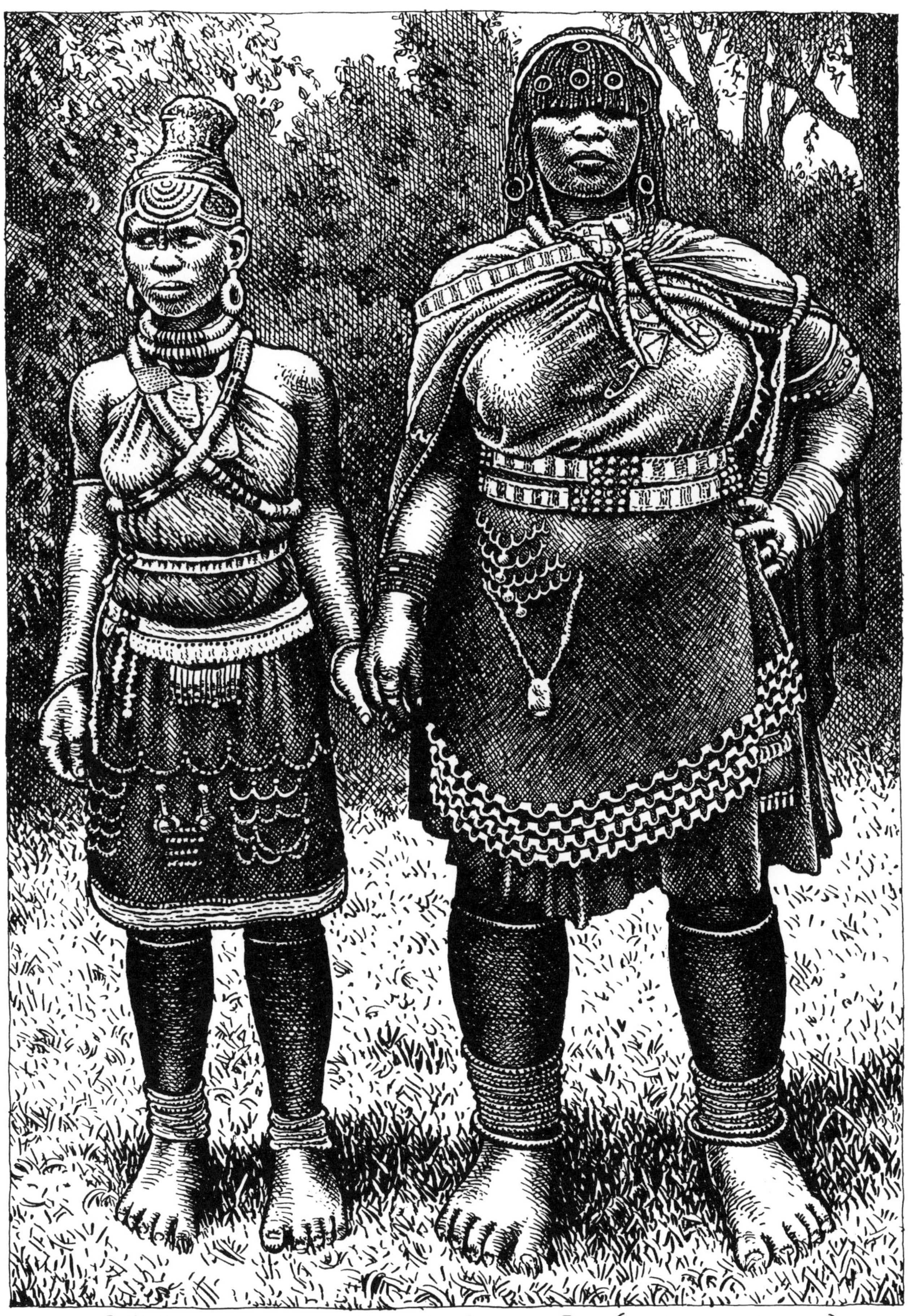

HANDSOME WOMEN OF THE FORMIDABLE ZULU RACE (SOUTH AFRICA, EARLY 1900s)
IN THOSE TIMES THE ZULU WOMAN'S HAIR WAS ARRANGED IN FANTASTIC FASHIONS, TWISTED AND PLASTERED INTO A HARD HIGH TOPKNOT OR WONDERFULLY WAXED INTO MYRIAD HANGING CURLS, WHILE MUCH BEAD AND BONE TRUMPERY ADORNED HER CLOTHING.

ANOTHER POINT OF VIEW

THE NOVEL, PROVOCATIVE COSTUME AND REARVIEW POSES OF THIS BLONDE CALIFORNIA GIRL OF NORDIC ANCESTRY, TOGETHER WITH HER SOLIDLY STRUCTURED, WELL-DEVELOPED PHYSIQUE, ARE CONVINCING PROOF THAT THE ABOUT-FACE VIEW OF A FINELY-SHAPED MODEL CAN BE OF EQUAL INTEREST TO THE ARTIST AS ANY FRONTAL, PROFILE, OR THREE-QUARTERS POSITION.

"I MUST CREATE A SYSTEM OR BE ENSLAVED BY ANOTHER MAN'S ... MY BUSINESS IS TO CREATE."
~~~ WILLIAM BLAKE

"OH YOUNG ARTISTS, YOU SEARCH FOR A SUBJECT — EVERYTHING IS A SUBJECT. YOUR SUBJECT IS YOURSELF, YOUR IMPRESSIONS, YOUR EMOTIONS IN THE PRESENCE OF NATURE."
~~~ EUGÈNE DELACROIX

"THE GREAT QUALITY OF TRUE ART IS THAT IT REDISCOVERS, GRASPS AND REVEALS TO US A REALITY FAR FROM THAT IN WHICH WE LIVE, AND FROM WHICH WE GET FARTHER AND FARTHER REMOVED AS THE CONVENTIONAL KNOWLEDGE WE SUBSTITUTE FOR IT BECOMES THICKER AND MORE IMPERMEABLE."
~~~ MARCEL PROUST

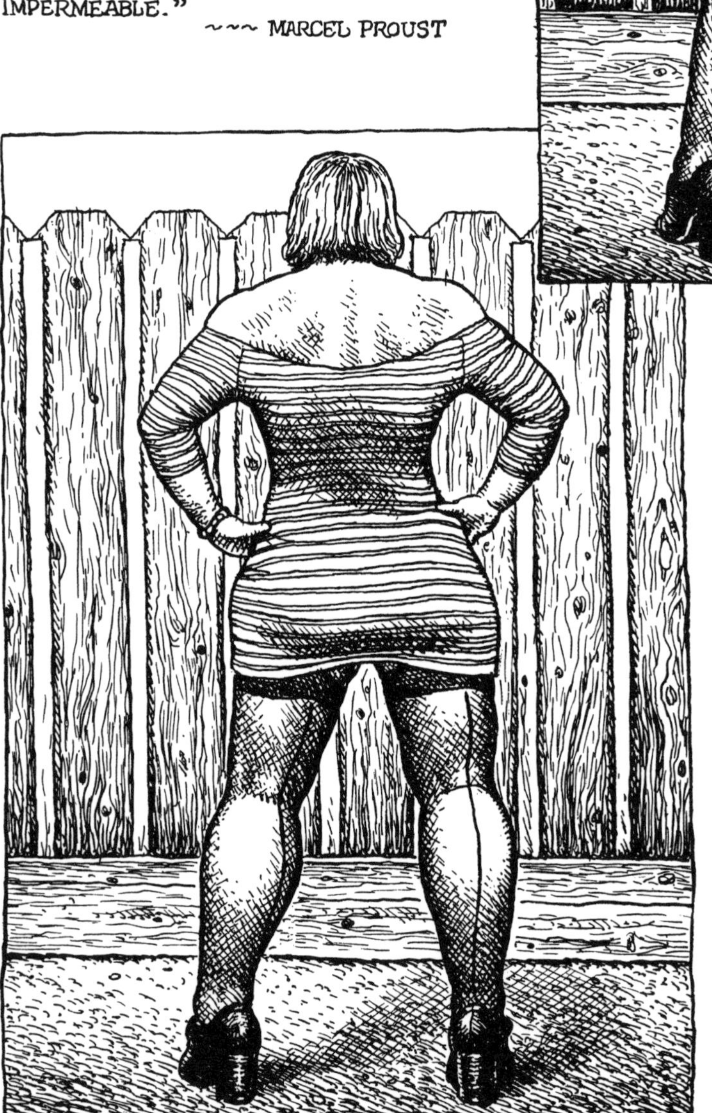

"ONE MUST KEEP RIGHT ON DRAWING. DRAW WITH YOUR EYES WHEN YOU CANNOT DRAW WITH A PENCIL. AS LONG AS YOU DO NOT HOLD A BALANCE BETWEEN YOUR SEEING OF THINGS AND YOUR EXECUTION, YOU WILL DO NOTHING THAT IS REALLY GOOD."
~~~ INGRES, 1780-1867

"PAINTING FROM NATURE IS NOT COPYING THE OBJECT, IT IS REALIZING ONE'S SENSATIONS."
~~~ JOHN CONSTABLE

"I MAINTAIN THAT ART IS COMPLETELY INDIVIDUAL, AND IS FOR EACH ARTIST NOTHING BUT THE TALENT ISSUING FROM HIS OWN INSPIRATION AND HIS OWN STUDIES OF TRADITION."
~~~ GUSTAVE COURBET

"ART IS ESSENTIALLY SERIOUS AND BENEFICIAL, A GAME PLAYED AGAINST CHAOS AND DEATH. ART BUILDS TEMPORARY WALLS AGAINST LIFE'S LEVELING FORCE, THE RUIN OF WHAT IS SPLENDIDLY UNNATURAL IN US; CONSCIOUSNESS.
A GOOD [WORK OF ART] IS ONE THAT, FOR ITS TIME, IS WISE, SANE, AND MAGICAL, ONE THAT CLARIFIES LIFE AND TENDS TO IMPROVE IT... TRUE ART TREATS IDEALS, AFFIRMING AND CLARIFYING THE GOOD, THE TRUE, AND THE BEAUTIFUL."
~~~ JOHN GARDNER
~~~

"THE IDEAL ARTIST IS THE SUPER-
MAN. HE USES EVERY POSSIBLE POW-
ER, SPIRIT, EMOTION, CONSCIOUS OR UN-
CONSCIOUS, TO ARRIVE AT HIS ENDS."
~~~ GEORGE BELLOWS

ADVICE TO THE PAINTER:
"O PAINTER, TAKE CARE LEST THE
GREED FOR GAIN PROVE A STRONGER
INCENTIVE THAN RENOWN IN ART, FOR
TO GAIN THIS RENOWN IS A FAR GREAT-
ER THING THAN IS THE PRESTIGE OF
RICHES."
~~~ LEONARDO DA VINCI

"PAINTING IS A VERY DIFFICULT
THING. IT ABSORBS THE WHOLE MAN,
BODY AND SOUL. THUS I HAVE PASSED
BLINDLY MANY THINGS WHICH BELONG
TO REAL AND POLITICAL LIFE."
~~~ MAX BECKMANN
—LONDON, JULY, 1938

"IT IS ONLY WELL WITH ME WHEN
I HAVE A CHISEL IN MY HAND."
~~~ MICHAELANGELO

"THE MEANING OF A GREAT WORK
OF ART, OR THE LITTLE OF IT THAT WE
CAN UNDERSTAND, MUST BE RELATED TO
OUR OWN LIFE IN SUCH A WAY AS TO IN-
CREASE OUR ENERGY OF SPIRIT."
~~~ KENNETH CLARK

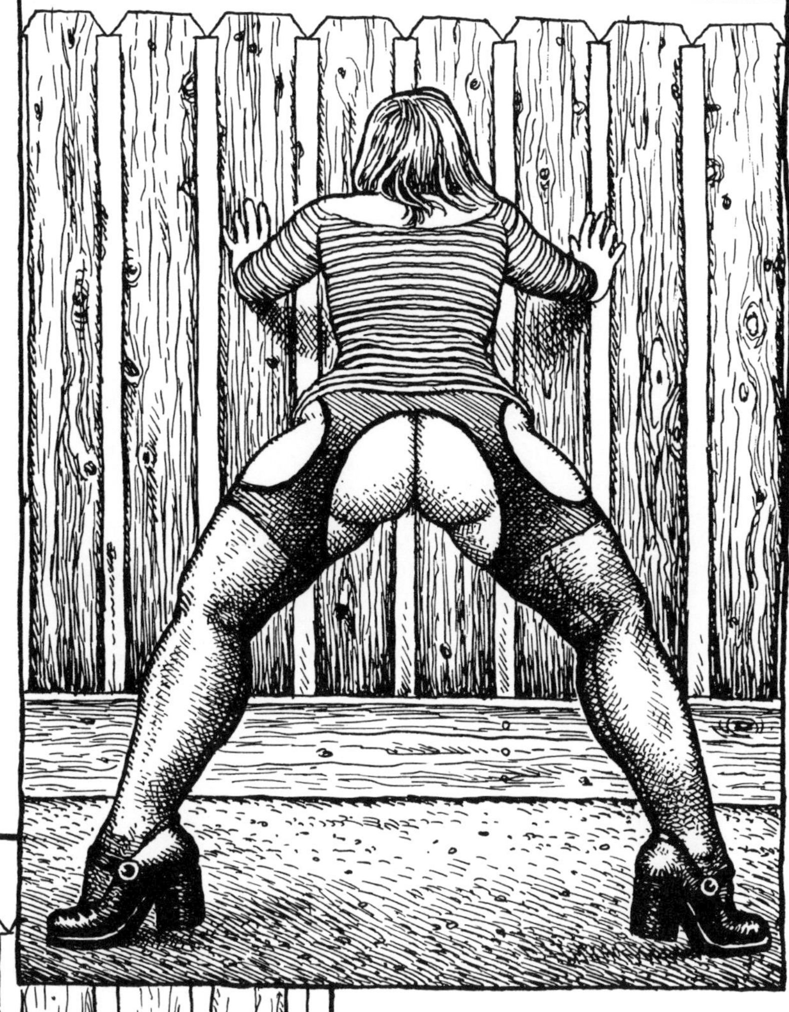

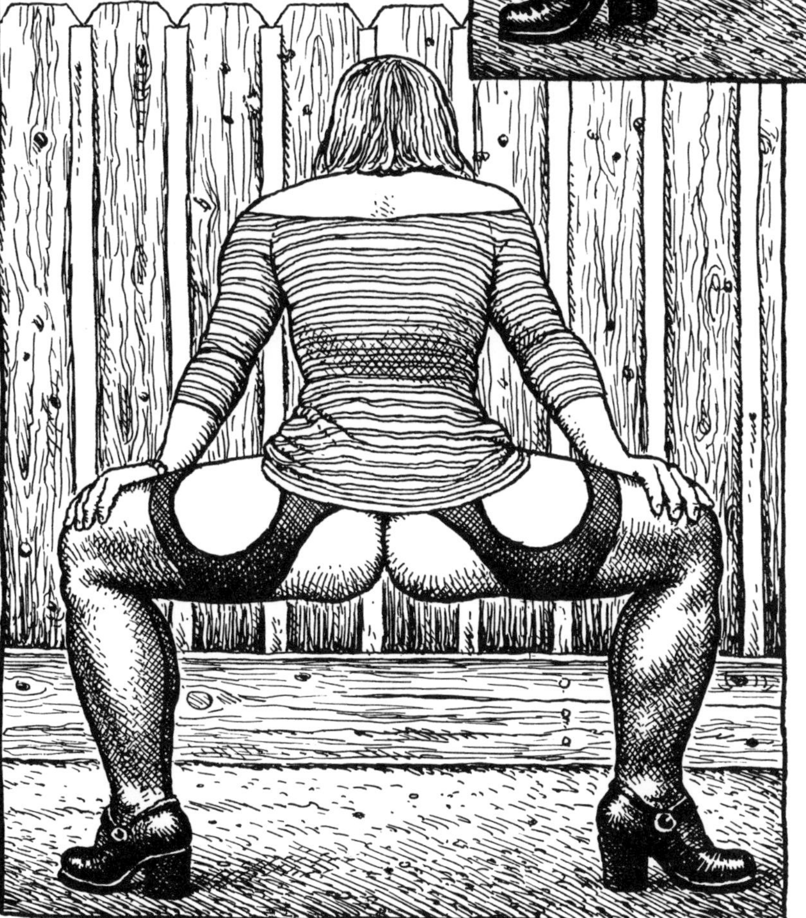

"TALENT IS LONG PATIENCE, AND
ORIGINALITY IS AN EFFORT OF
WILL AND INTENSE OBSERVATION."
~~~ GUSTAVE FLAUBERT

"NARROW MINDS DEMAND OLD
BEGINNINGS, IDENTICAL CONTINUA-
TIONS. THE ARTIST MUST REPEAT
HIS LITTLE WORKS, AND ALL ELSE
IS CONDEMNED."
~~~ JAMES ENSOR, 1915

"EVERYTHING DEPENDS ON ONE'S
SELF... THE WORK ONE DOES IS A
WAY OF KEEPING A DIARY."
~~~ PICASSO

"THE SOONER YOU MAKE YOUR FIRST
FIVE-THOUSAND MISTAKES, THE SOONER
YOU WILL BE ABLE TO CORRECT THEM."
~~~ KIMON NICOLAIDES

CAN ANYTHING IN MAN'S INVEN-
TION COMPARE WITH THE GLORY OF
LINE WHICH A PERFECT CURVE FURN-
ISHES? NOTE THE PROFUSION, THE
ABUNDANCE OF PLEASING CURVES
AND SHAPES! THE GENIUS THAT CRE-
ATED SUCH A BOUNTY OF SENSUOUS
BEAUTY IS MOTHER NATURE HERSELF,
AND TO HER SUPERIOR ART ALL EARTH-
LY ARTISTS MUST STAND IN AWE.
~~~

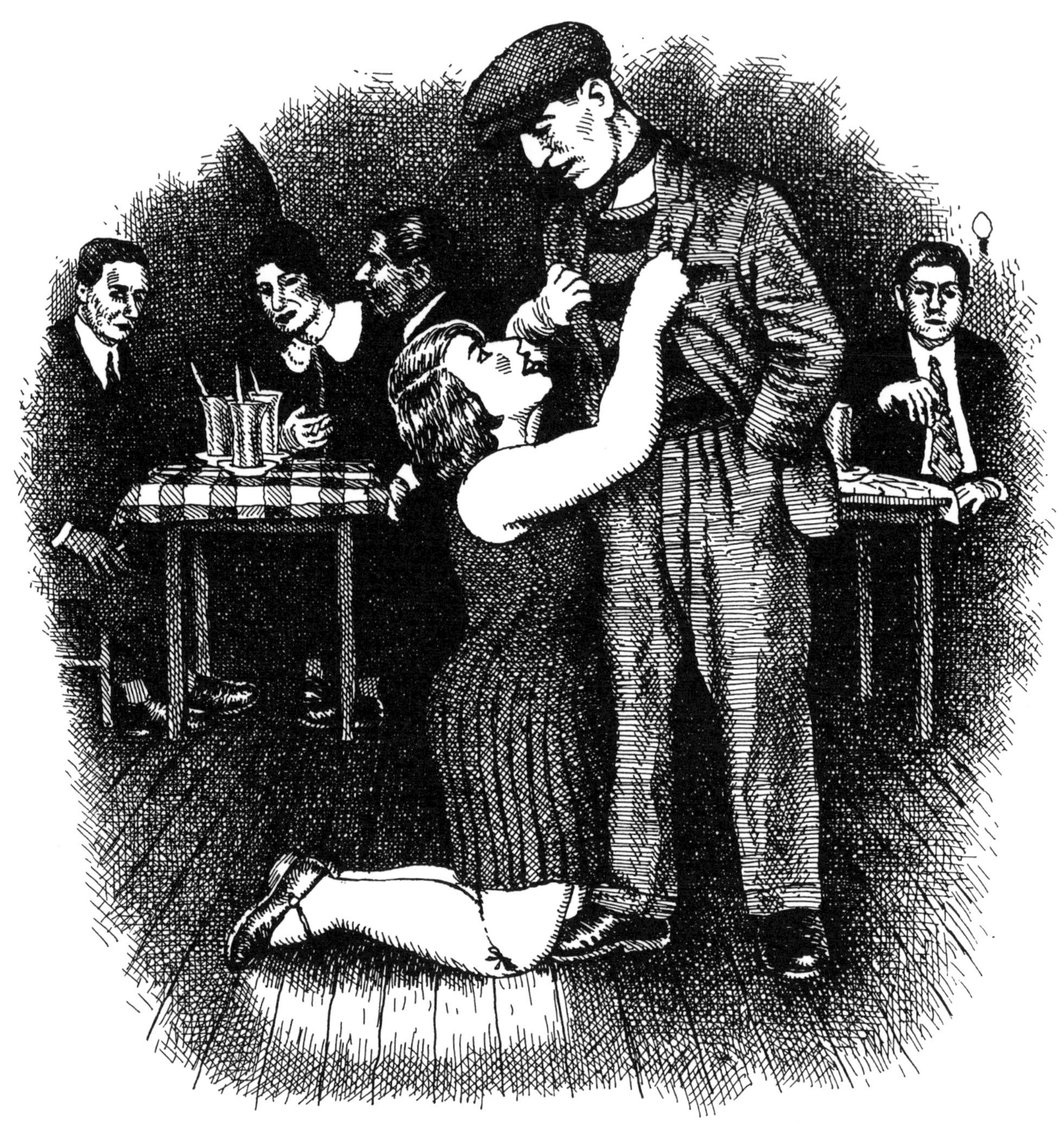

"THE APACHE DANCE"

A QUINTESSENTIAL EXPRESSION OF FRENCH IDEAS ABOUT LOVE AND ROMANCE, THE APACHE DANCE FLOURISHED AS A POPULAR NIGHT-CLUB ENTERTAINMENT IN GAY PAREE IN THE 1920s AND '30s. THE "MAU-VAIS GARÇONS", OR "BAD BOYS" OF THE PARIS STREETS, HOT-BLOODED AND KNIFE-WIELDING, WERE CALLED, AMONG OTHER THINGS, "APACHES", AFTER THE NOTORIOUSLY VIOLENT AMERICAN INDIAN TRIBE. THE APACHE DANCE WAS A SORT OF SADO-MASOCHISTIC BALLET IN WHICH THE WOMAN WAS THROWN ACROSS THE FLOOR BY THE SWAGGERING HOODLUM, CAME CRAWLING BACK, WAS KICKED AWAY, AND SO ON, TO THE MUSIC OF A REEDY ACCORDION.   ONLY THE BLASÉ, UNSHOCKABLE FRENCH COULD HAVE TURNED THE BATTLE OF THE SEXES INTO AN OPEN, ACCEPTED, PUBLIC, NIGHT-TIME AMUSEMENT FOR ALL TO BEHOLD, AND REAFFIRMING ONCE AGAIN THE ETERNAL TRUTH THAT IT DOESN'T PAY FOR A MAN TO BE TOO GOOD, BECAUSE WOMEN, ALWAYS AND EVER, ARE ATTRACTED TO THE *DANGEROUS* ONES!

"ART ITSELF MAY BE DEFINED AS A SINGLE-MINDED ATTEMPT TO RENDER THE HIGHEST KIND OF JUSTICE TO THE VISIBLE UNIVERSE, BY BRINGING TO LIGHT THE TRUTH, MANIFOLD AND ONE, UNDERLYING EVERY ASPECT."

~~~ JOSEPH CONRAD

"I COULD ACCEPT ANY HUMILIATION MYSELF, BUT MY PURE AREA WAS ART, AND THERE IT WAS THE TRUTH. I TOLD THE TRUTH THE BEST I WAS ABLE.... I WAS ALWAYS MUCH MORE TRUTHFUL AND COURAGEOUS ON CANVAS."

~~~ ALICE NEEL

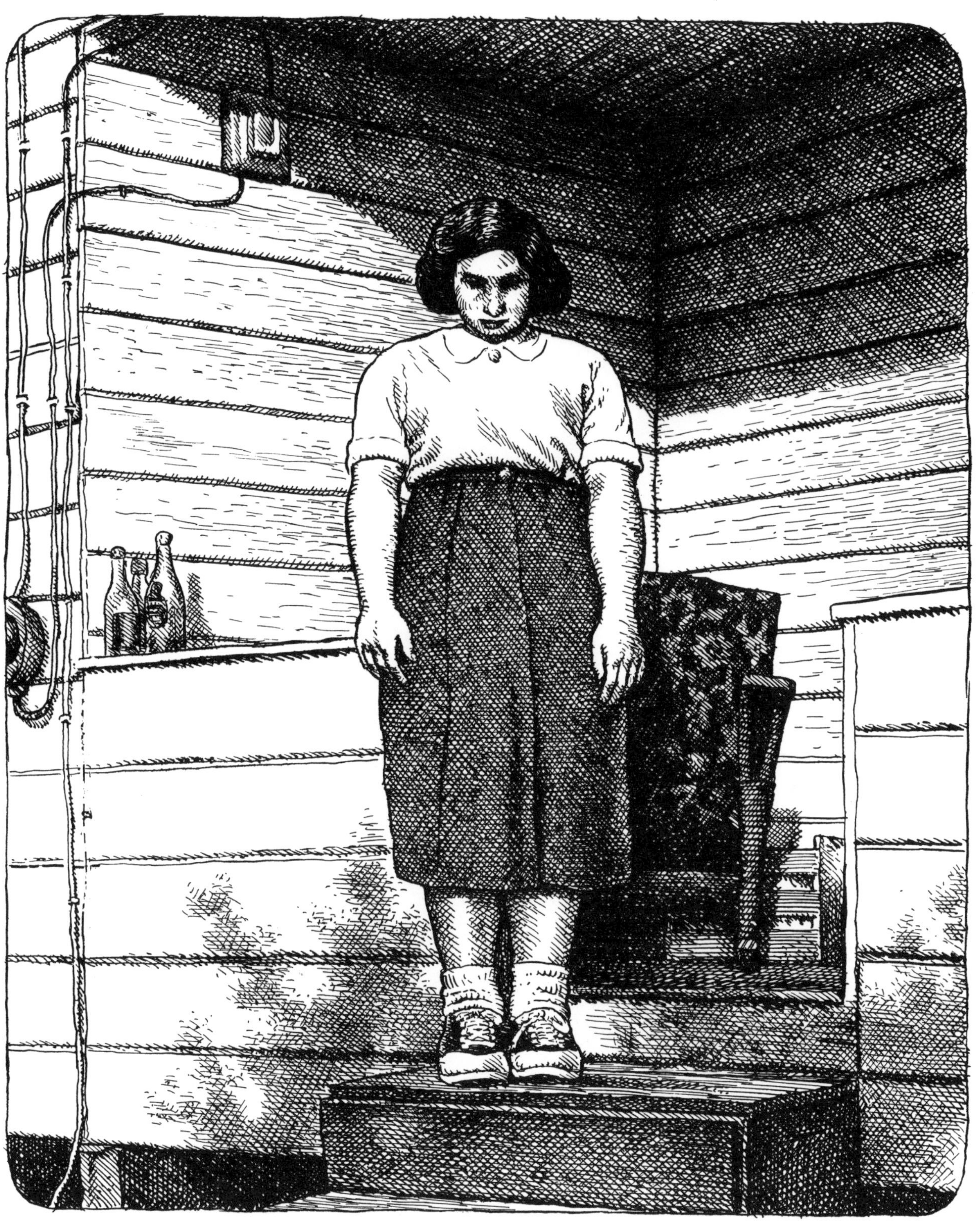

A DRAWING RENDERED FROM A SNAPSHOT FOUND IN A FORGOTTEN BOX OF OLD PHOTOGRAPHS... A CAPTION ON THE BACK READS, "GRAND-DAUGHTER VIRGINIA LEE, COAL FORK, W. VA.", PROBABLY TAKEN IN THE 1940S. THE ARTIST FOUND IN THIS STRAY SNAPSHOT THE EMBODIMENT OF THE PAINFULLY SHY RURAL GIRL. SHE IS DEEPLY MORTIFIED, HEAD BOWED, AS SHE STANDS BE- FORE THE CAMERA. SUCH AN IMAGE INDUCES REFLECTIONS; WHAT BECAME OF VIRGINIA LEE? DID SHE EVER FIND A SOUL MATE? IS SHE PERHAPS STILL LIVING SOMEWHERE? HELLO, SWEET SHY VIRGINIA LEE, WHERE EVER YOU MAY BE!

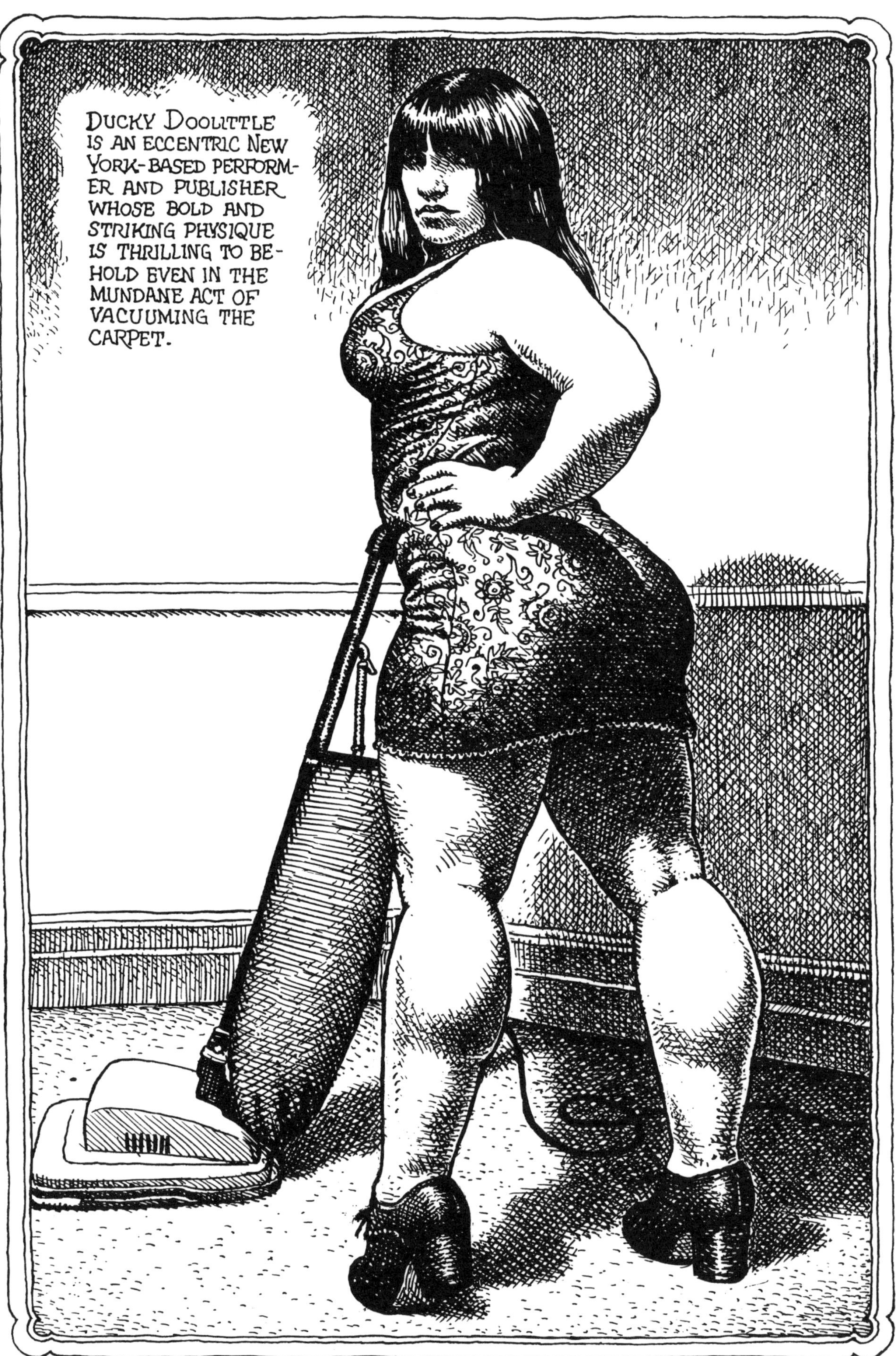

DUCKY DOOLITTLE
IS AN ECCENTRIC NEW
YORK-BASED PERFORM-
ER AND PUBLISHER
WHOSE BOLD AND
STRIKING PHYSIQUE
IS THRILLING TO BE-
HOLD EVEN IN THE
MUNDANE ACT OF
VACUUMING THE
CARPET.

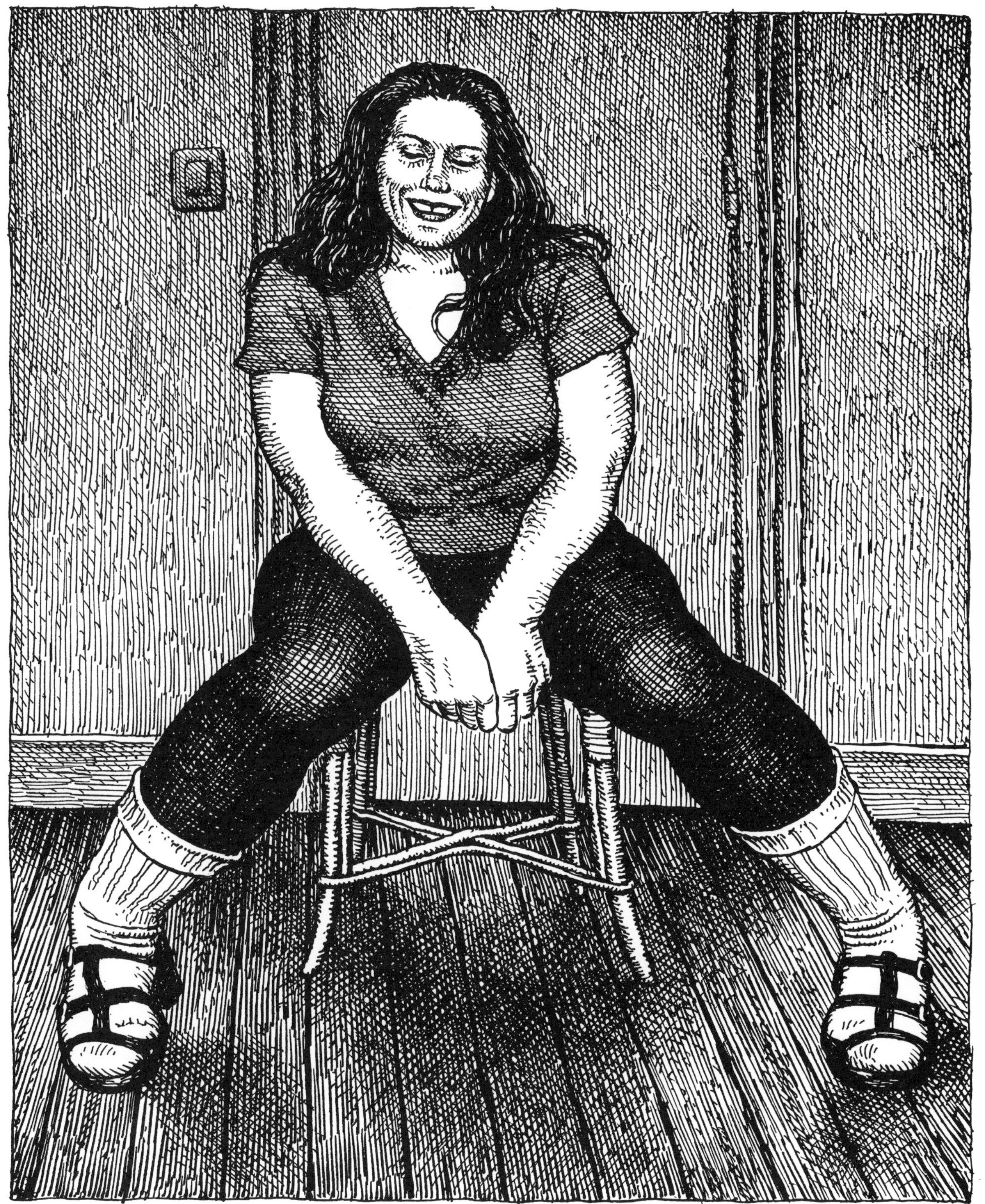

Here is a model who endears but at the same time arouses the animal passions of the male viewer, with her shy, awkward, girlish self-consciousness combined with the striking proportions of her sensuous, shapely body. Her unstudied pose speaks volumes about woman's strength and vulnerability. The effect achieved is one of artless charm.

"One thing is sure — we have to transform the three-dimensional world of objects into the two-dimensional world of canvas... To transform three into two dimensions is for me an experience full of magic in which I glimpse for a moment that fourth dimension which my whole being is seeking."
~~~ Max Beckman, July, 1938
~~~

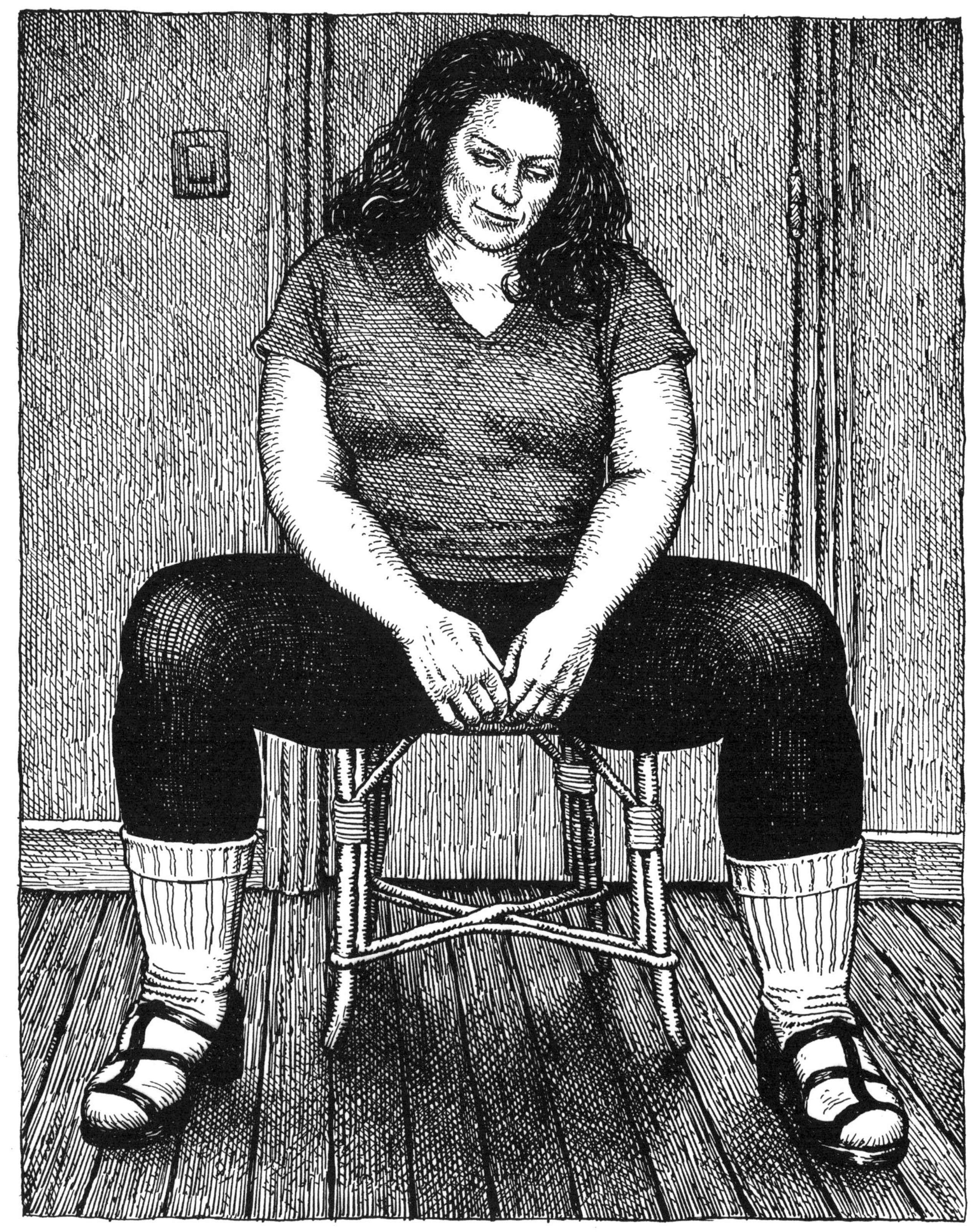

AGAIN THIS "ARTLESS" MODEL UNINTENTIONALLY REVEALS THE GENUINE ESSENCE OF HER BEING, AND A PICTURE SUCH AS THIS SUCCEEDS WHERE WORDS FAIL, BEING AS IT IS THE WORK OF A SKILLED AND SENSITIVE ARTIST. IN THE DELICACY AND SUBTLETY OF HIS LINES, THE DISCERNING VIEWER IS INVITED TO PLUMB THE DEPTHS OF THE SUBJECT'S CHARACTER. NOT THE MALE'S PROJECTED FANTASY, BUT THE TRUE NATURE OF THE FEMALE, IT IS THIS THAT FOREVER MAGNETIZES AND INTRIGUES, AND IS ETERNALLY UNFATHOMABLE.

"OUR PICTORIAL SENSATIONS CANNOT BE WHISPERED. WE SING THEM AND SHOUT THEM IN OUR CANVASES, WHICH RING WITH DEAFENING AND TRIUMPHAL FANFARES!"
— UMBERTO BOCCIONI, ITALIAN FUTURIST, FEB. 11, 1910

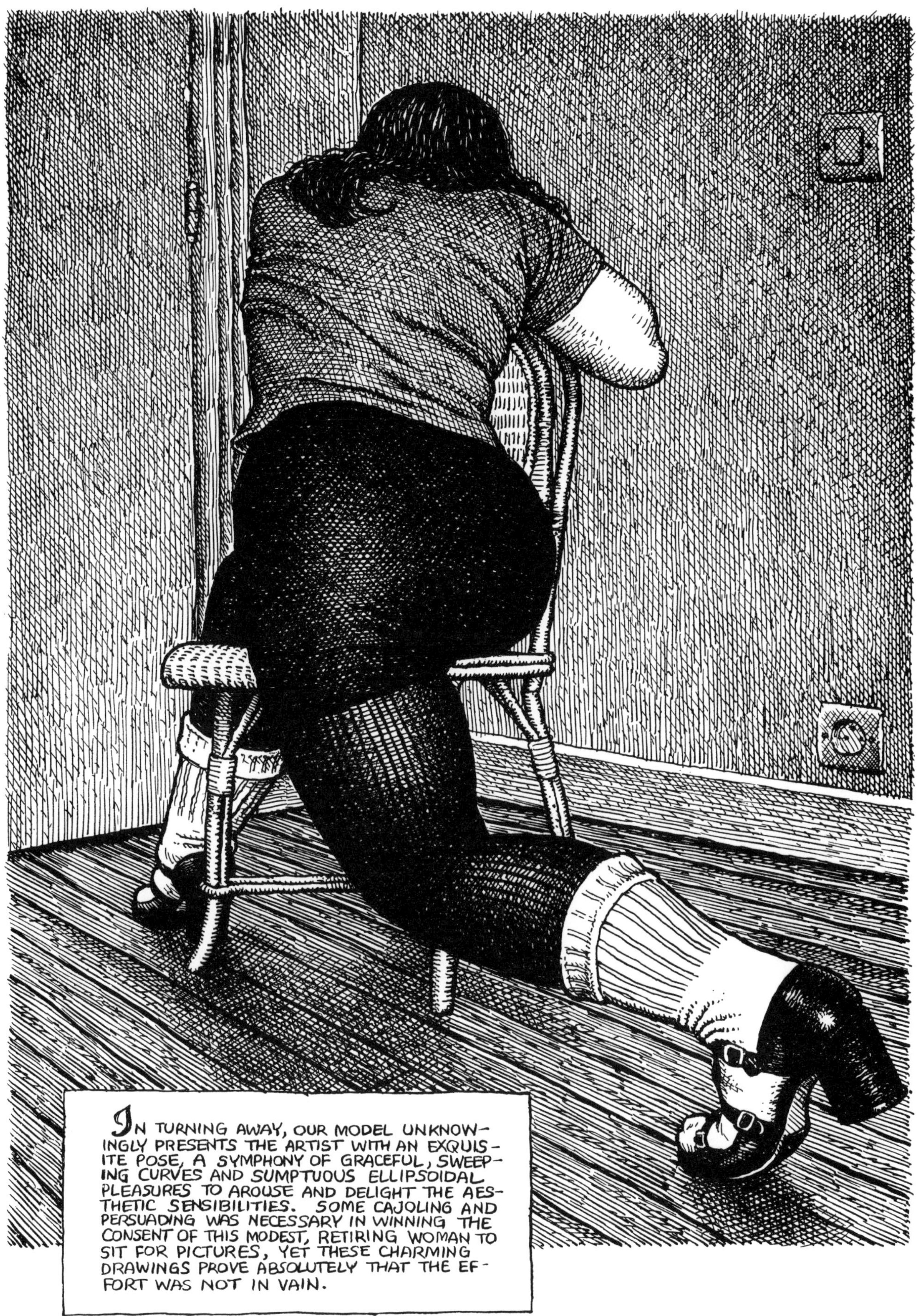

IN TURNING AWAY, OUR MODEL UNKNOW-
INGLY PRESENTS THE ARTIST WITH AN EXQUIS-
ITE POSE, A SYMPHONY OF GRACEFUL, SWEEP-
ING CURVES AND SUMPTUOUS ELLIPSOIDAL
PLEASURES TO AROUSE AND DELIGHT THE AES-
THETIC SENSIBILITIES. SOME CAJOLING AND
PERSUADING WAS NECESSARY IN WINNING THE
CONSENT OF THIS MODEST, RETIRING WOMAN TO
SIT FOR PICTURES, YET THESE CHARMING
DRAWINGS PROVE ABSOLUTELY THAT THE EF-
FORT WAS NOT IN VAIN.

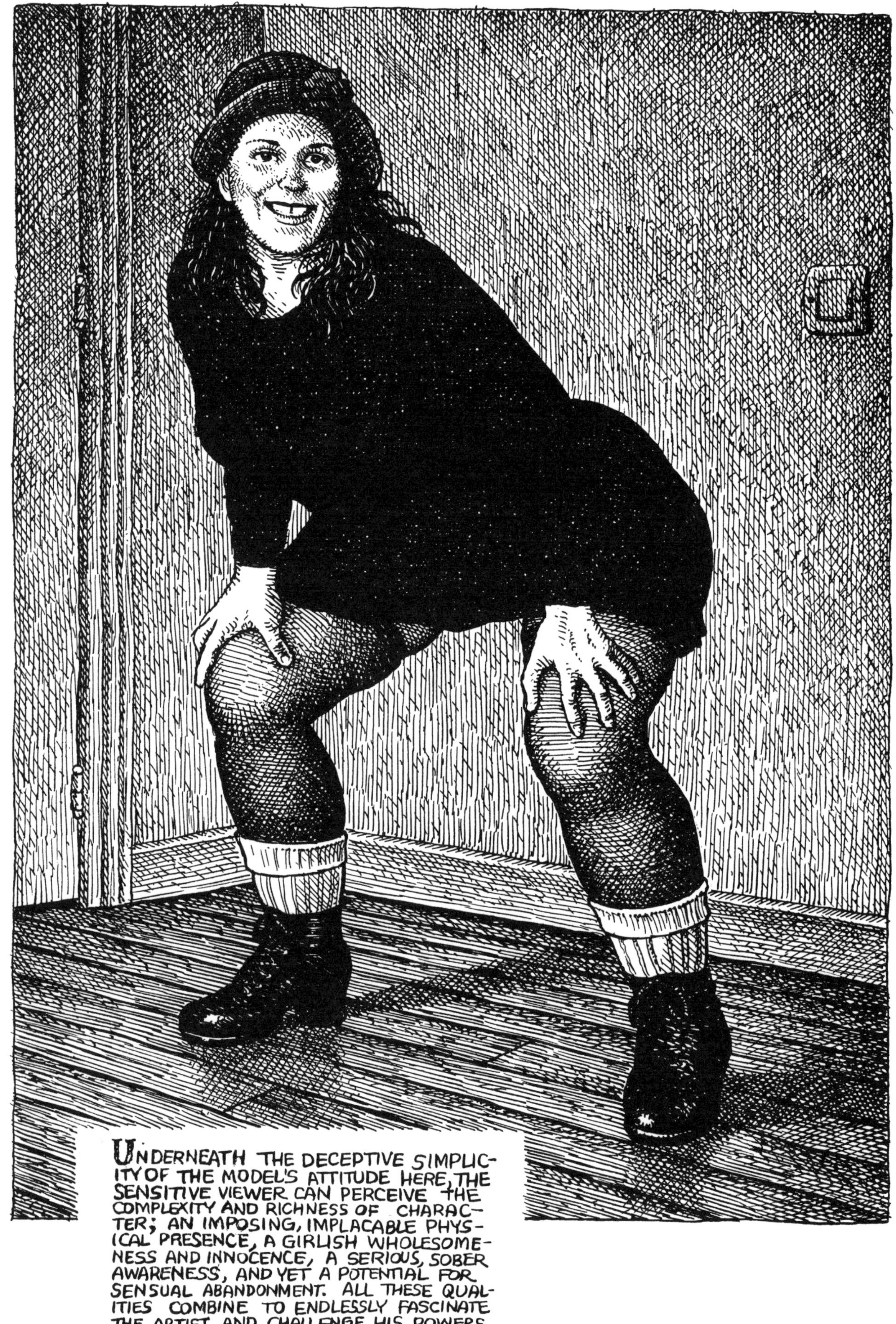

UNDERNEATH THE DECEPTIVE SIMPLIC-
ITY OF THE MODEL'S ATTITUDE HERE, THE
SENSITIVE VIEWER CAN PERCEIVE THE
COMPLEXITY AND RICHNESS OF CHARAC-
TER; AN IMPOSING, IMPLACABLE PHYS-
ICAL PRESENCE, A GIRLISH WHOLESOME-
NESS AND INNOCENCE, A SERIOUS, SOBER
AWARENESS, AND YET A POTENTIAL FOR
SENSUAL ABANDONMENT. ALL THESE QUAL-
ITIES COMBINE TO ENDLESSLY FASCINATE
THE ARTIST AND CHALLENGE HIS POWERS
OF EXPRESSION IN HIS CHOSEN MEDIUM.

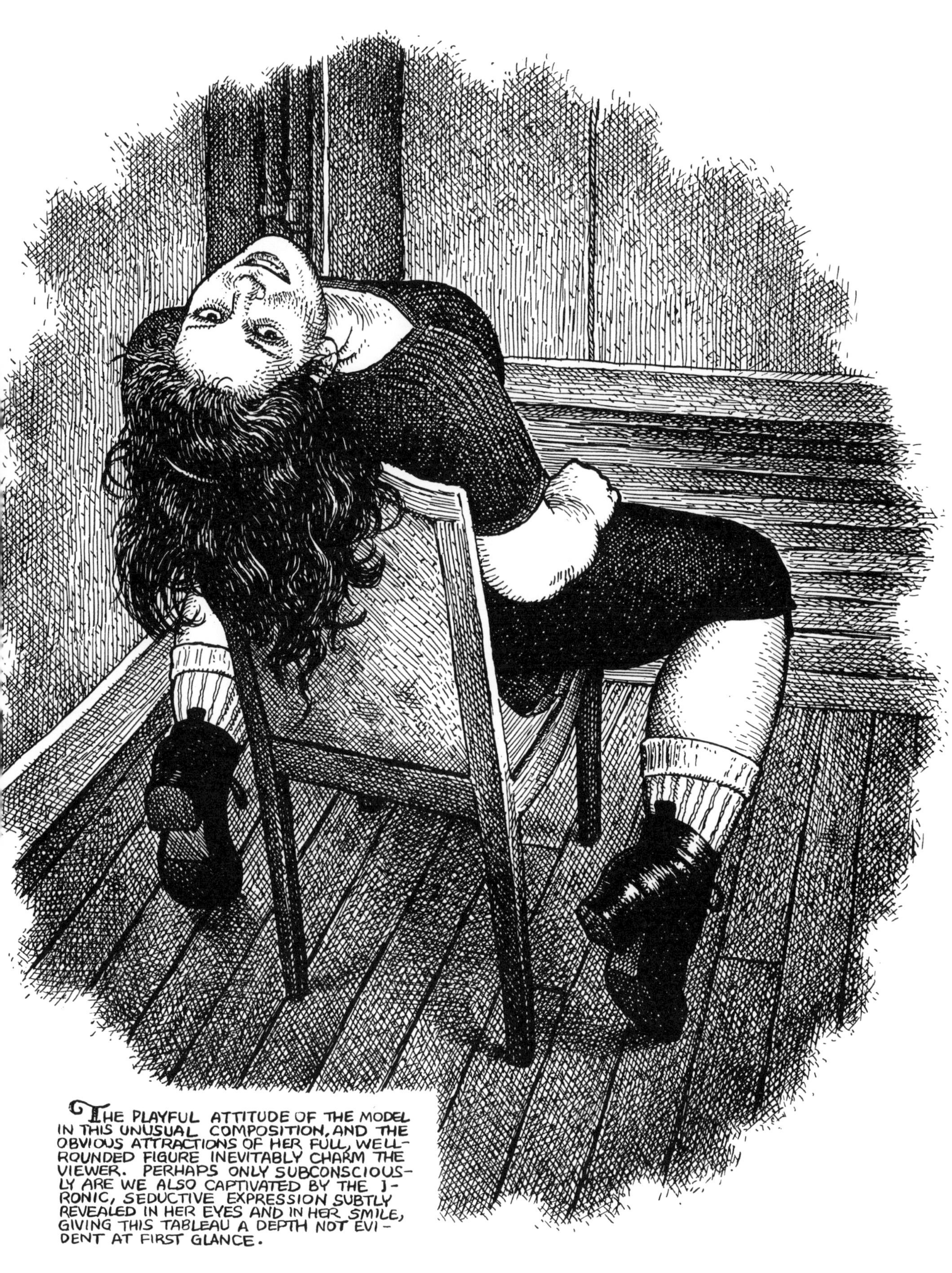

THE PLAYFUL ATTITUDE OF THE MODEL IN THIS UNUSUAL COMPOSITION, AND THE OBVIOUS ATTRACTIONS OF HER FULL, WELL-ROUNDED FIGURE INEVITABLY CHARM THE VIEWER. PERHAPS ONLY SUBCONSCIOUS-LY ARE WE ALSO CAPTIVATED BY THE I-RONIC, SEDUCTIVE EXPRESSION SUBTLY REVEALED IN HER EYES AND IN HER SMILE, GIVING THIS TABLEAU A DEPTH NOT EVI-DENT AT FIRST GLANCE.

"GAUGUIN MADE A MISTAKE WHEN HE IMITATED NEGRO SCULPTURE. HE SHOULD HAVE DONE HIS SCULPTURE IN THE SAME WAY AS HIS PAINTINGS, BY DRAWING FROM NATURE, WHILE INSTEAD HE MADE WOMEN WITH LARGE HEADS AND LITTLE LEGS."
~~~ARISTIDE MAILLOL

"VISION CHANGES WHILE IT OBSERVES. REASON IS THE ENEMY OF ART."
~~~JAMES ENSOR

"TO BECOME TRULY IMMORTAL A WORK OF ART MUST ESCAPE ALL HUMAN LIMITS; LOGIC AND COMMON SENSE WILL ONLY INTERFERE. BUT ONCE THESE BARRIERS ARE BROKEN, IT WILL ENTER THE REGION OF CHILDHOOD VISION AND DREAM."
~~~GIORGIO DE CHIRICO, PARIS, 1913

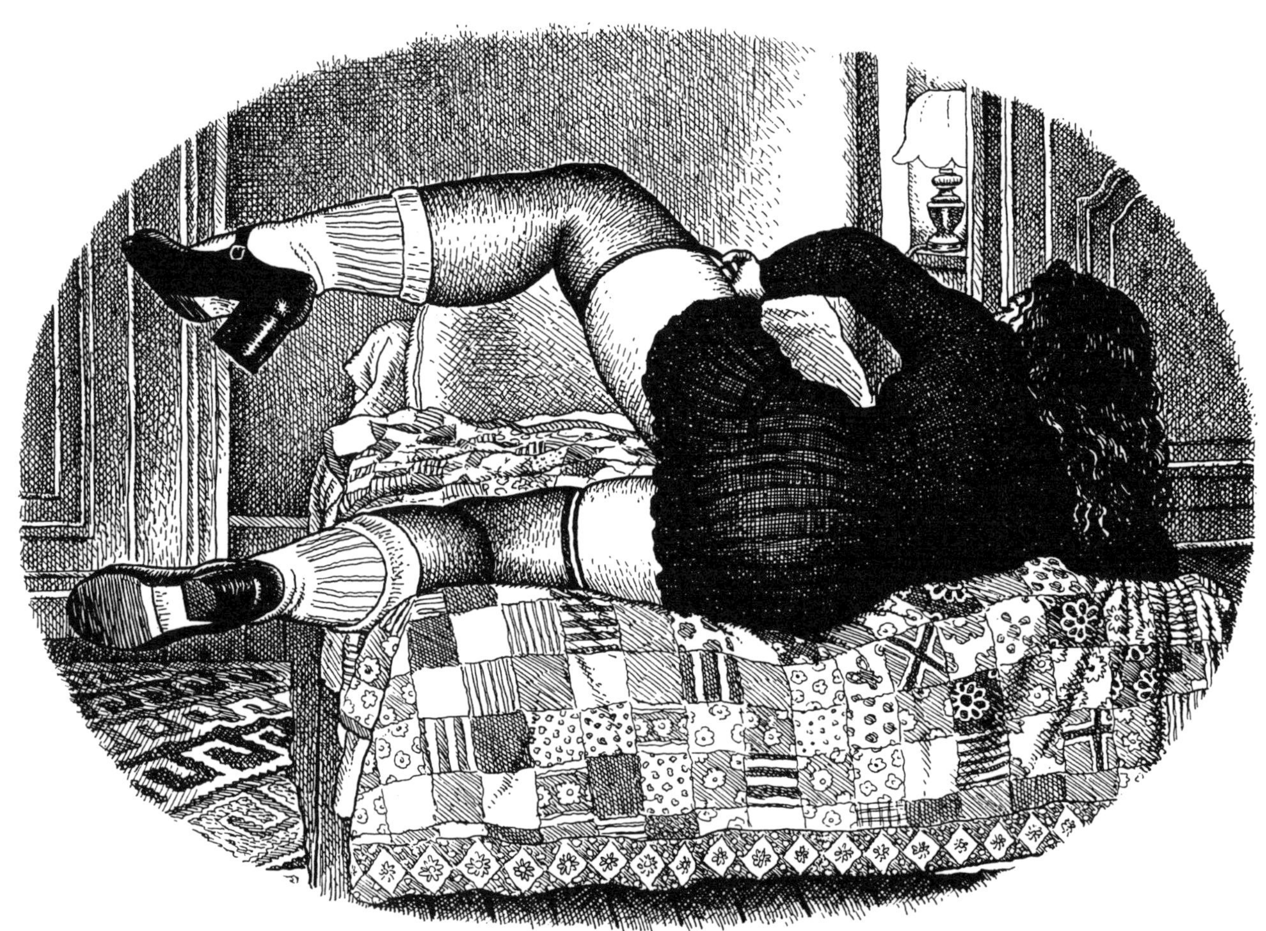

CAUGHT IN AN OFF-GUARD MOMENT AS SHE PULLS UP HER STOCKING, THIS FAIR DAUGHTER OF THE NORTHWEST STRIKES A DELIGHTFUL POSE, SHOWING AN EXQUISITE ARRANGEMENT OF FULL, GENEROUS BODILY CURVES. SHE POSSESSES THE TYPE OF FEMALE FIGURE THAT IS EVER AND ALWAYS SOUGHT AFTER BY THE TRUE, DEDICATED ARTIST.

"A PICTURE IS SOMETHING WHICH REQUIRES AS MUCH KNAVERY, TRICKERY, AND DECEIT AS THE PERPETRATION OF A CRIME. PAINT FALSELY, AND THEN ADD THE ACCENT OF NATURE. THE ARTIST DOES NOT DRAW WHAT HE SEES, BUT WHAT HE MUST MAKE OTHERS SEE. ONLY WHEN HE NO LONGER KNOWS WHAT HE IS DOING DOES THE PAINTER DO GOOD THINGS."
~~~DEGAS

— THE TRIUMPH OF INSPIRATION OVER THEORY —

"I FEEL MYSELF WASHED BY ALL THE COLORS OF INFINITY. I BECOME ONE WITH MY PAINTING. WE LIVE IN A RAINBOW CHAOS. I STAND IN FRONT OF MY SUBJECT, LOSE MYSELF IN IT, I DREAM HAZILY. THE SUN, LIKE A DISTANT FRIEND, SECRETLY WARMS MY IDLENESS AND MAKES IT FRUITFUL. WE GERMINATE."
~~~PAUL CÉZANNE
~~~

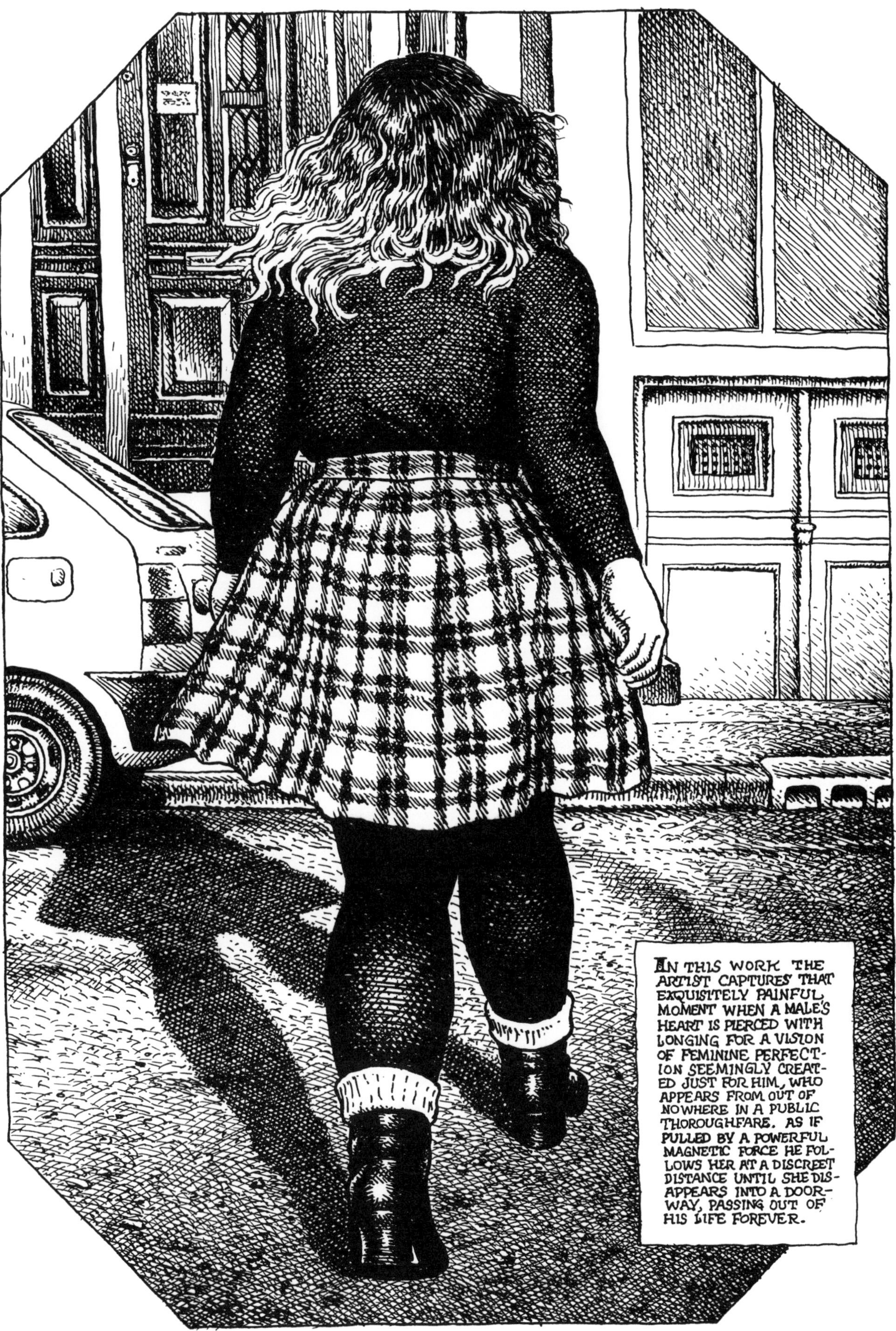

IN THIS WORK THE ARTIST CAPTURES THAT EXQUISITELY PAINFUL MOMENT WHEN A MALE'S HEART IS PIERCED WITH LONGING FOR A VISION OF FEMININE PERFECTION SEEMINGLY CREATED JUST FOR HIM, WHO APPEARS FROM OUT OF NOWHERE IN A PUBLIC THOROUGHFARE. AS IF PULLED BY A POWERFUL MAGNETIC FORCE HE FOLLOWS HER AT A DISCREET DISTANCE UNTIL SHE DISAPPEARS INTO A DOORWAY, PASSING OUT OF HIS LIFE FOREVER.

"IN ART, INTENTIONS ARE NOT SUFFICIENT, AND, AS WE SAY IN SPANISH, LOVE MUST BE PROVED BY FACTS AND NOT BY REASONS."

~~~ PICASSO

"WE ARE FAR REMOVED FROM THE GREAT FRESCO PAINTERS OF THE PAST, BESIDE WHOM WE OFTEN APPEAR SO SMALL..."

~~~ GEORGES ROUALT

"THE GREAT ARTIST SPENDS HIS LIFE TURNING HIMSELF INSIDE OUT."

~~~ KENNETH CLARK, *PIONEERS OF MODERN PAINTING*

"OUR PURPOSE IS TO EVOLVE. WE EVOLVE THROUGH OUR PERCEPTION OF BEAUTY. THE MORE WE UNDERSTAND AND APPRECIATE BEAUTY, THE MORE WE EVOLVE."

~~~ PETE POPLASKI

"ART IS TWO THINGS: A SEARCH FOR A ROAD AND A SEARCH FOR FREEDOM. IT'S VERY HARD TO GET FREEDOM. YOU KNOW, ALL THESE THINGS IN LIFE KEEP CRAWLING OVER YOU ALL THE TIME, SO IT'S VERY HARD TO FEEL FREE."

~~~ ALICE NEEL

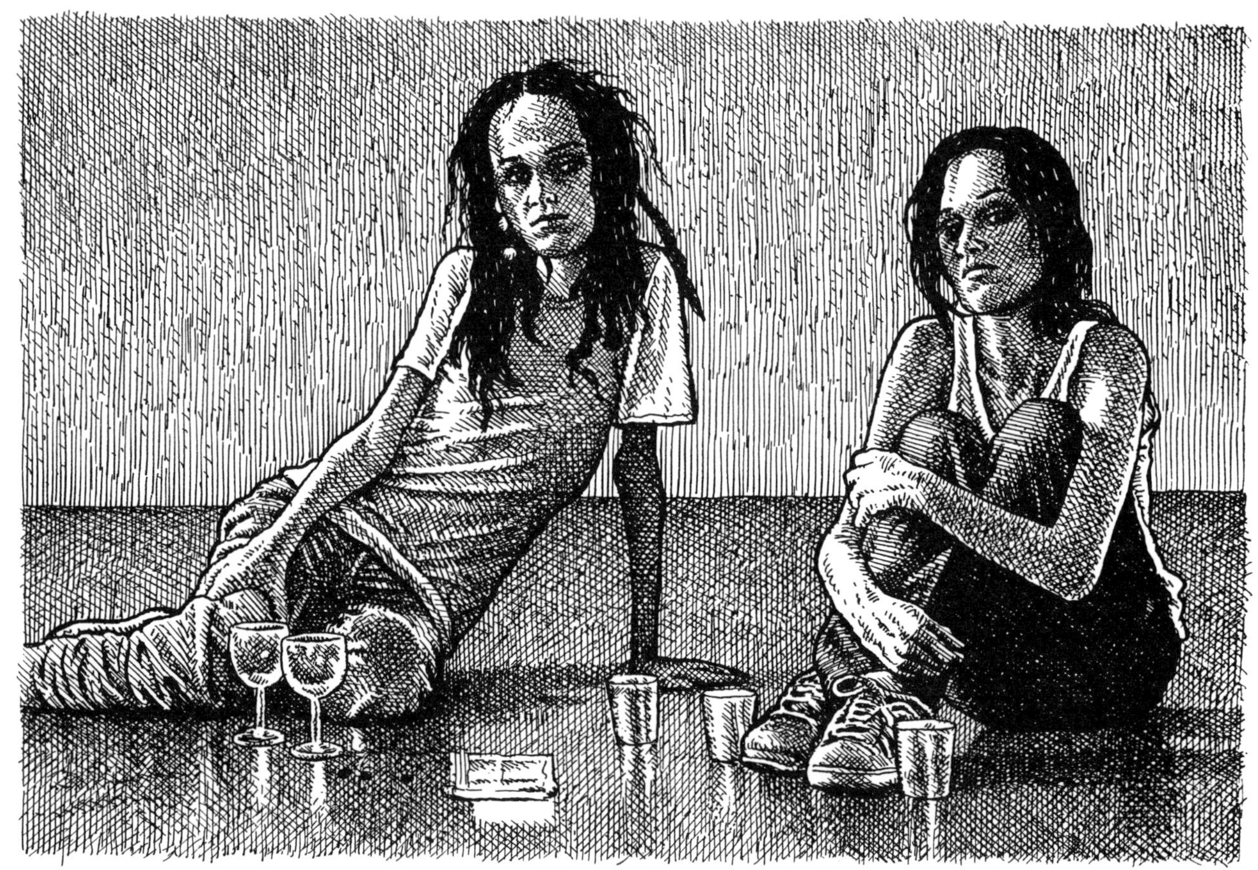

TWO YOUNG ARTISTS FROM HOLLAND, WHO CALL THEMSELVES "L. A. RAEVEN" ('L' FOR LIESBETH, 'A' FOR ANGELIQUE), CAPTURED IN A MOMENT FROM A VIDEO "INSTALLATION" RECENTLY SHOWN AT THE INSTITUTE OF CONTEMPORARY ARTS IN LONDON. A FAR CRY FROM THE ROBUST FEMALE AESTHETIC NORMALLY PREFERRED BY THE EDITOR OF THIS MAGAZINE, STILL, GIRLS OF THIS TYPE HOLD A MYSTERIOUS FASCINATION FOR MANY MEN. A REVIEW OF THE VIDEO INSTALLATION BY ONE BARRY SCHWABSKY, FROM THE SUMMER, 2002 NUMBER OF *ART FORUM* REFLECTS ON THE WORK THUSLY: "L. A. RAEVEN, A PAIR OF ARTISTS FROM AMSTERDAM, ...SEEM TO HAVE FOUND IN THEIR OWN TWINHOOD THE PERFECT METAPHOR AND MECHANISM FOR THE MODERNIST IDEAL OF SELF-REFERENTIALITY: A CLOSED COMMUNICATIVE CIRCUIT IN WHICH NO VIEWER NEED BE ADDRESSED... THE TWO WOMEN DO VERY LITTLE OVER THE COURSE OF THE VIDEOS. THEY SIP FROM WINE GLASSES, THEY MOVE AROUND A BIT, BUT BASICALLY THEY JUST HANG OUT, SITTING ON THE FLOOR OF A NEARLY EMPTY ROOM. ...THE WOMEN, THE ARTISTS THEMSELVES,... ARE SHOWN AS ART OBJECTS... GAZING OUT IMPASSIVELY AT THE VIEWER, DISAFFECTED AND SULLEN LOOKING... IN A STRANGE WAY THE PAIR REPRESENT THE STANCE OF THE PARADIGMATIC WORKS OF THE MODERNIST AVANT-GARDES— OF DUCHAMP, OF COURSE, BUT ALSO ARTISTS LIKE BARNETT NEWMAN OR CARL ANDRE, WHICH THE PUBLIC STILL TENDS TO FIND INFURIATINGLY INCOMMUNICATIVE; WORKS IN WHICH, AS BORIS CROYS ONCE SAID, 'IT IS NOT THE OBSERVER WHO JUDGES THE ARTWORK, BUT RATHER THE ARTWORK THAT JUDGES—AND OFTEN CONDEMNS—ITS PUBLIC.'" IT APPEARS THAT MR. SCHWABSKY, THE CRITIC HIMSELF, HAS BEEN BEWITCHED BY THESE TWO BLOODLESS, EMACIATED FEMALES. HE SEEMS TO EMBRACE WHOLE-HEARTEDLY THEIR "SULLEN" JUDGMENT, THEIR "SELF-REFERENTIALITY."
~~~

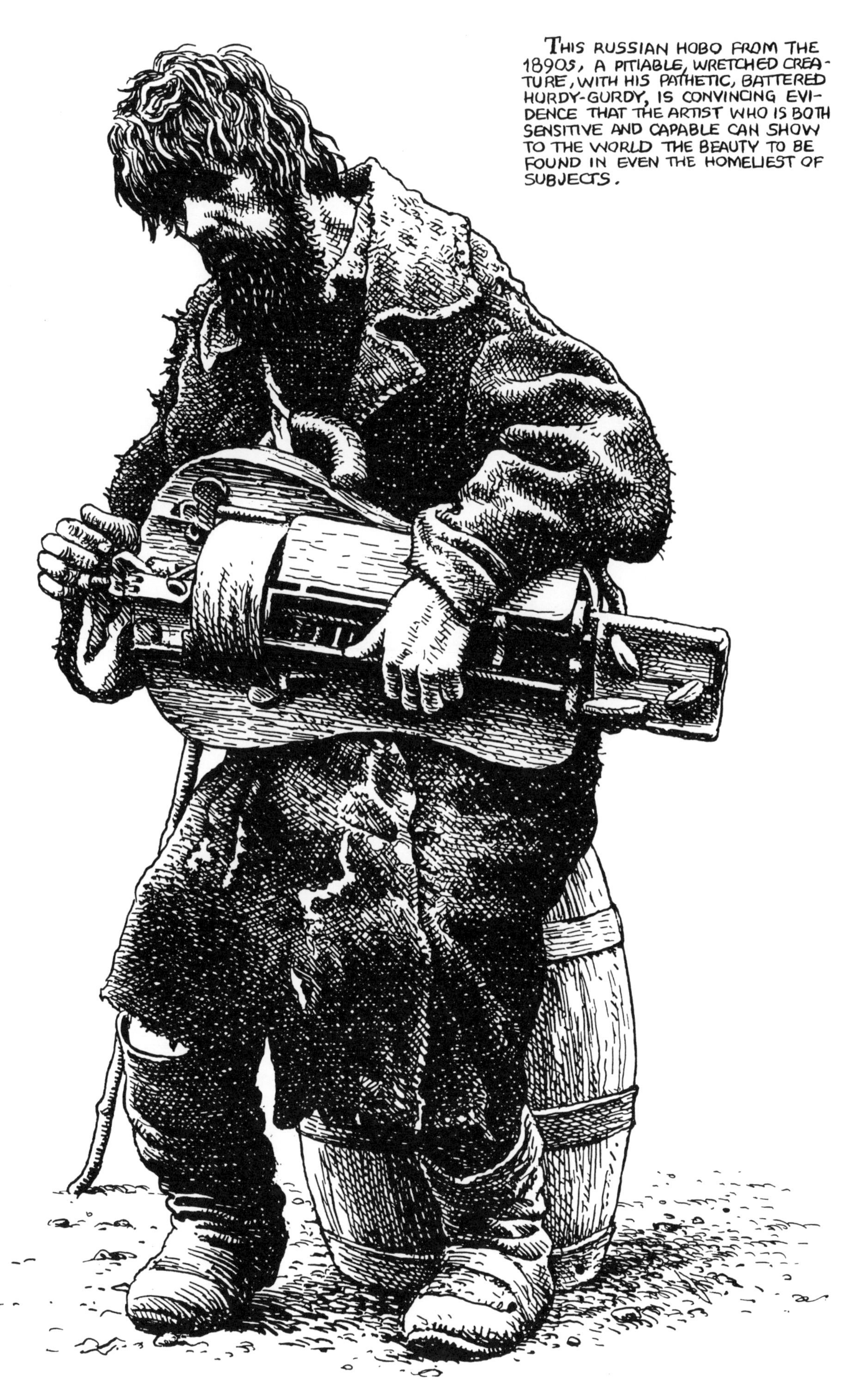

THIS RUSSIAN HOBO FROM THE
1890S, A PITIABLE, WRETCHED CREA-
TURE, WITH HIS PATHETIC, BATTERED
HURDY-GURDY, IS CONVINCING EVI-
DENCE THAT THE ARTIST WHO IS BOTH
SENSITIVE AND CAPABLE CAN SHOW
TO THE WORLD THE BEAUTY TO BE
FOUND IN EVEN THE HOMELIEST OF
SUBJECTS.

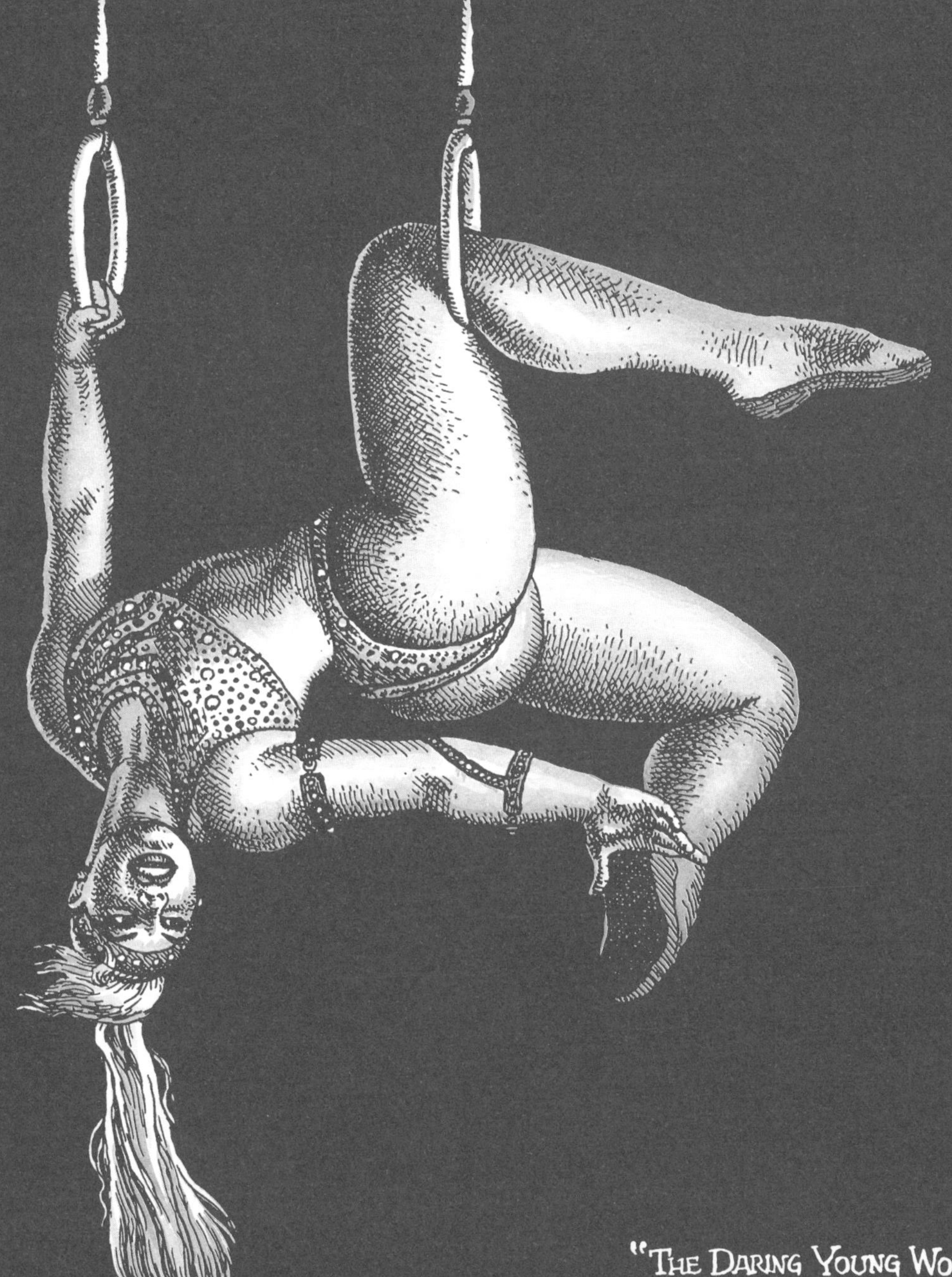

"THE DARING YOUNG WOMAN"

ACROBATS AND TRAPEZE ARTISTS HAVE BEEN AN ATTRACTION TO MANY LOVERS OF BEAUTY. WITH HER FINELY-TONED FIGURE AND ATHLETIC SKILLS SHE IS AN IDEAL MODEL AND POSSESSES LONG BLONDE HAIR.

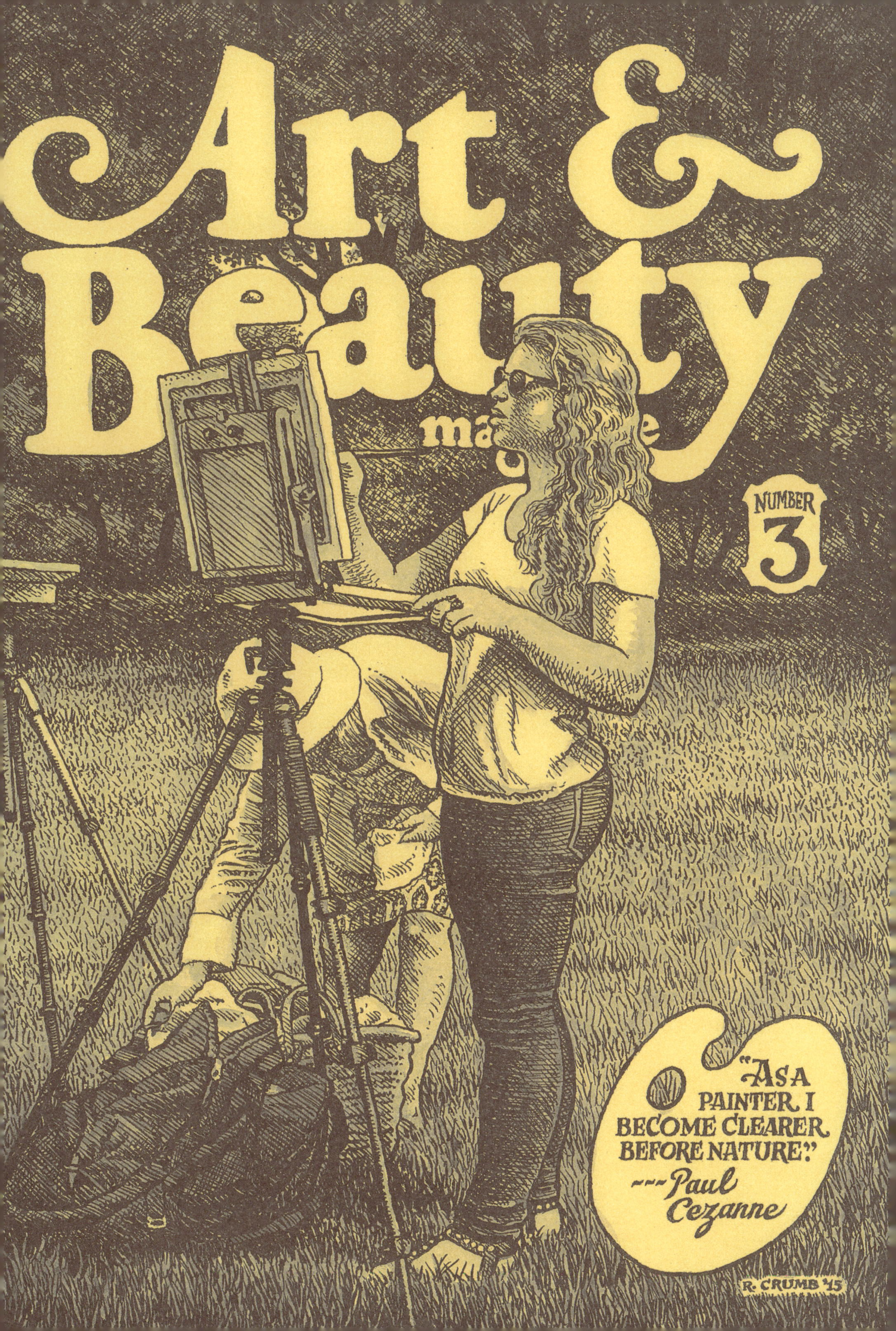

Art &
Beauty
magazine
NUMBER
3
"As a
painter I
become clearer
before nature."
~~~ Paul
Cezanne
R. Crumb '15
~~~

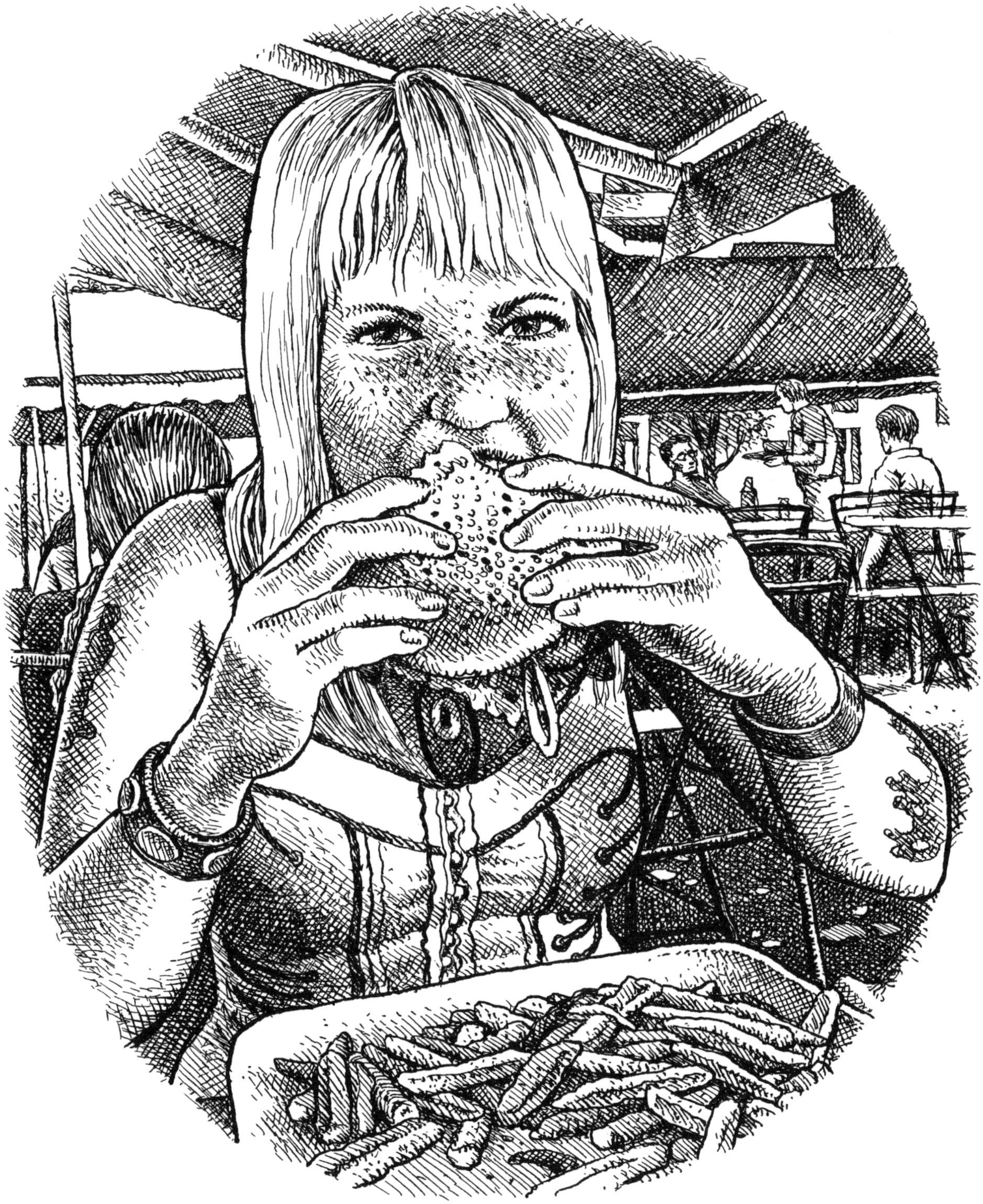

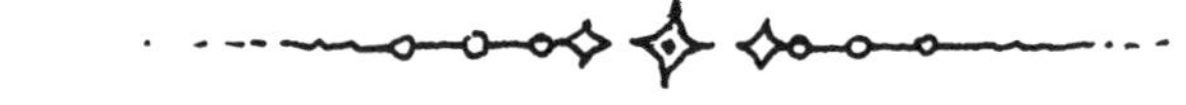

BEAUTY COMBINED WITH INNOCENCE AND SPONTANEITY ARE ACHIEVED IN THIS STUDY AND THE ONE ON THE NEXT PAGE, AS A WHOLESOME YOUNG WOMAN OF TODAY UNABASHEDLY ATTACKS THE EVER POPULAR HAMBURGER AND FRENCH FRIES.

"DRAWING ISN'T FORM; IT IS A WAY OF SEEING FORM."
~~~EDGAR DEGAS
~~~

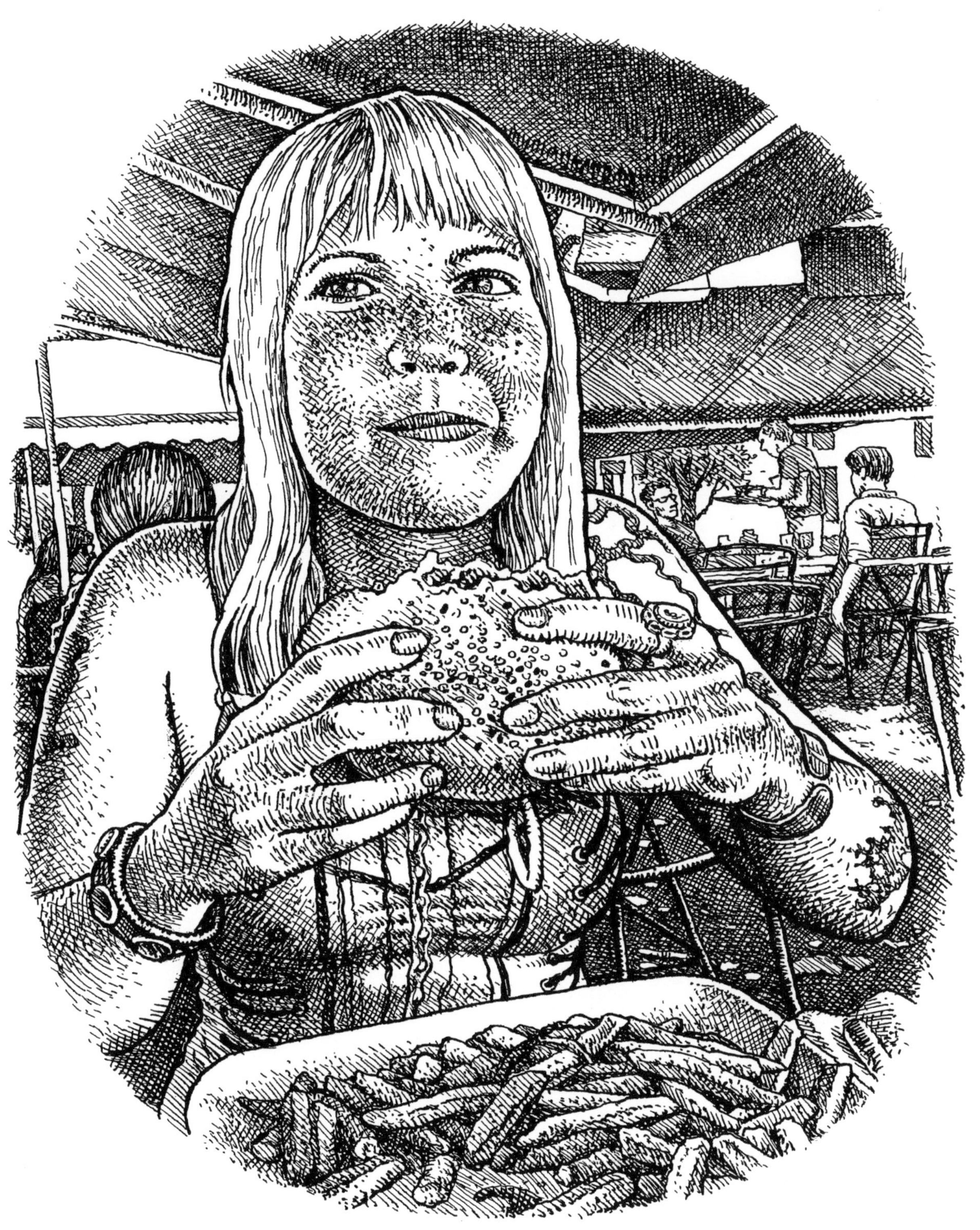

A SPOT OF KETCHUP AT THE CORNER OF HER MOUTH IN NO WAY MARS THE EXQUISITE CHARM OF THIS VIBRANT, SENSUOUS GIRL, WHOSE VERY ARTLESSNESS ONLY INCREASES HER VALUE AS AN INSPIRING SUBJECT FOR THE PEN OR THE BRUSH.

Art & Beauty

magazine
~ NUMBER 3 ~

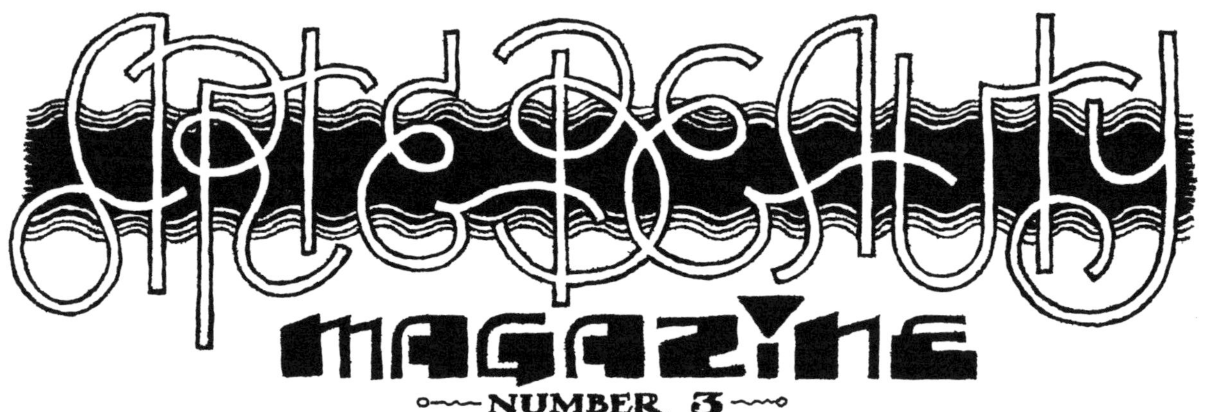

DRAWN FROM LIFE IN ONE
OF THOSE PUBLIC LIFE DRAW-
ING CLASSES IN WHICH EVERY-
ONE CONTRIBUTES TO PAY FOR
THE MODEL'S TIME.

EDITORIALLY SPEAKING
BY EDITOR-IN-CHIEF R. CRUMB

IT IS REALLY RATHER FUNNY, THIS QUESTION ABOUT ART. WHAT *IS* ART ANYWAY? WE HAVE ATTEMPTED TO READ SOME OF THE MAJOR CONTEMPORARY ART MAGAZINES, BUT IN GENERAL WE HAVE FOUND THESE JOURNALS CONFUSING AND INCOMPREHENSIBLE. PERHAPS WE ARE INADEQUATELY EDUCATED, OUR IN- TELLECT TOO PLEBIAN, FOR THE SOPHISTICATED LANGUAGE USED BY THE WRITERS TO EXPRESS THEIR COMPLEX THEORIES ABOUT ART. WE WOULD BE THE FIRST TO ADMIT THAT ART WITH A CAPITAL "A" DEFIES ANY TERSE OR SIMPLE DEFINI- TION, AND THERE-IN LIES THE DIFFICULTY, LEAVING THE FIELD OPEN TO ALL MAN- NER OF OBFUSCATION. IN ANY CASE, BEAUTY IS IN THE EYE OF THE BEHOLDER, AND SO WE CARRY ON WITH OUR OWN ARTISTIC ENDEAVORS AND HOPE FOR THE BEST.

ART & BEAUTY MAGAZINE Number 3, ©2016 by R. Crumb. Published by Fanta- graphics Books, 7563 Lake City Way N.E., Seattle, Washington, 98115, U.S.A.

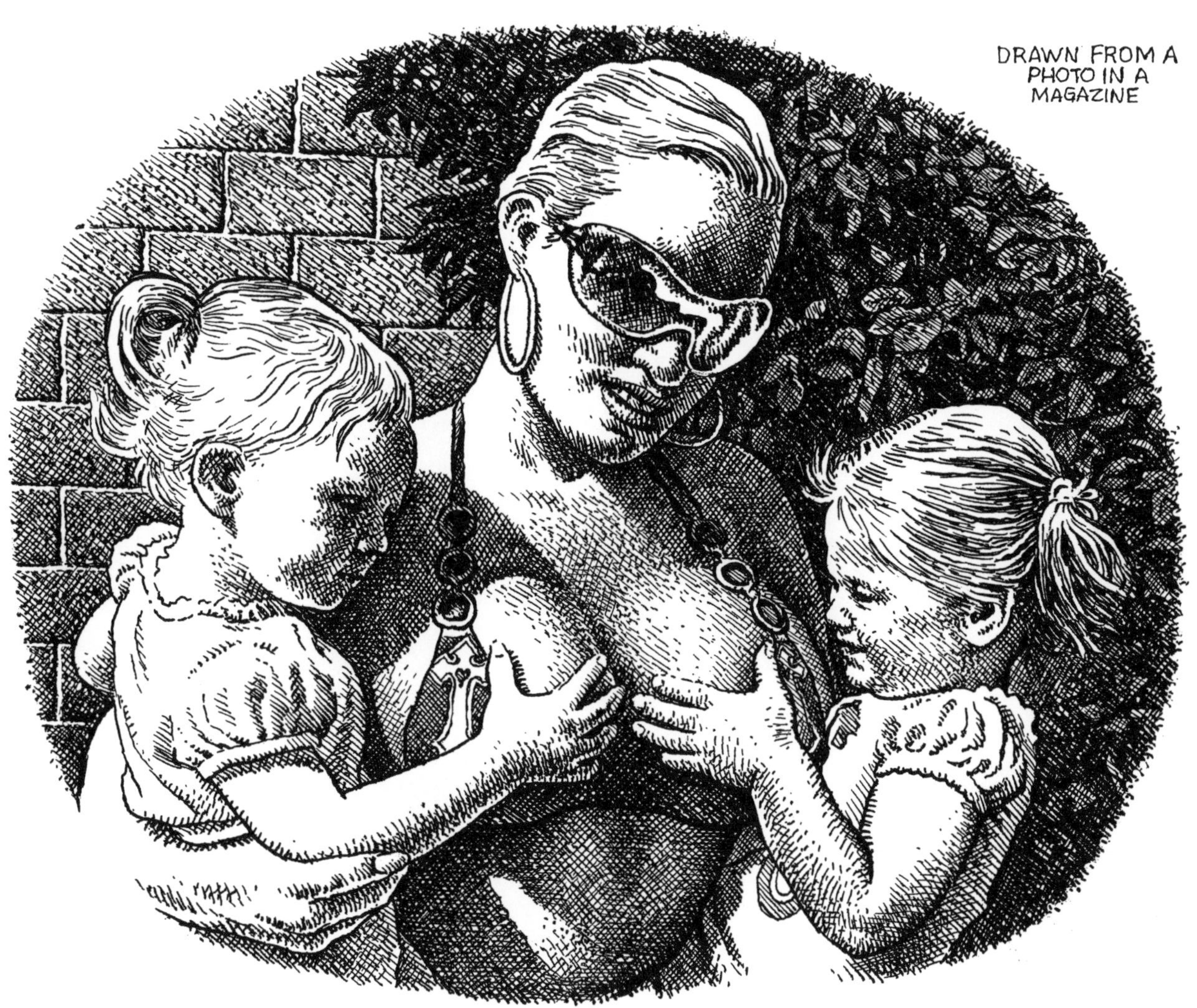

In this curious yet somehow poignant tableau, twin girls of toddler age are innocently fascinated by the extraordinarily spheroid, pneumatic quality of the breasts of the well-known photographer's model Coco Austin. Yet Ms. Austin conveys not an image of sweet, soft, nurturing motherliness but rather calls to mind something more akin to the ancient Egyptian goddess Sekhmet, "at whose wish the arts were born," "lady of intoxication," "giver of ecstasies," "inspirer of males," "ruler of serpents and dragons," "destroyer of rebellions," and so on and so forth, a formidable force in the human firmament.

While the question "what is art?" can never be answered satisfactorily, a more pointed question relevant to this publication might be, is the copying of photographs an inferior form of artistic expression to drawing or painting directly from life? Once again, there seems to be no simple answer. Copying from photos may well be inferior to working directly from life. Intuitively, it "feels" like "cheating," but then one can point to the example of Vermeer with his camera obscura. Was the great 17th century painter "cheating"? Who's to judge? Art in our technological age exists in a vastly different context from the art of previous times, and the validity or originality of any contemporary work of art must be judged according to a very different set of criteria. You, dear reader, must use your own eyes and trust to your own judgment.

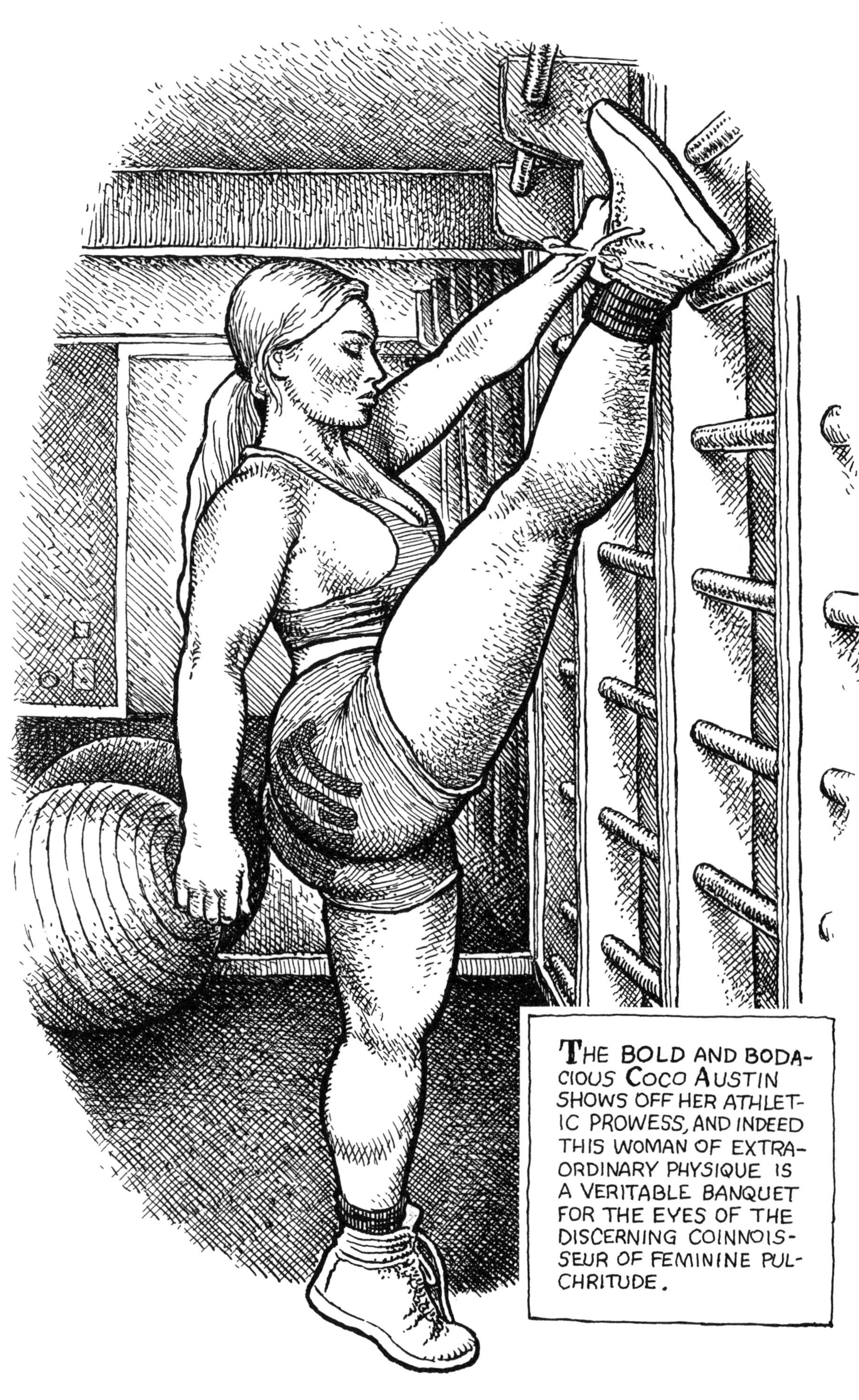

THE BOLD AND BODA-
CIOUS COCO AUSTIN
SHOWS OFF HER ATHLET-
IC PROWESS, AND INDEED
THIS WOMAN OF EXTRA-
ORDINARY PHYSIQUE IS
A VERITABLE BANQUET
FOR THE EYES OF THE
DISCERNING COINNOIS-
SEUR OF FEMININE PUL-
CHRITUDE.

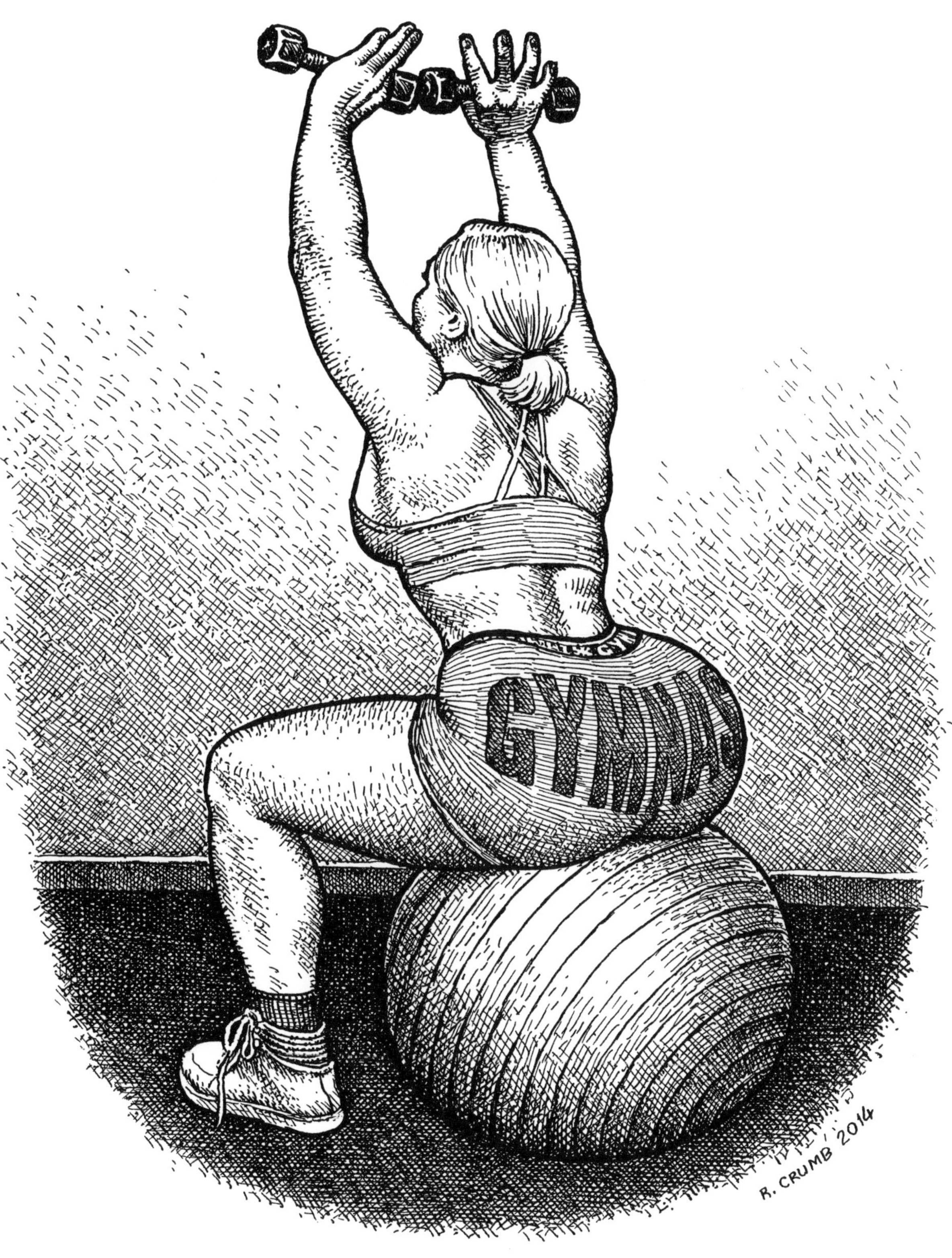

THE LOVELY COCO IS RENOWNED THE WORLD OVER AS A WHITE GIRL WHO IS THE PROUD POSSESSER OF A STRIKING PHYSICAL ATTRIBUTE MOST OFTEN CLAIMED BY WOMEN OF AFRICAN DESCENT, AS SHE SO OFFHANDEDLY REVEALS IN THIS EXERCISE POSE.

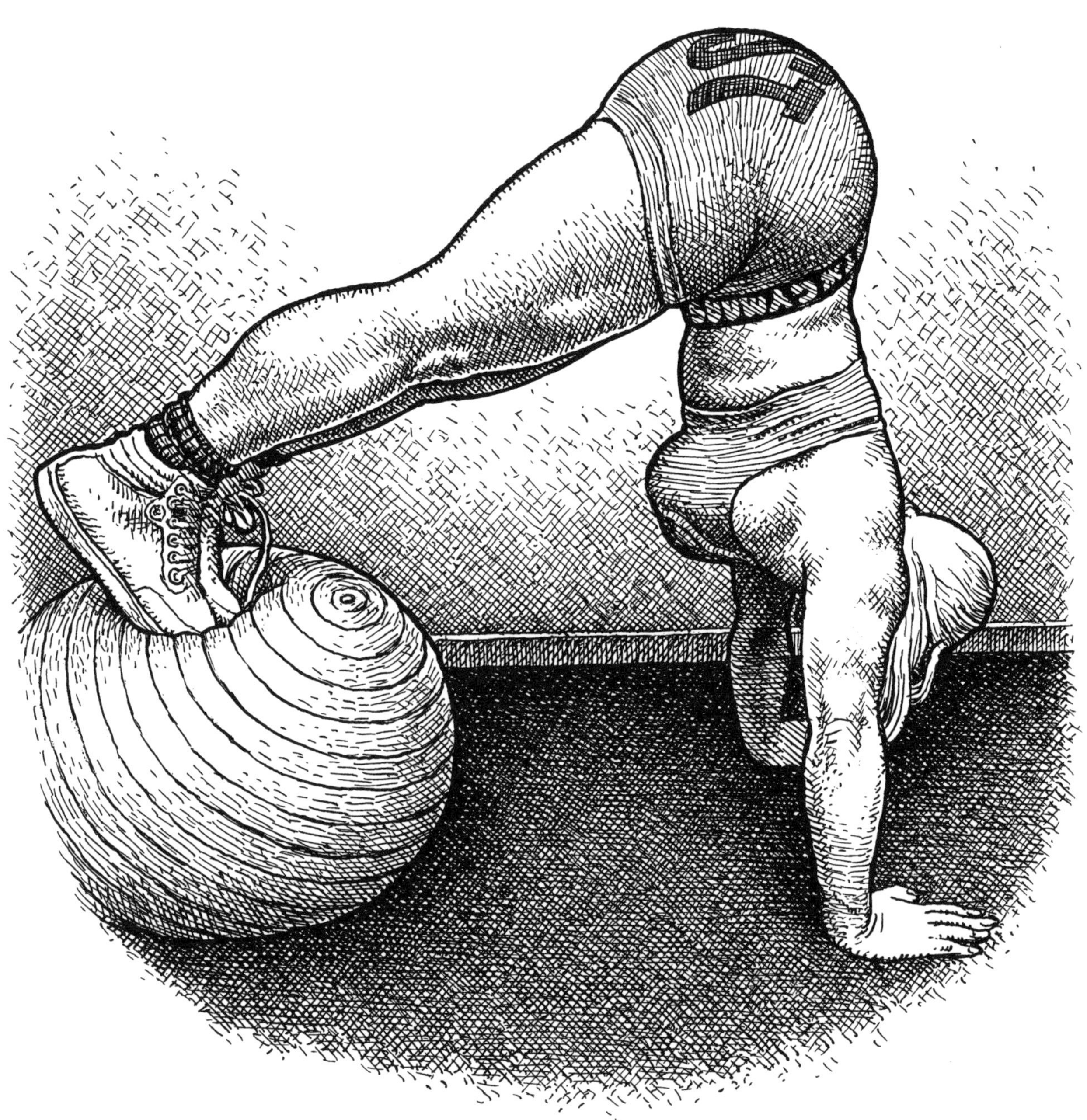

HERE WE SEE ANOTHER EXERCISE POSITION WHICH AFFORDS COCO THE OPPORTUNITY TO DISPLAY HER GRACEFUL STRENGTH, AT THE SAME TIME, PERHAPS UNKNOWINGLY, CREATING A PERFECT COMPOSITION OF SPHERES AND ELLIPSES, A TOTALITY OF DELIGHT FOR THE EYE OF THE BEHOLDER.

"NO MATTER IF THE ARTIST HIMSELF IS A PHYSICAL WEAKLING, YET HE STRIVES TO PORTRAY THE BODY IN ITS MOST IDEAL, BEAUTIFUL FORM." — GEORGE F. JOWETT, PHYSICAL CULTURIST, PITTSBURGH, PA.

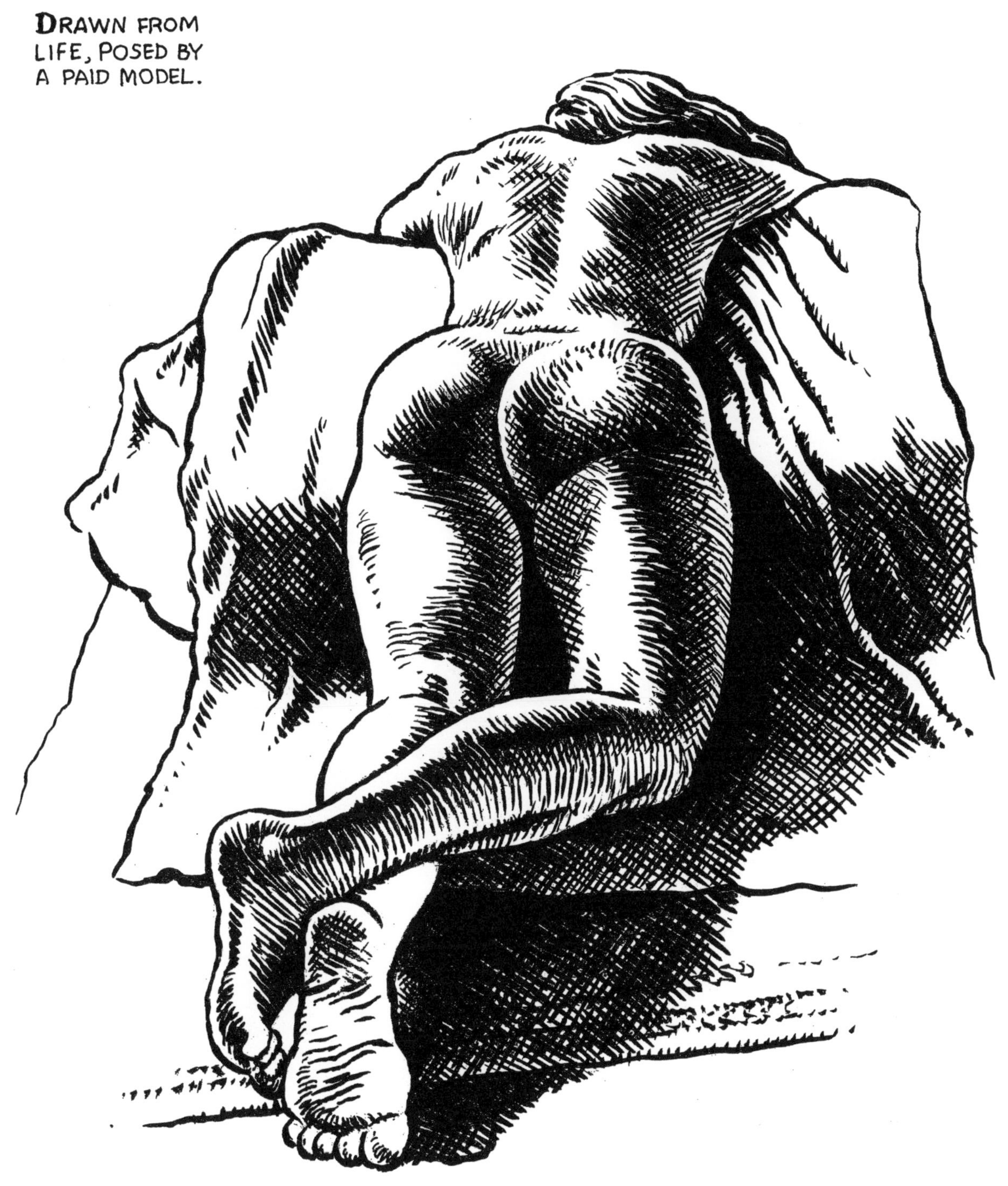

"*If a good form is not intended to be seen, why is it? The perfume of flowers was meant to be smelled, delicious fruits should be eaten, for the same reason a beautiful form is wasted when not revealed.*"
—— *Rubie Stevens, artist's model and cabaret dancer in New York, 1926*

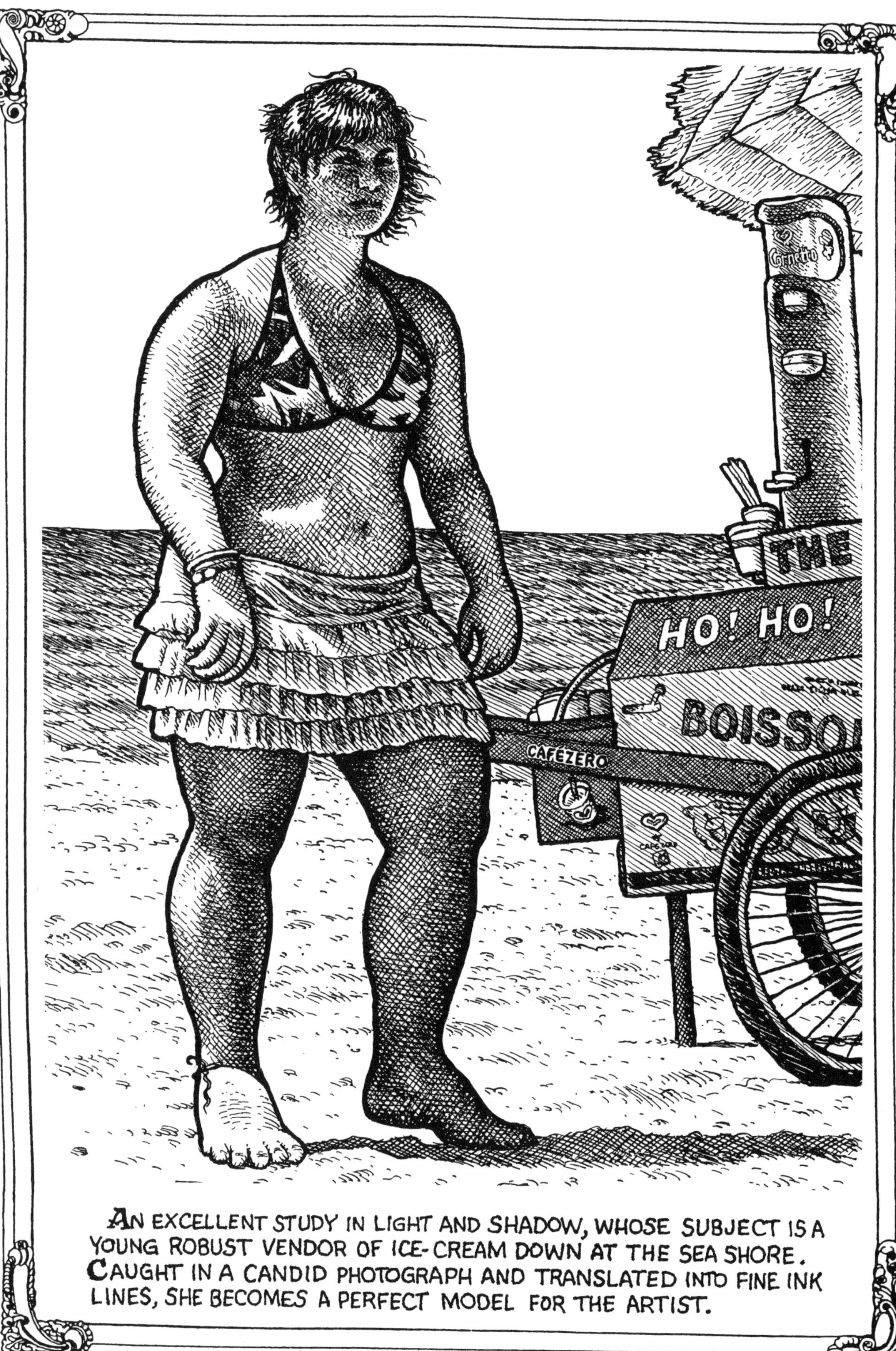

An excellent study in light and shadow, whose subject is a young robust vendor of ice-cream down at the sea shore. Caught in a candid photograph and translated into fine ink lines, she becomes a perfect model for the artist.

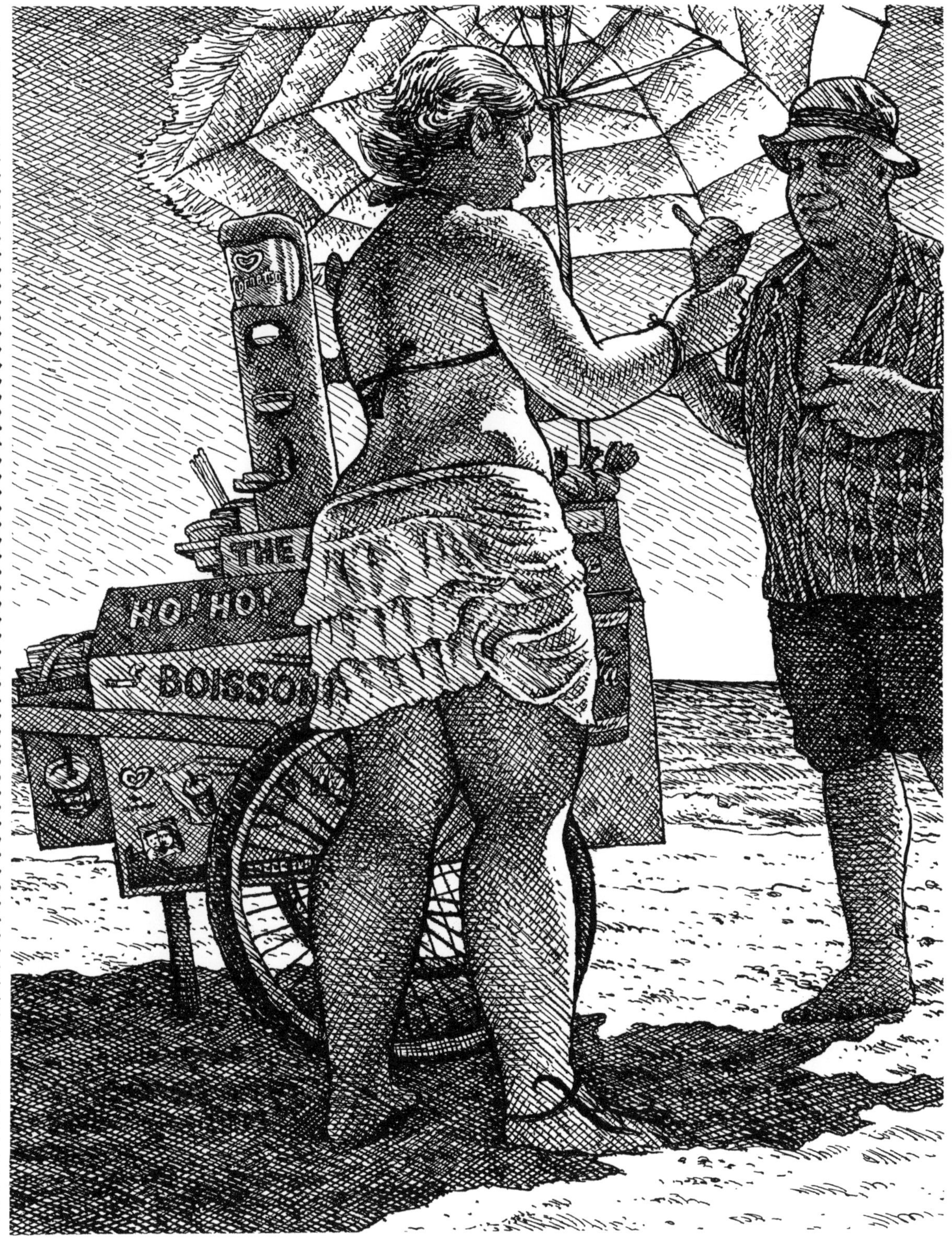

THE YOUNG ICE-CREAM VENDOR, AS PORTRAYED ON THE PREVIOUS PAGE, IS RENDERED ONCE AGAIN, THIS TIME IN THE ACT OF PLYING HER WARES TO A TYPICAL VACATIONER. AN IRRESISTABLE INSPIRATION TO THE ARTIST, WHO IS COMPELLED TO MEET THE CHALLENGE OF CAPTURING THE PLAY OF LIGHT AND SHADOW ON THE VOLUPTUOUSLY ROUNDED CURVES OF THE GIRL'S SOLIDLY RUBENESQUE FIGURE.

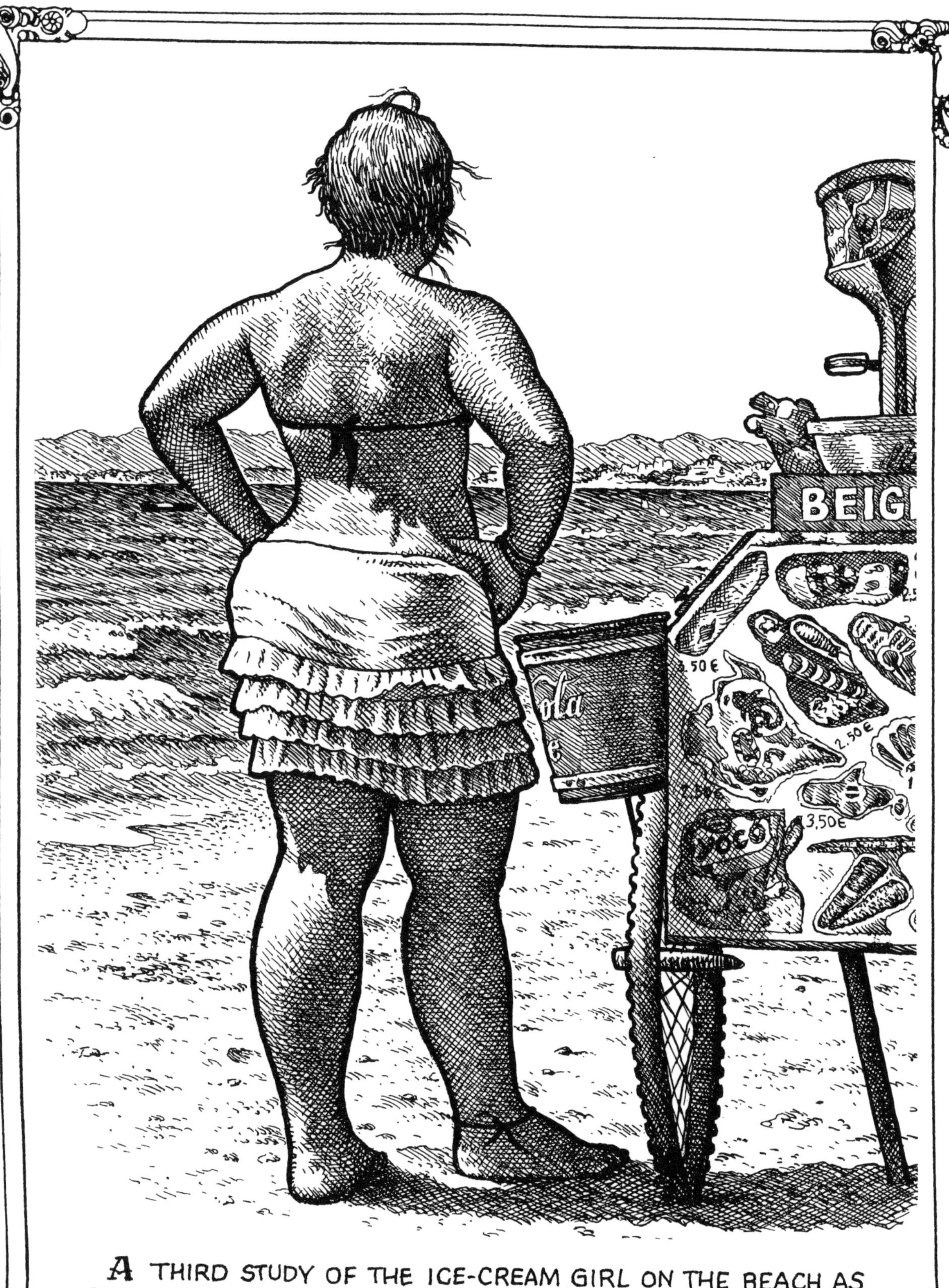

A THIRD STUDY OF THE ICE-CREAM GIRL ON THE BEACH AS SHE GAZES OUT AT THE SEA, DREAMING HER OWN DREAMS, THE HOT SUMMER SUN CREATING GLEAMING HIGH-LIGHTS ON HER SHINY, TANNED YOUNG BODY. SHE STANDS AS IF ON THE BRINK OF LIFE, HER DESTINY, HER FATE, AS YET UNDECIDED.

DRAWN
FROM
LIFE.

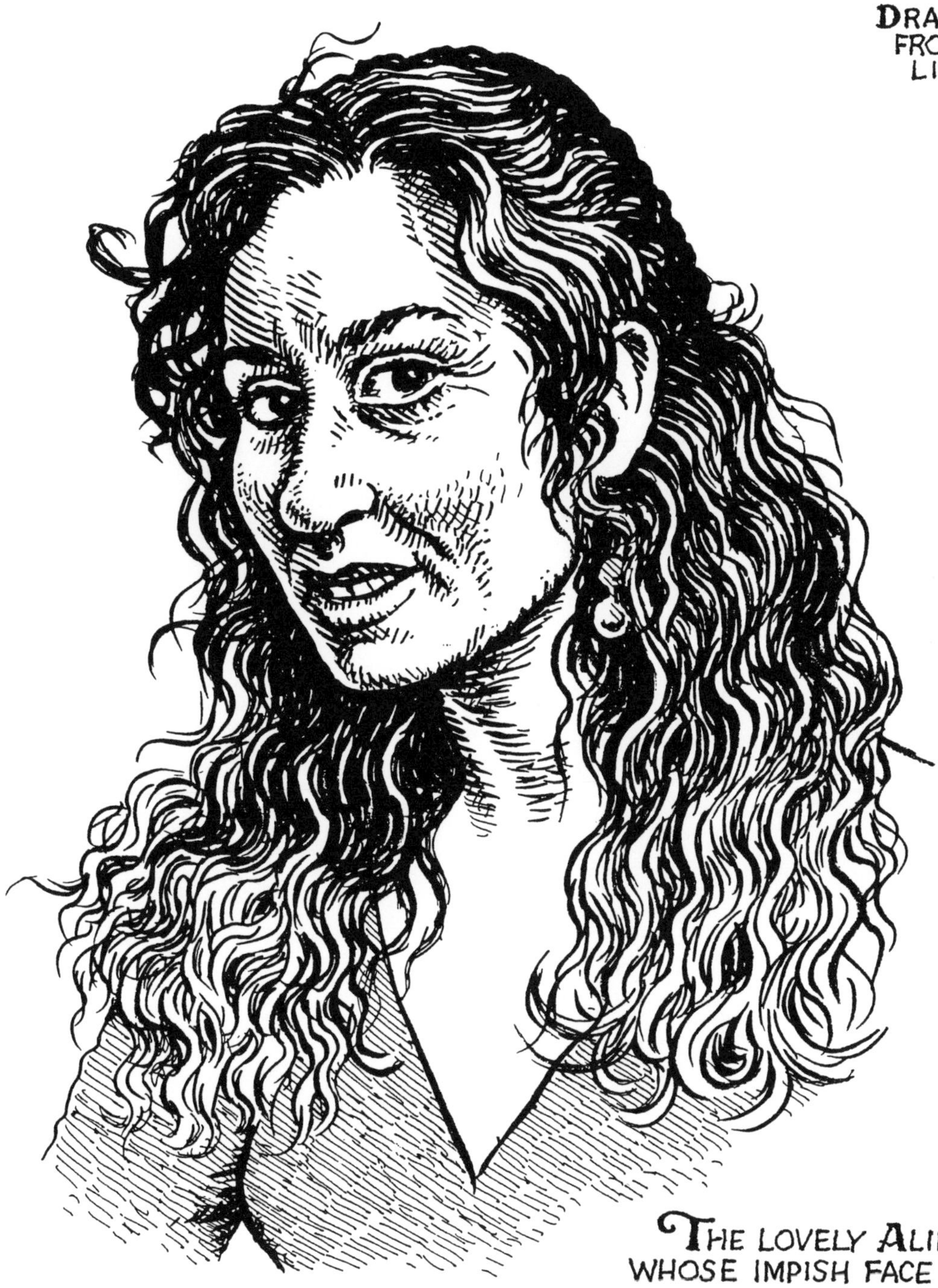

THE LOVELY ALINE, WHOSE IMPISH FACE AND FORM HAVE GRACED THE PAGES OF *ART & BEAUTY* IN PREVIOUS ISSUES. SHE ALSO HAPPENS TO BE THE ARTIST'S WIFE, AND AN ARTIST OF RENOWN IN HER OWN RIGHT.

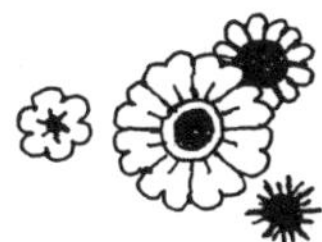

"IT IS THE NATURE OF WOMAN TO WISH TO BE GLORIFIED, IN PAINT AS MUCH AS SEXUALLY... MANY A GIRL WHO WOULD HESITATE TO 'GIVE' HERSELF TO A MAN SHE LIKED WOULD BE QUITE HAPPY A-BOUT 'GIVING' HERSELF TO HIM BY POSING NUDE." ~~~ JAMES McINTYRE, PAINTER

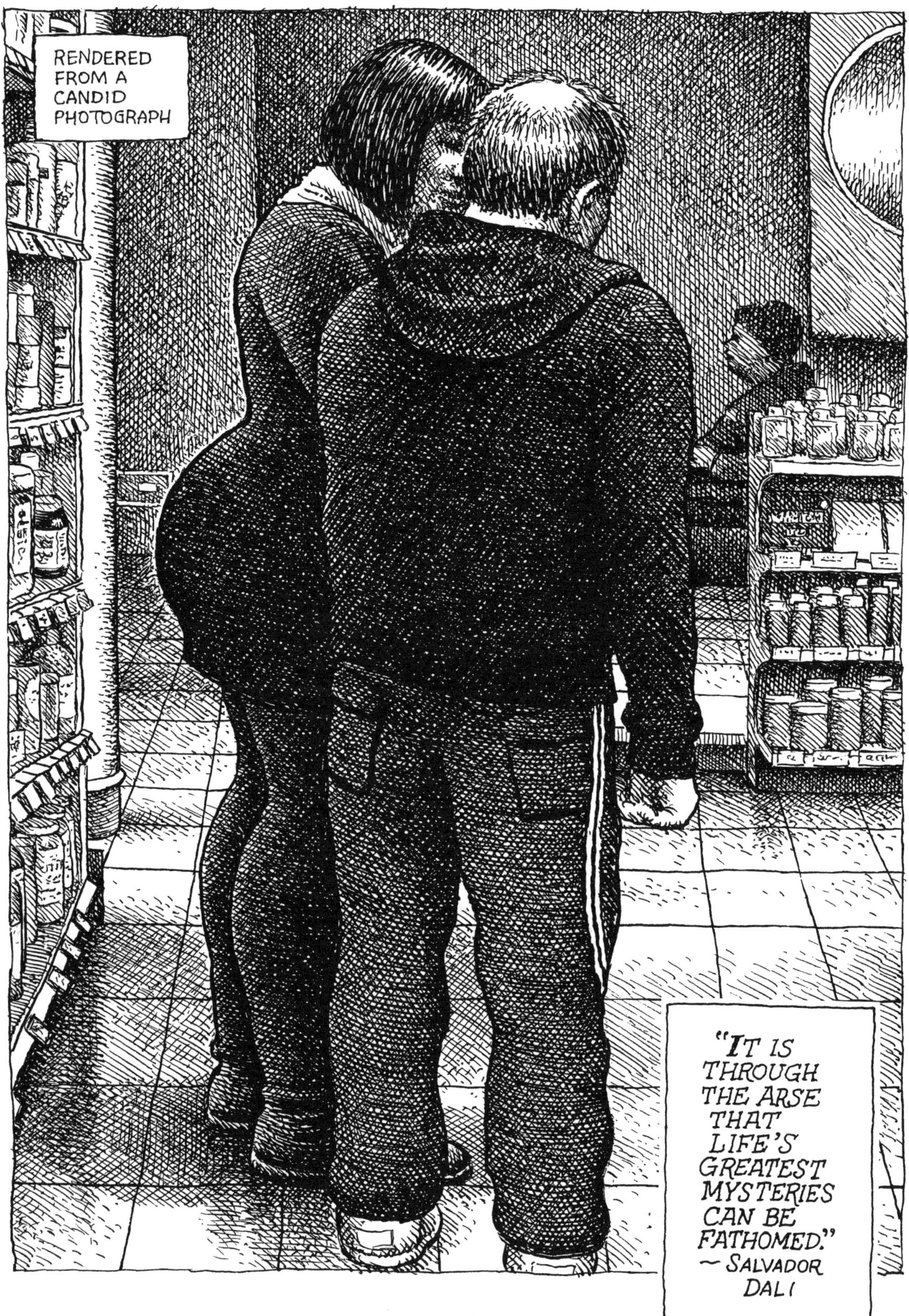

RENDERED
FROM A
CANDID
PHOTOGRAPH

"IT IS
THROUGH
THE ARSE
THAT
LIFE'S
GREATEST
MYSTERIES
CAN BE
FATHOMED."
~ SALVADOR
DALI

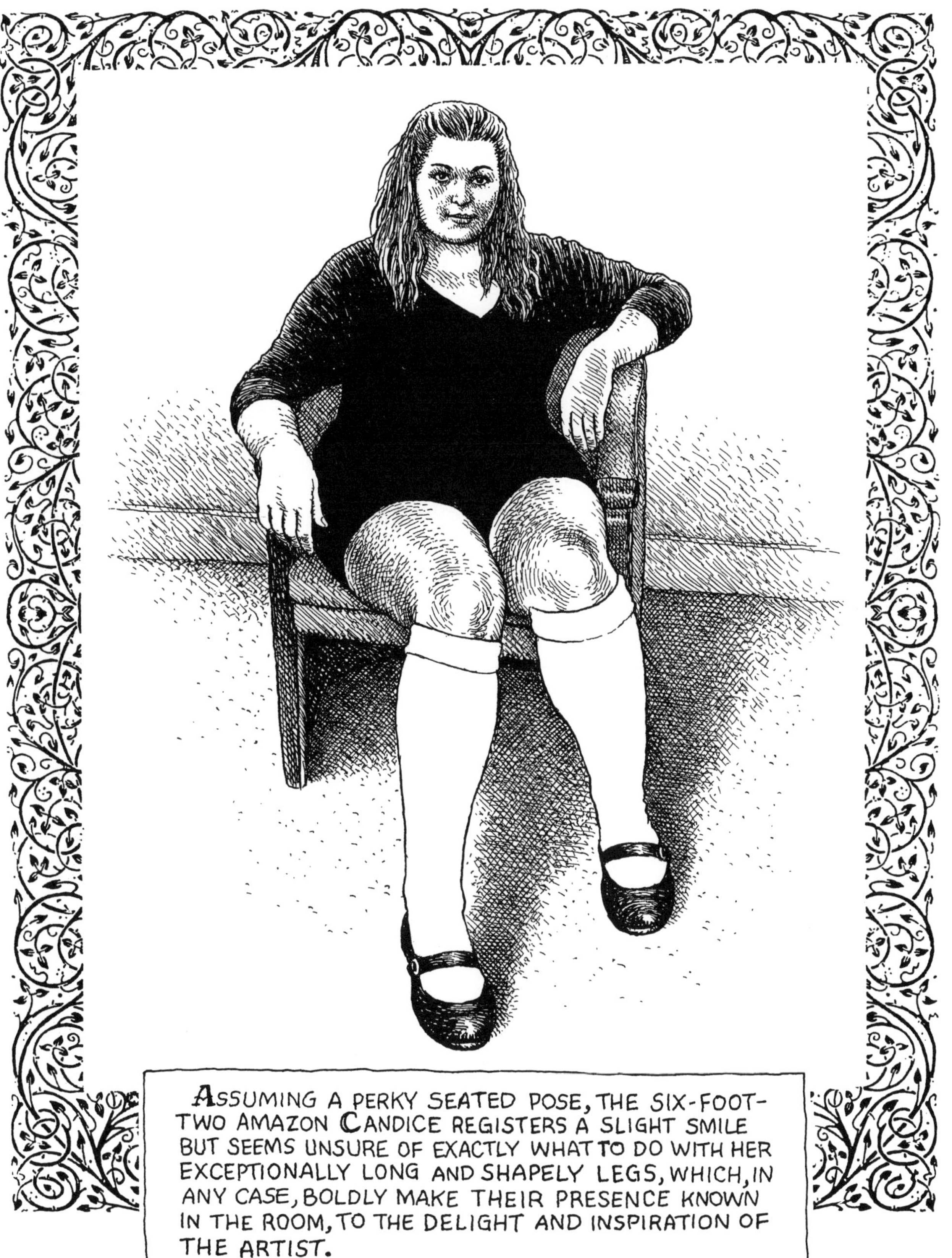

ASSUMING A PERKY SEATED POSE, THE SIX-FOOT-TWO AMAZON CANDICE REGISTERS A SLIGHT SMILE BUT SEEMS UNSURE OF EXACTLY WHAT TO DO WITH HER EXCEPTIONALLY LONG AND SHAPELY LEGS, WHICH, IN ANY CASE, BOLDLY MAKE THEIR PRESENCE KNOWN IN THE ROOM, TO THE DELIGHT AND INSPIRATION OF THE ARTIST.

"THE MORE YOU LOOK AT THE SAME EXACT THING, THE MORE THE MEANING GOES AWAY, AND THE BETTER AND EMPTIER YOU FEEL."
—— ANDY WARHOL

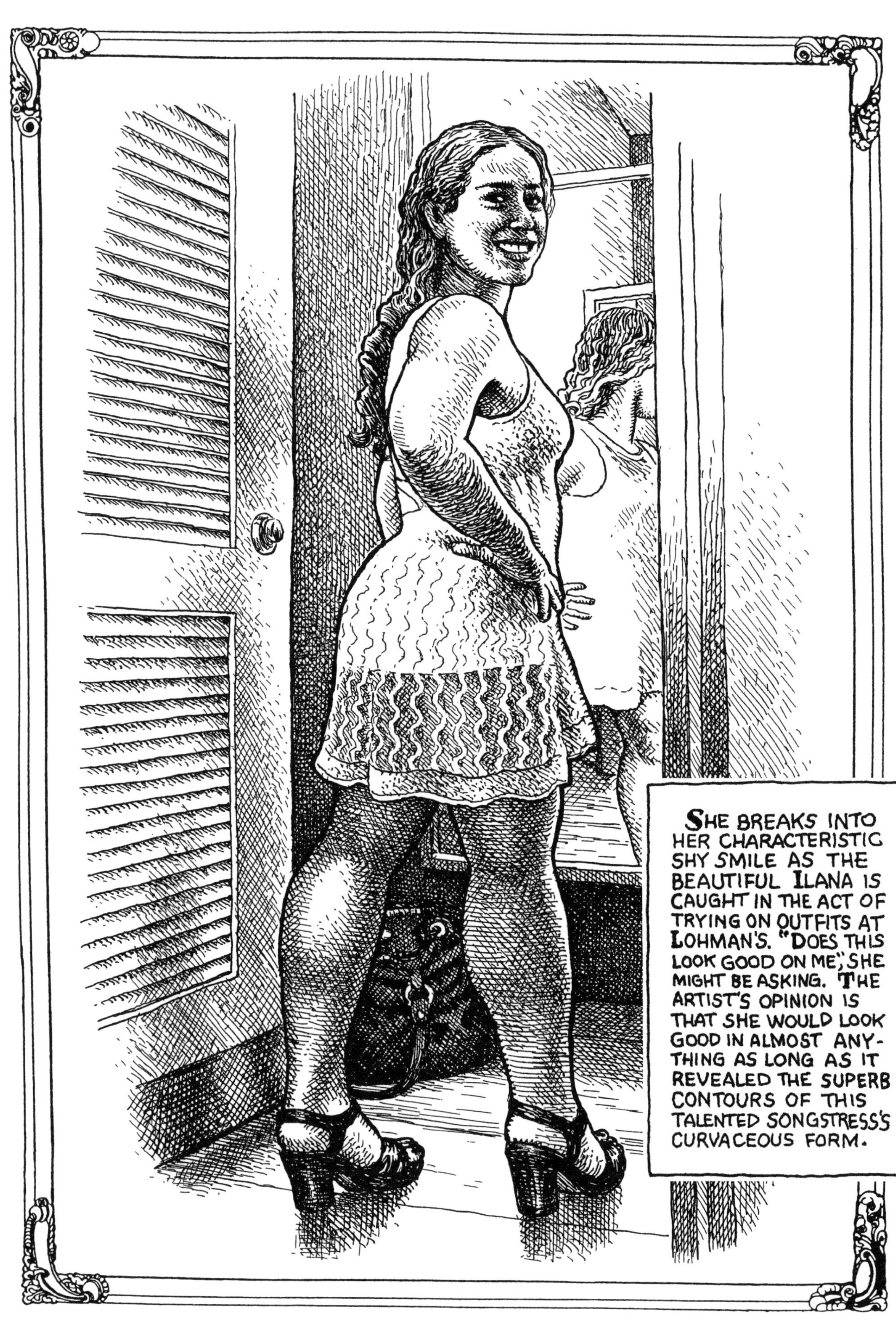

SHE BREAKS INTO HER CHARACTERISTIC SHY SMILE AS THE BEAUTIFUL ILANA IS CAUGHT IN THE ACT OF TRYING ON OUTFITS AT LOHMAN'S. "DOES THIS LOOK GOOD ON ME", SHE MIGHT BE ASKING. THE ARTIST'S OPINION IS THAT SHE WOULD LOOK GOOD IN ALMOST ANYTHING AS LONG AS IT REVEALED THE SUPERB CONTOURS OF THIS TALENTED SONGSTRESS'S CURVACEOUS FORM.

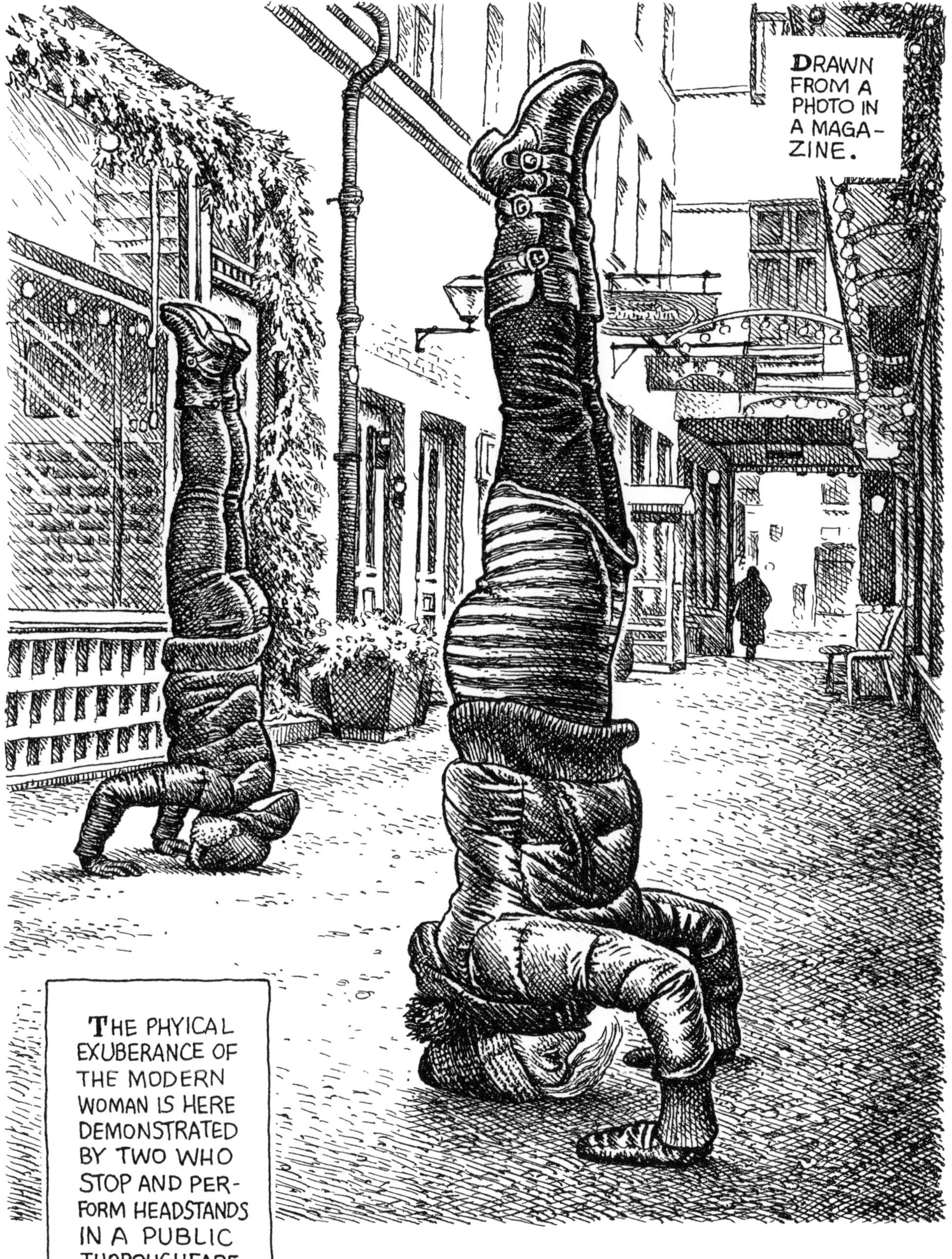

DRAWN FROM A PHOTO IN A MAGAZINE.
THE PHYICAL EXUBERANCE OF THE MODERN WOMAN IS HERE DEMONSTRATED BY TWO WHO STOP AND PERFORM HEADSTANDS IN A PUBLIC THOROUGHFARE, PERHAPS ON A DARE FROM THE PHOTOGRAPHER.
"THE ROAD ONE MUST TRAVEL TO REACH THE PINNACLE OF ART IS BESET WITH DAYS AND NIGHTS OF WORK, WITH DEPRIVATIONS AND FATIGUE." ~ RENÈE REBANÉ, PARISIAN ARTIST'S MODEL

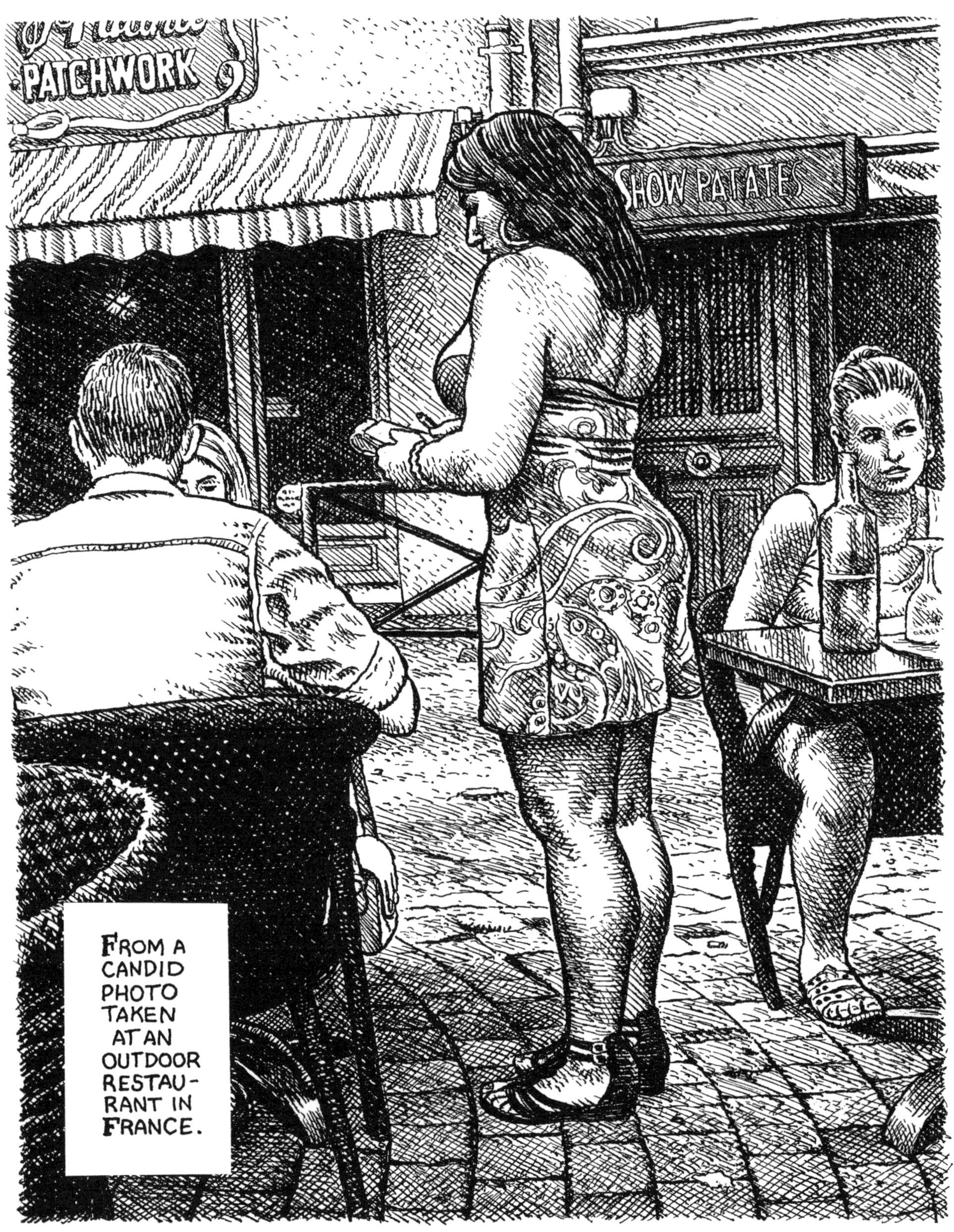

"THOSE WHO SUCCEED IN ART DO SO BECAUSE THEY CANNOT QUIT, BECAUSE THEY POSSESS PATIENCE AND A GENIUNE LOVE FOR THE WORK. MOST ASPIRANTS IN THIS DIRECTION DO NOT REALLY LOVE ART WORK; THEY LOVE THE FAME AND FORTUNE THAT ARE SUPPOSED TO COME TO ARTISTS. THE PROCESS OF BECOMING AN ARTIST IS ONE OF SLOW SPIRITUAL AND MENTAL DEVELOPMENT." ⸺ H. L. McCLEOD, "FIGURE DRAWING", 1924

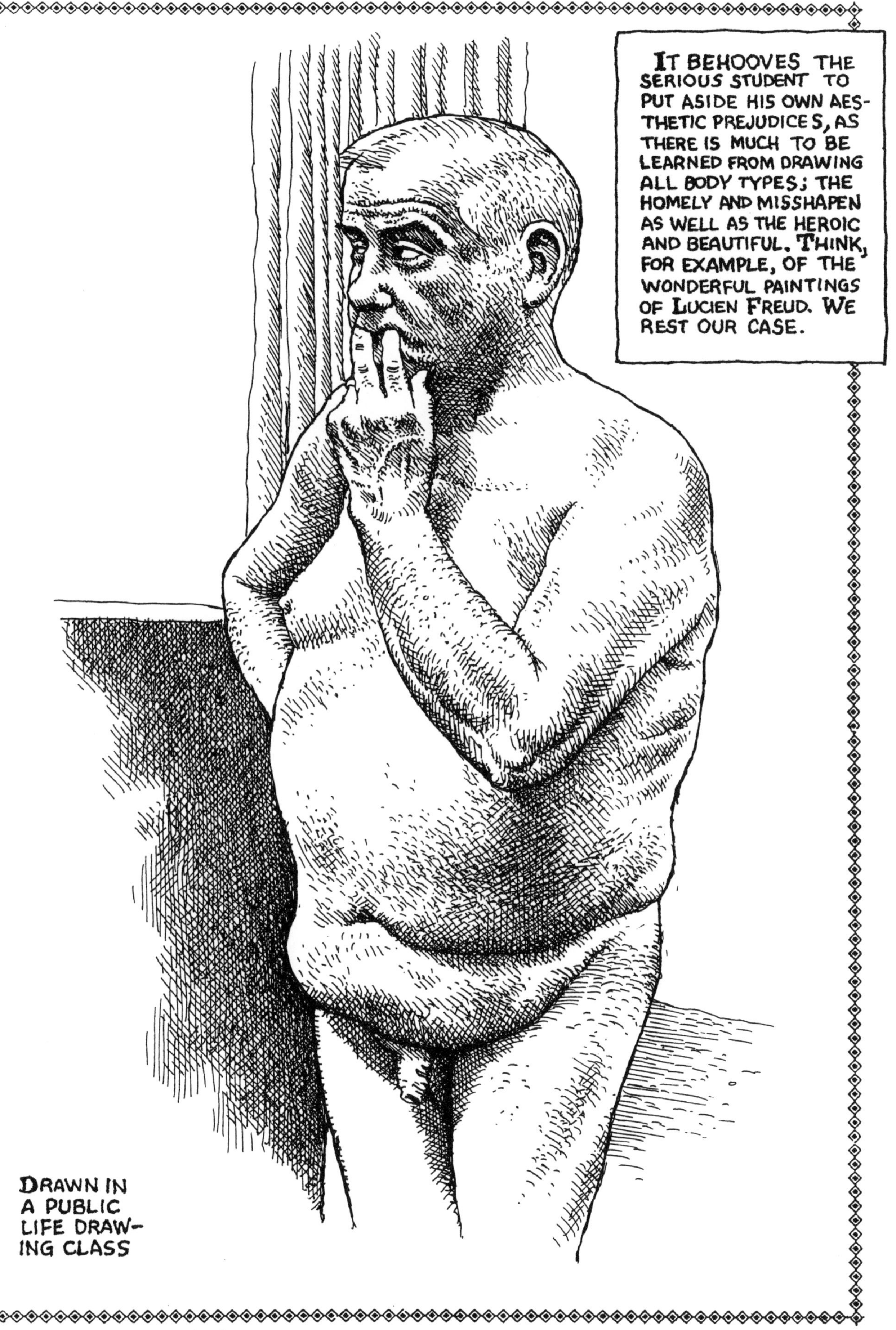

IT BEHOOVES THE SERIOUS STUDENT TO PUT ASIDE HIS OWN AESTHETIC PREJUDICES, AS THERE IS MUCH TO BE LEARNED FROM DRAWING ALL BODY TYPES; THE HOMELY AND MISSHAPEN AS WELL AS THE HEROIC AND BEAUTIFUL. THINK, FOR EXAMPLE, OF THE WONDERFUL PAINTINGS OF LUCIEN FREUD. WE REST OUR CASE.
DRAWN IN A PUBLIC LIFE DRAWING CLASS

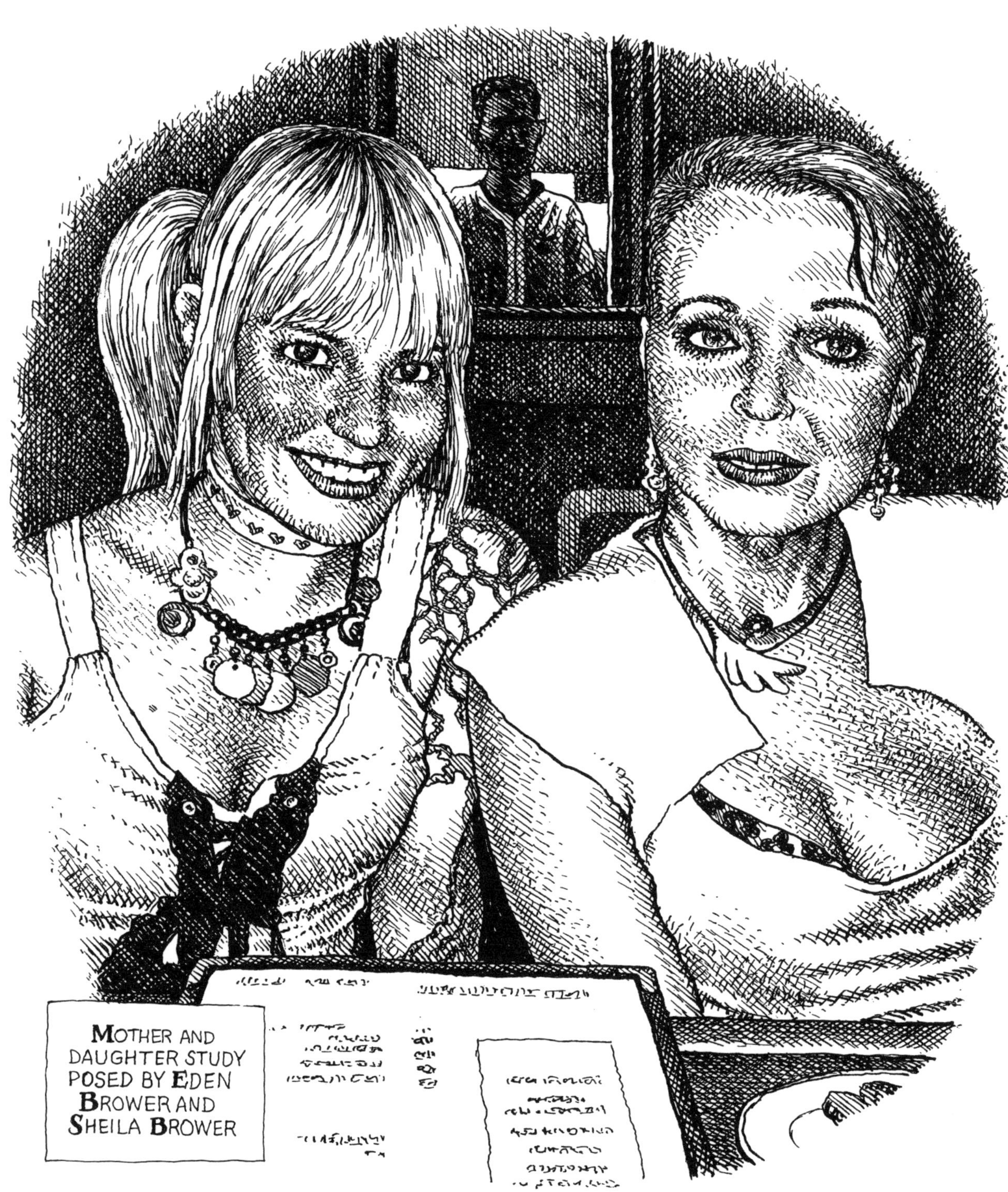

THE EXCELLENT SYMMETRY OF EDEN'S FLAWLESS FEATURES, AS EVIDENCED BY THIS STUDY FROM A PHOTO TAKEN AT A RESTAURANT, WOULD SEEM TO BE AN INHERITED TRAIT—OR PERHAPS IT IS THE LUCK OF THE GENETIC DRAW. WHO ARE WE TO SAY? EDEN, A POPULAR AND CHARISMATIC ENTERTAINER ON THE FOLK MUSIC CIRCUIT IN AND AROUND THE NEW YORK AREA, IS NOT ONLY THRILLING TO WATCH ON STAGE, BUT A GREAT PLEASURE TO LISTEN TO AS WELL.

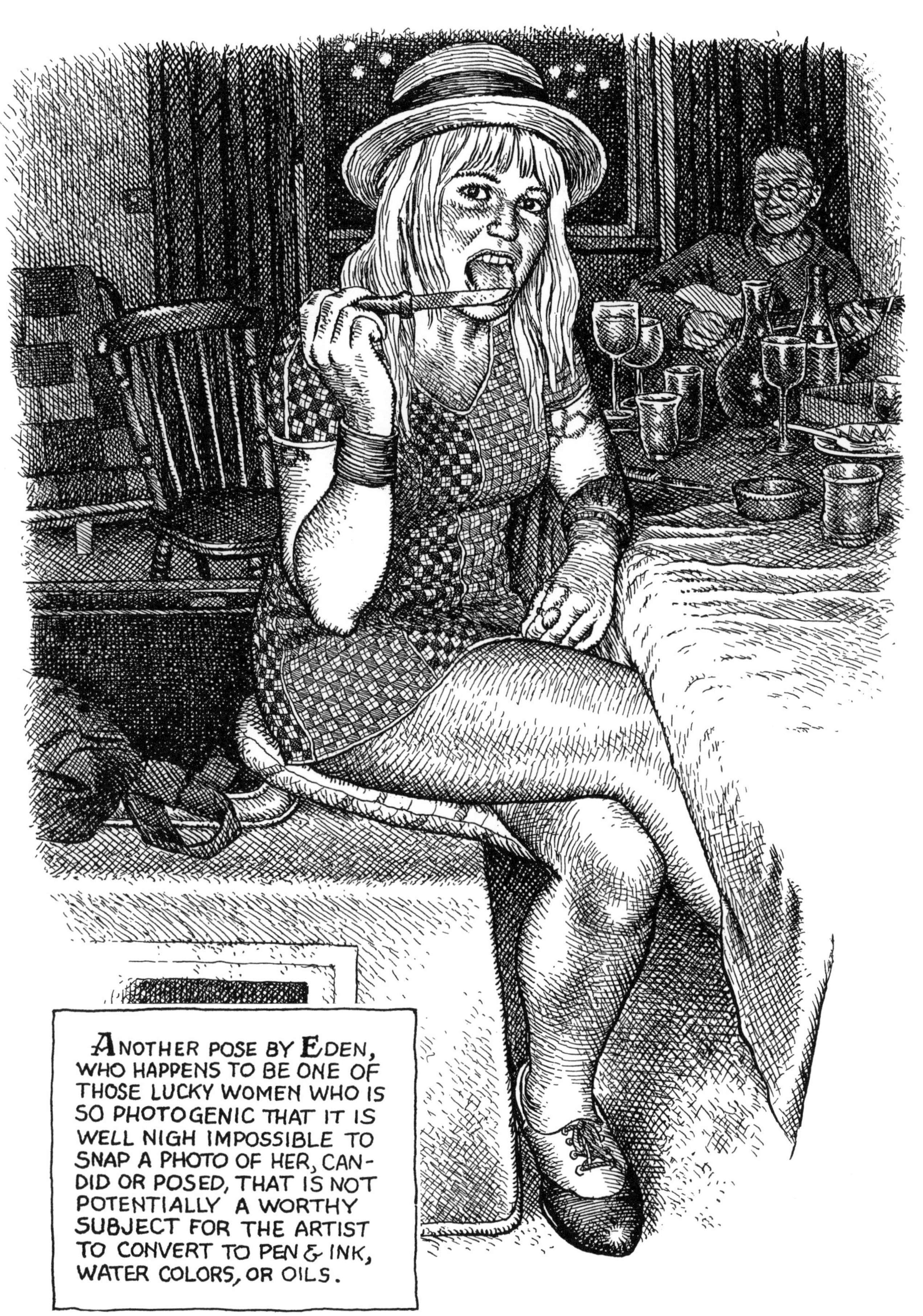

ANOTHER POSE BY EDEN,
WHO HAPPENS TO BE ONE OF
THOSE LUCKY WOMEN WHO IS
SO PHOTOGENIC THAT IT IS
WELL NIGH IMPOSSIBLE TO
SNAP A PHOTO OF HER, CAN-
DID OR POSED, THAT IS NOT
POTENTIALLY A WORTHY
SUBJECT FOR THE ARTIST
TO CONVERT TO PEN & INK,
WATER COLORS, OR OILS.

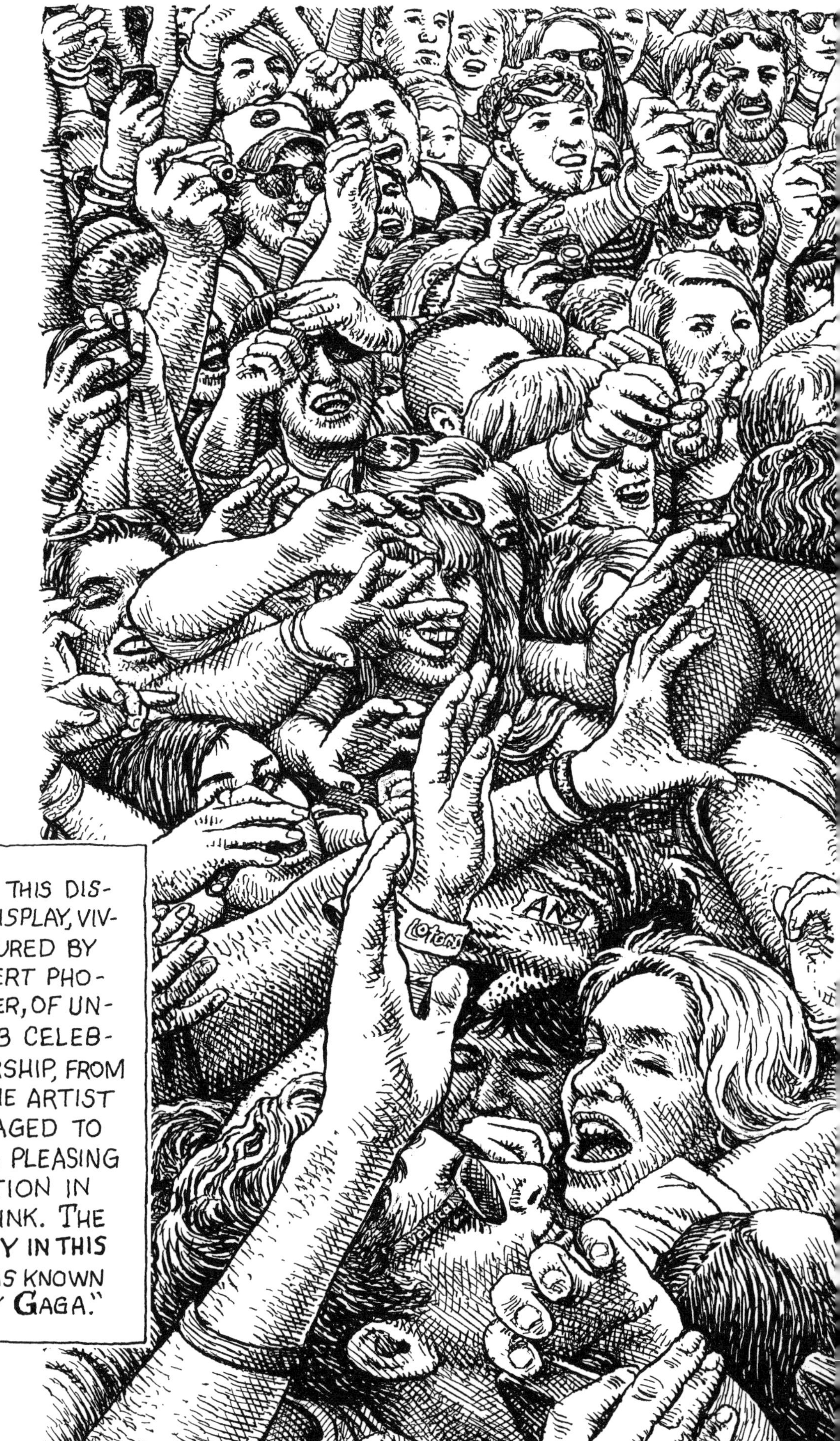

COPIED FROM A PHOTO IN A MAGAZINE
BEHOLD THIS DISGUSTING DISPLAY, VIVIDLY CAPTURED BY SOME ALERT PHOTOGRAPHER, OF UNRULY MOB CELEBRITY WORSHIP, FROM WHICH THE ARTIST HAS MANAGED TO CREATE A PLEASING COMPOSITION IN PEN AND INK. THE CELEBRITY IN THIS INSTANCE IS KNOWN AS "LADY GAGA."

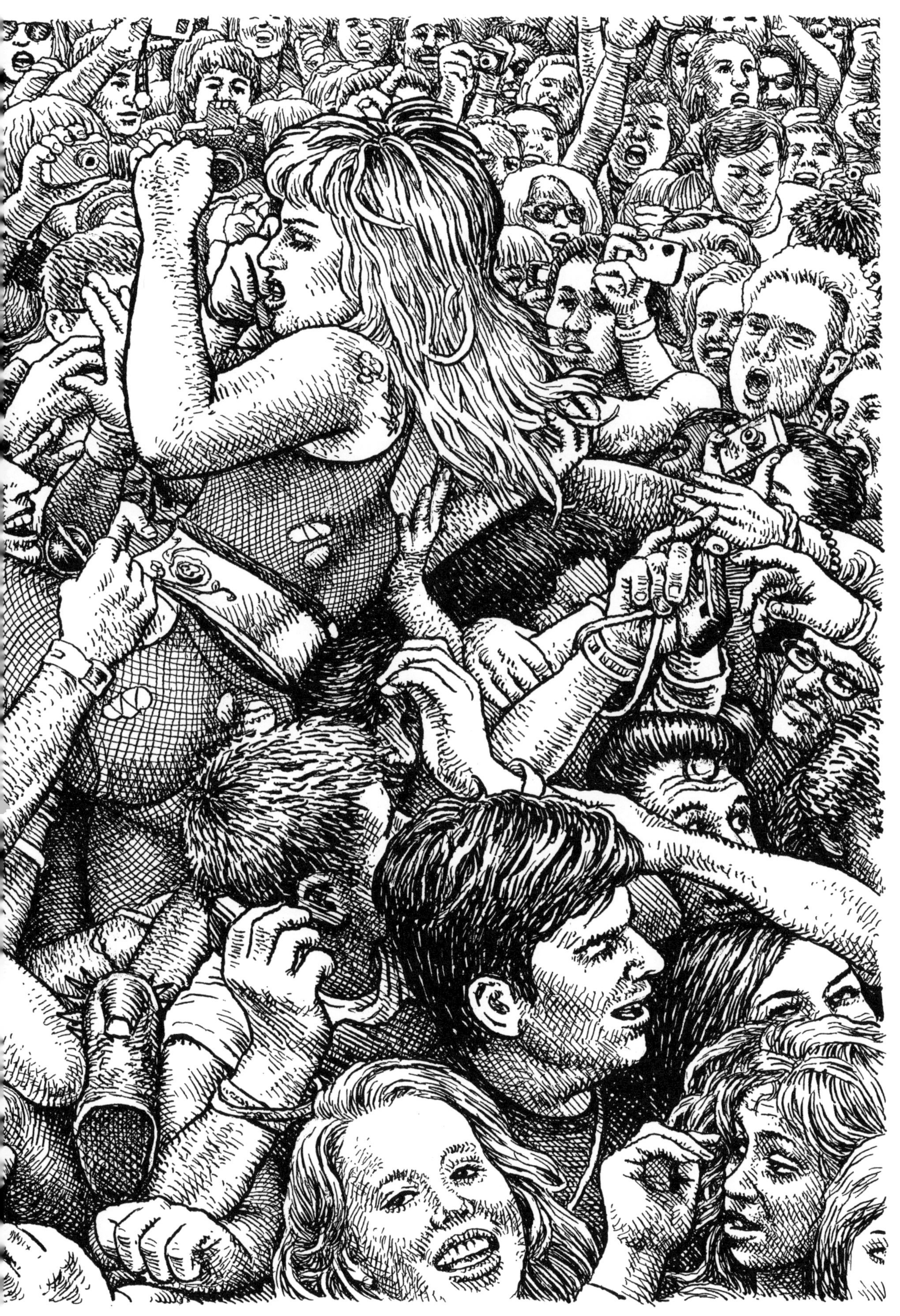

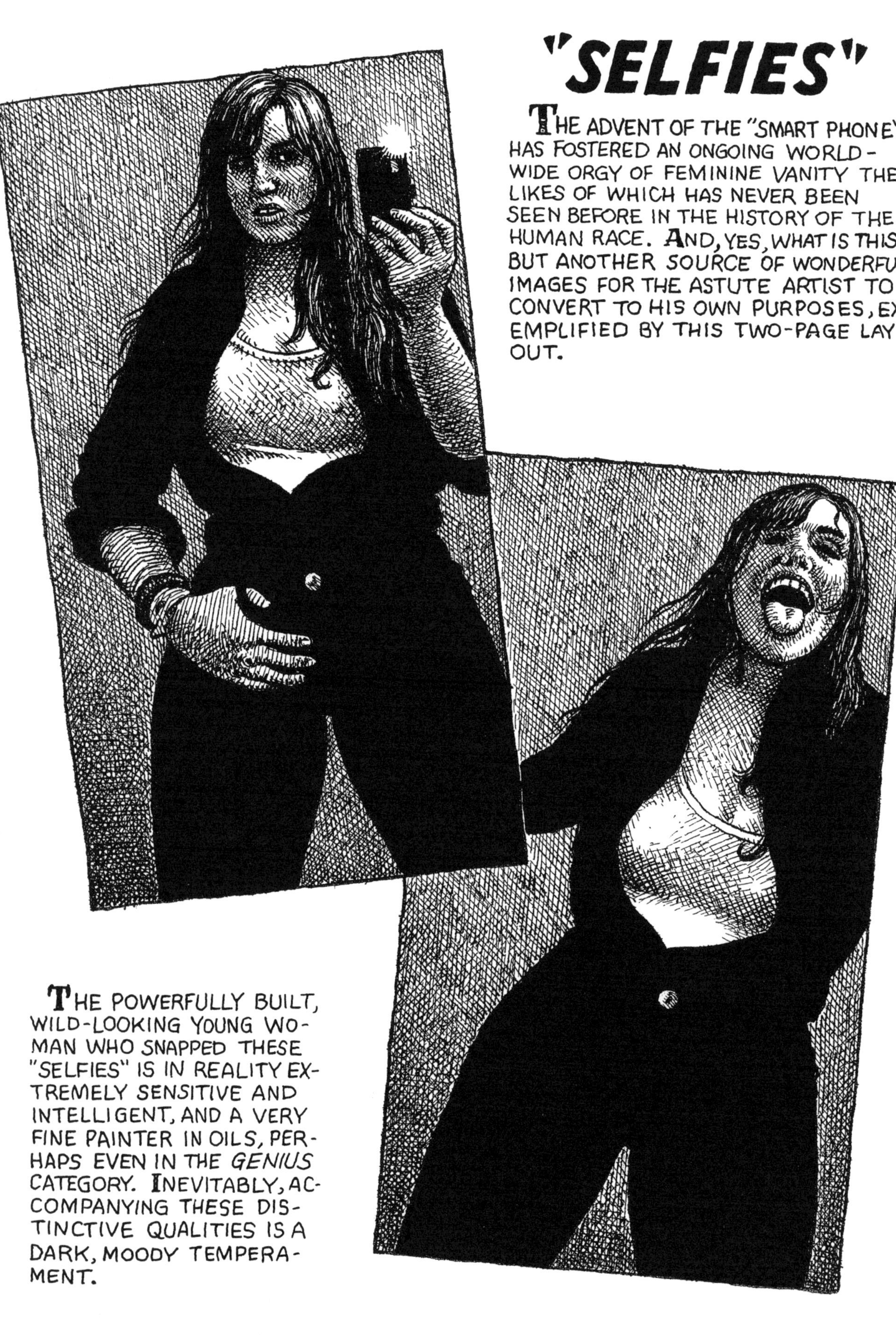

"SELFIES"

THE ADVENT OF THE "SMART PHONE" HAS FOSTERED AN ONGOING WORLD-WIDE ORGY OF FEMININE VANITY THE LIKES OF WHICH HAS NEVER BEEN SEEN BEFORE IN THE HISTORY OF THE HUMAN RACE. AND, YES, WHAT IS THIS BUT ANOTHER SOURCE OF WONDERFUL IMAGES FOR THE ASTUTE ARTIST TO CONVERT TO HIS OWN PURPOSES, EXEMPLIFIED BY THIS TWO-PAGE LAYOUT.

THE POWERFULLY BUILT, WILD-LOOKING YOUNG WOMAN WHO SNAPPED THESE "SELFIES" IS IN REALITY EXTREMELY SENSITIVE AND INTELLIGENT, AND A VERY FINE PAINTER IN OILS, PERHAPS EVEN IN THE GENIUS CATEGORY. INEVITABLY, ACCOMPANYING THESE DISTINCTIVE QUALITIES IS A DARK, MOODY TEMPERAMENT.

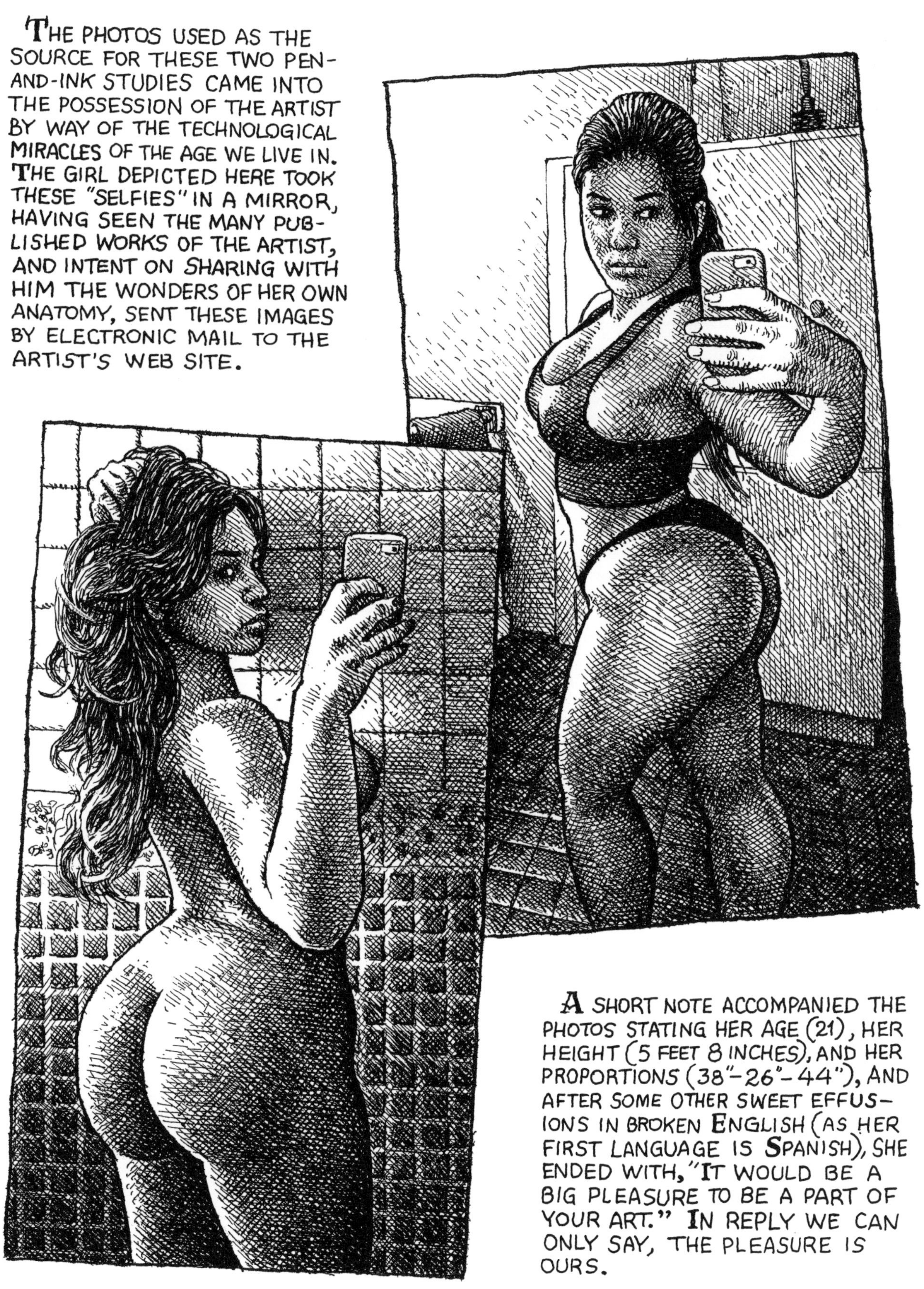

THE PHOTOS USED AS THE SOURCE FOR THESE TWO PEN-AND-INK STUDIES CAME INTO THE POSSESSION OF THE ARTIST BY WAY OF THE TECHNOLOGICAL MIRACLES OF THE AGE WE LIVE IN. THE GIRL DEPICTED HERE TOOK THESE "SELFIES" IN A MIRROR, HAVING SEEN THE MANY PUBLISHED WORKS OF THE ARTIST, AND INTENT ON *SHARING* WITH HIM THE WONDERS OF HER OWN ANATOMY, SENT THESE IMAGES BY ELECTRONIC MAIL TO THE ARTIST'S WEB SITE.

A SHORT NOTE ACCOMPANIED THE PHOTOS STATING HER AGE (21), HER HEIGHT (5 FEET 8 INCHES), AND HER PROPORTIONS (38"-26"-44"), AND AFTER SOME OTHER SWEET EFFUSIONS IN BROKEN ENGLISH (AS HER FIRST LANGUAGE IS SPANISH), SHE ENDED WITH, "IT WOULD BE A BIG PLEASURE TO BE A PART OF YOUR ART." IN REPLY WE CAN ONLY SAY, THE PLEASURE IS OURS.

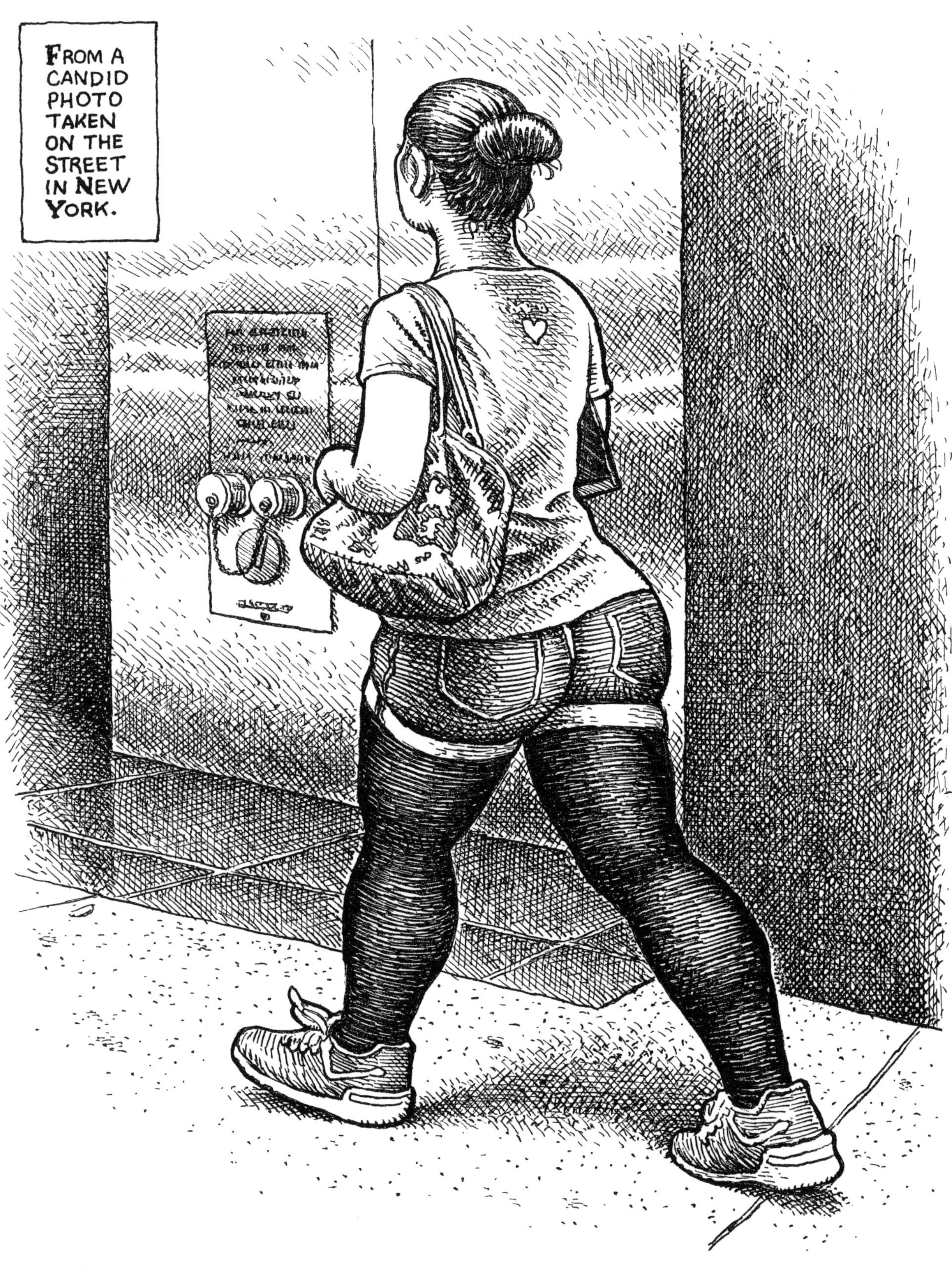

"*ANY PROSPECTIVE ART STUDENT WHO TAKES UP ART BECAUSE HE THINKS IT WILL BE AN EASY WAY OF MAKING BIG MONEY IS DISQUALIFIED BEFORE HE STARTS.*"
·······~ G. H. LOCKWOOD, "*ART AND LIFE*", 1924

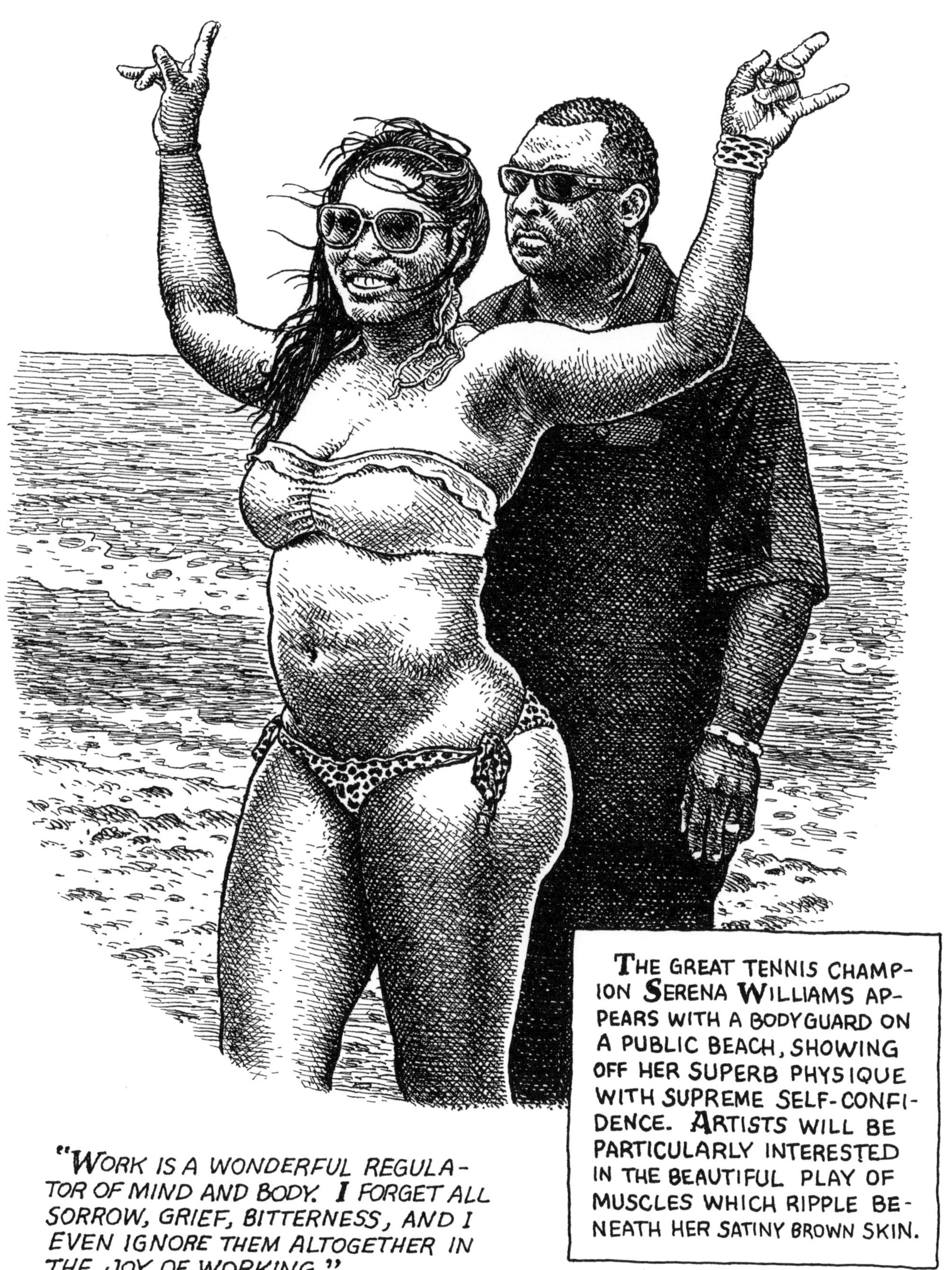

THE GREAT TENNIS CHAMP-
ION SERENA WILLIAMS AP-
PEARS WITH A BODYGUARD ON
A PUBLIC BEACH, SHOWING
OFF HER SUPERB PHYSIQUE
WITH SUPREME SELF-CONFI-
DENCE. ARTISTS WILL BE
PARTICULARLY INTERESTED
IN THE BEAUTIFUL PLAY OF
MUSCLES WHICH RIPPLE BE-
NEATH HER SATINY BROWN SKIN.

"WORK IS A WONDERFUL REGULA-
TOR OF MIND AND BODY. I FORGET ALL
SORROW, GRIEF, BITTERNESS, AND I
EVEN IGNORE THEM ALTOGETHER IN
THE JOY OF WORKING."
—— C. PISARRO

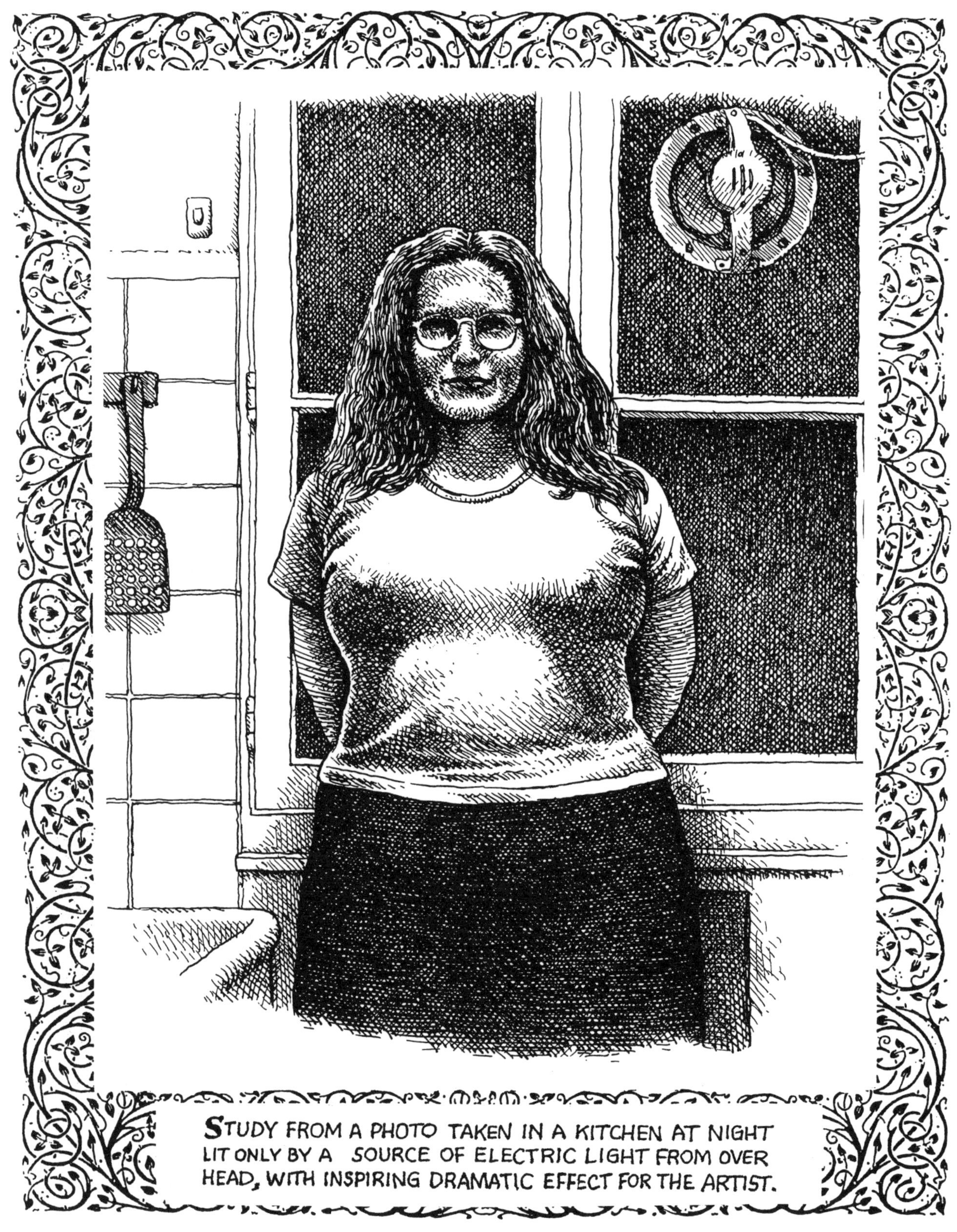

STUDY FROM A PHOTO TAKEN IN A KITCHEN AT NIGHT LIT ONLY BY A SOURCE OF ELECTRIC LIGHT FROM OVER HEAD, WITH INSPIRING DRAMATIC EFFECT FOR THE ARTIST.

"ART IS A LIE THAT MAKES US REALIZE TRUTH." — PICASSO

"THE REAL ARTIST IS LARGELY A PRODUCT OF SELF-TEACHING" — G.H. LOCKWOOD, ART & LIFE, 1924

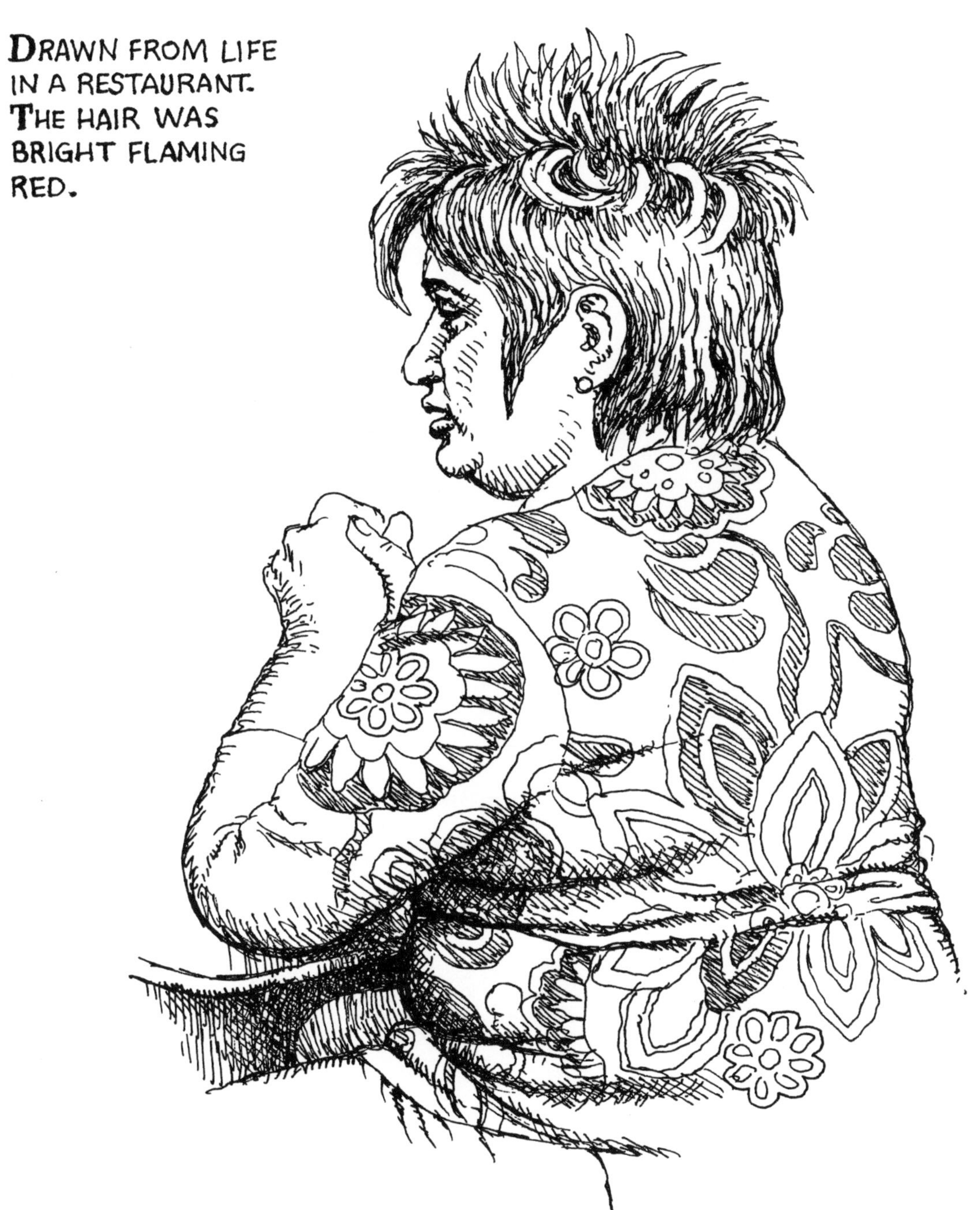

The American College Dictionary defines ART as: 1. The production or expression of what is beautiful, or of more than ordinary significance. 2. Any illustration in a newspaper or magazine. 3. A department of skilled performance: industrial art. 4 (PL.). A branch of learning or university study. 5 (PL.). Liberal arts. 6. Skilled workmanship, execution, or agency (often opposed to nature). These definitions will suffice for our purposes.

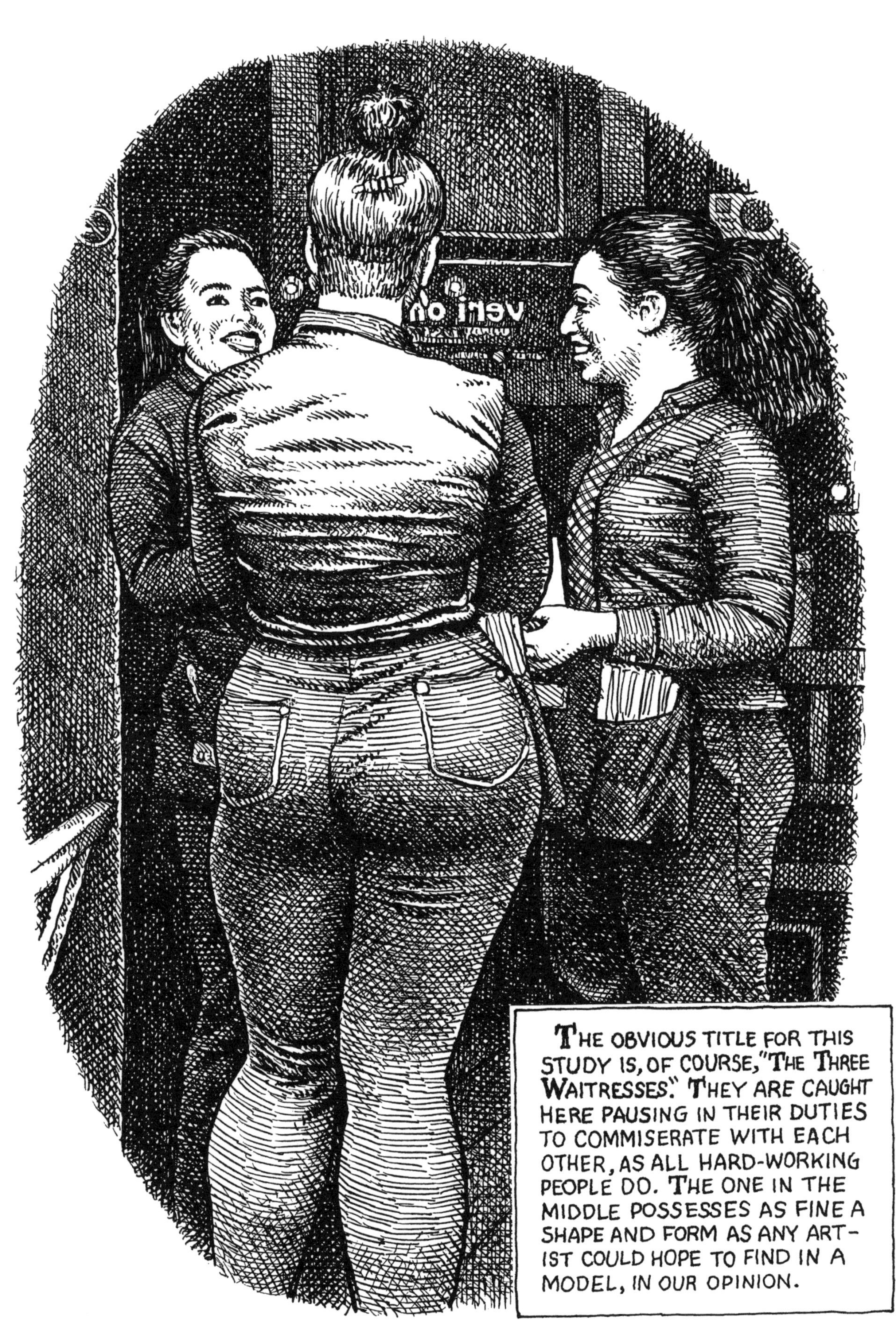

THE OBVIOUS TITLE FOR THIS STUDY IS, OF COURSE, "THE THREE WAITRESSES." THEY ARE CAUGHT HERE PAUSING IN THEIR DUTIES TO COMMISERATE WITH EACH OTHER, AS ALL HARD-WORKING PEOPLE DO. THE ONE IN THE MIDDLE POSSESSES AS FINE A SHAPE AND FORM AS ANY ARTIST COULD HOPE TO FIND IN A MODEL, IN OUR OPINION.

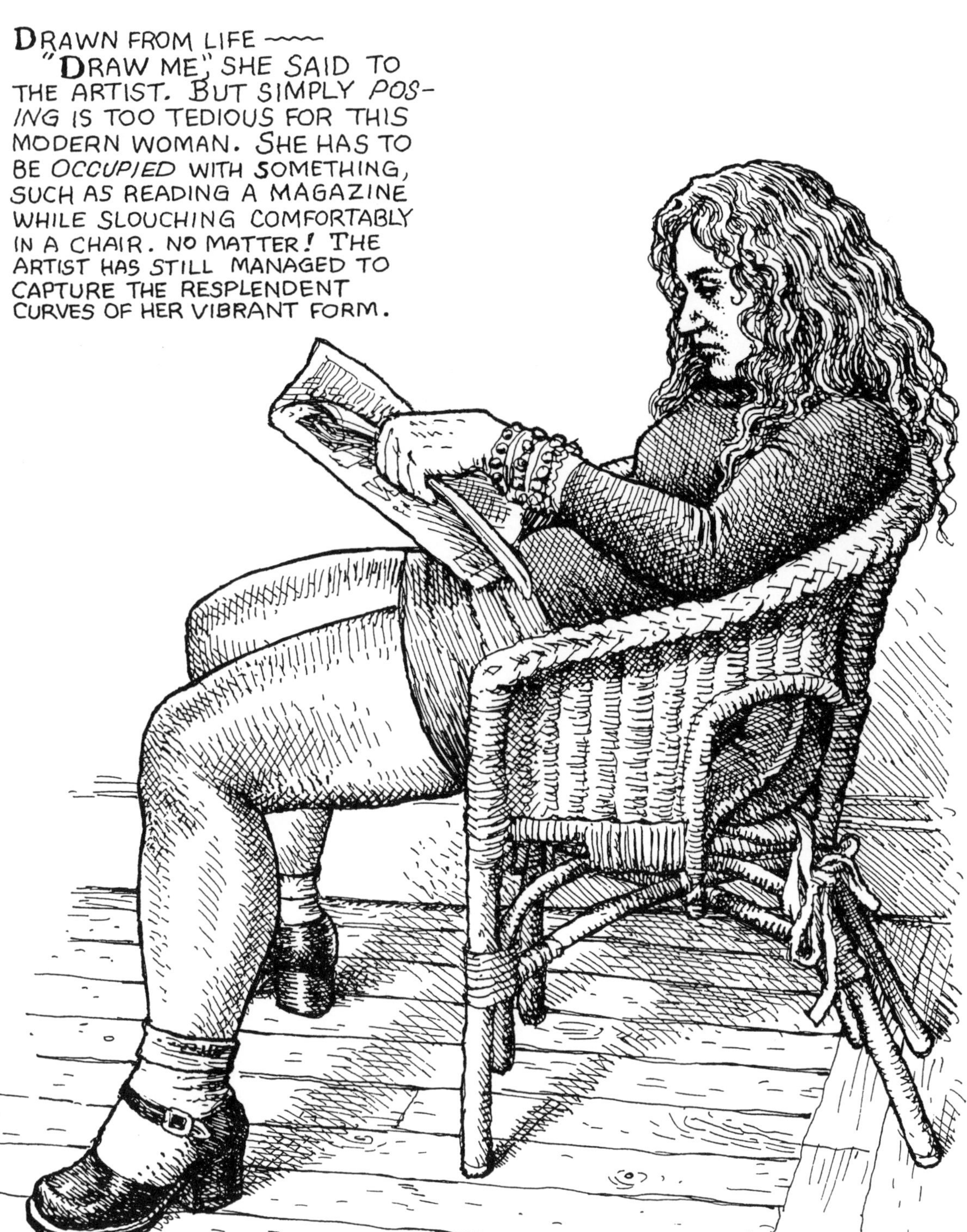

Drawn from life ——
"Draw me," she said to the artist. But simply *posing* is too tedious for this modern woman. She has to be *occupied* with something, such as reading a magazine while slouching comfortably in a chair. No matter! The artist has still managed to capture the resplendent curves of her vibrant form.

"The artist's technical problem is how to transform the material with which he works back into the sphere of the spirit." —— Hans Hofmann

"Art never seems to make me peaceful or pure. I always seem to be wrapped up in the melodrama of vulgarity." —— Willem de Kooning

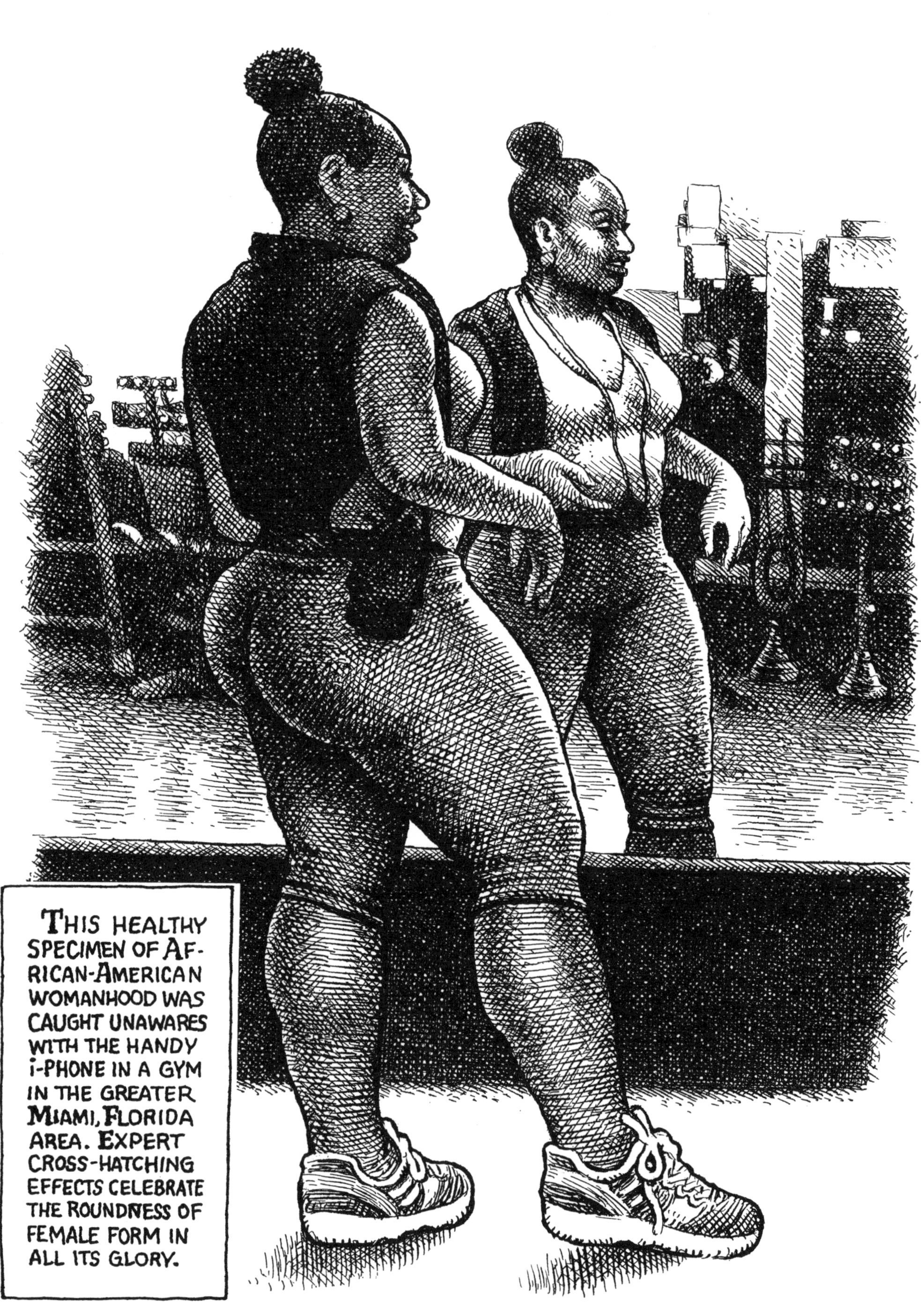

THIS HEALTHY
SPECIMEN OF AF-
RICAN-AMERICAN
WOMANHOOD WAS
CAUGHT UNAWARES
WITH THE HANDY
i-PHONE IN A GYM
IN THE GREATER
MIAMI, FLORIDA
AREA. EXPERT
CROSS-HATCHING
EFFECTS CELEBRATE
THE ROUNDNESS OF
FEMALE FORM IN
ALL ITS GLORY.

"IF I HAVE A THEORY AT ALL, IT IS THAT OF THE SIMPLE PRIN-
CIPLE: THERE IS GOOD ART AND BAD ART. THE BEST THING FOR
ART IS FOR IT TO BE TREATED AS A HOBBY, AN INCIDENTAL THING.
FOR AFTER ALL, WHAT DO WE ARTISTS, WE INSIGNIFICANT LITTLE
ANTS, HAVE TO SAY? WE, WHO ARE NOTHING MORE THAN BLOWN
UP FROGS? WHERE IS OUR INFLUENCE? WHERE, OUR SIGNIF-
ICANCE?...MY FAITH HAS BEEN SHATTERED." ~GEORGE GROSZ, 1946

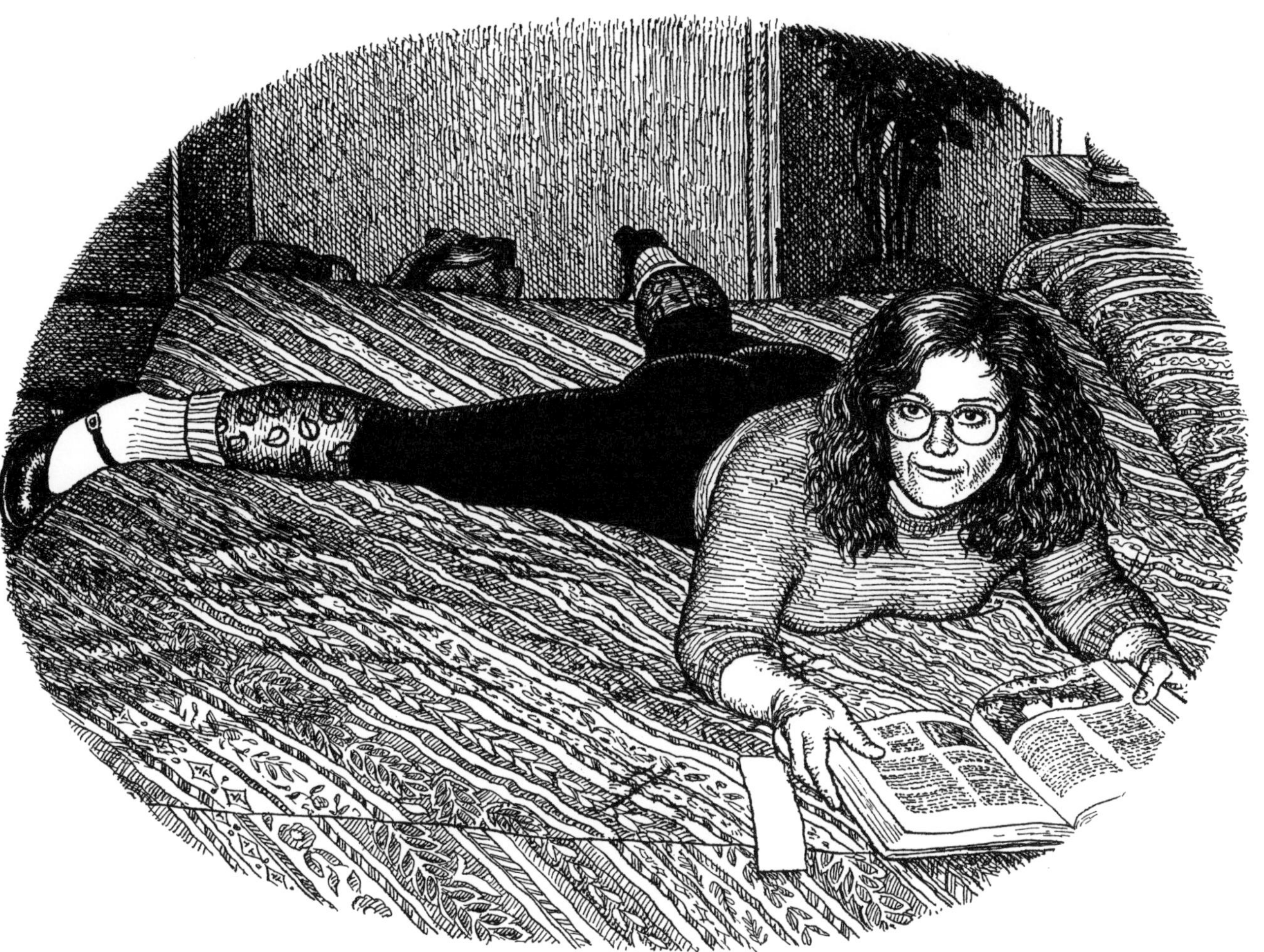

A MAN CANNOT READ A WOMAN'S MIND. THE MAN GAZES AT THE
WOMAN AS SHE SPRAWLS CARELESSLY ACROSS THE BED, ABSORBED
IN A BOOK. SUDDENLY THE MAN SAYS, "JUST LOOK UP HERE FOR A
SECOND." SHE LOOKS UP, AND THE MAN TAKES A PHOTO OF HER.
LATER, EXAMINING THE PHOTO, AND WHILE MAKING THE DRAWING
FROM IT, HE ATTEMPTS TO FATHOM THE UNFATHOMABLE EXPRESSION
ON HER FACE. WHAT IS SHE THINKING? WHAT IS SHE FEELING? WHAT
LIES BEHIND THOSE CLEAR, KNOWING EYES, THAT SLIGHT SMIRK OF
HER MOUTH? IMPOSSIBLE TO KNOW. ALL THE MAN CAN KNOW IS
THAT, TAKEN ALL TOGETHER, THE FACE, THE FINE FORM, THE ATTITUDE
OF THE WOMAN, HER VERY ESSENCE STIMULATES THE MALE INSTINCTS
TO A HIGH DEGREE. BEYOND THAT SHE IS A MYSTERY.

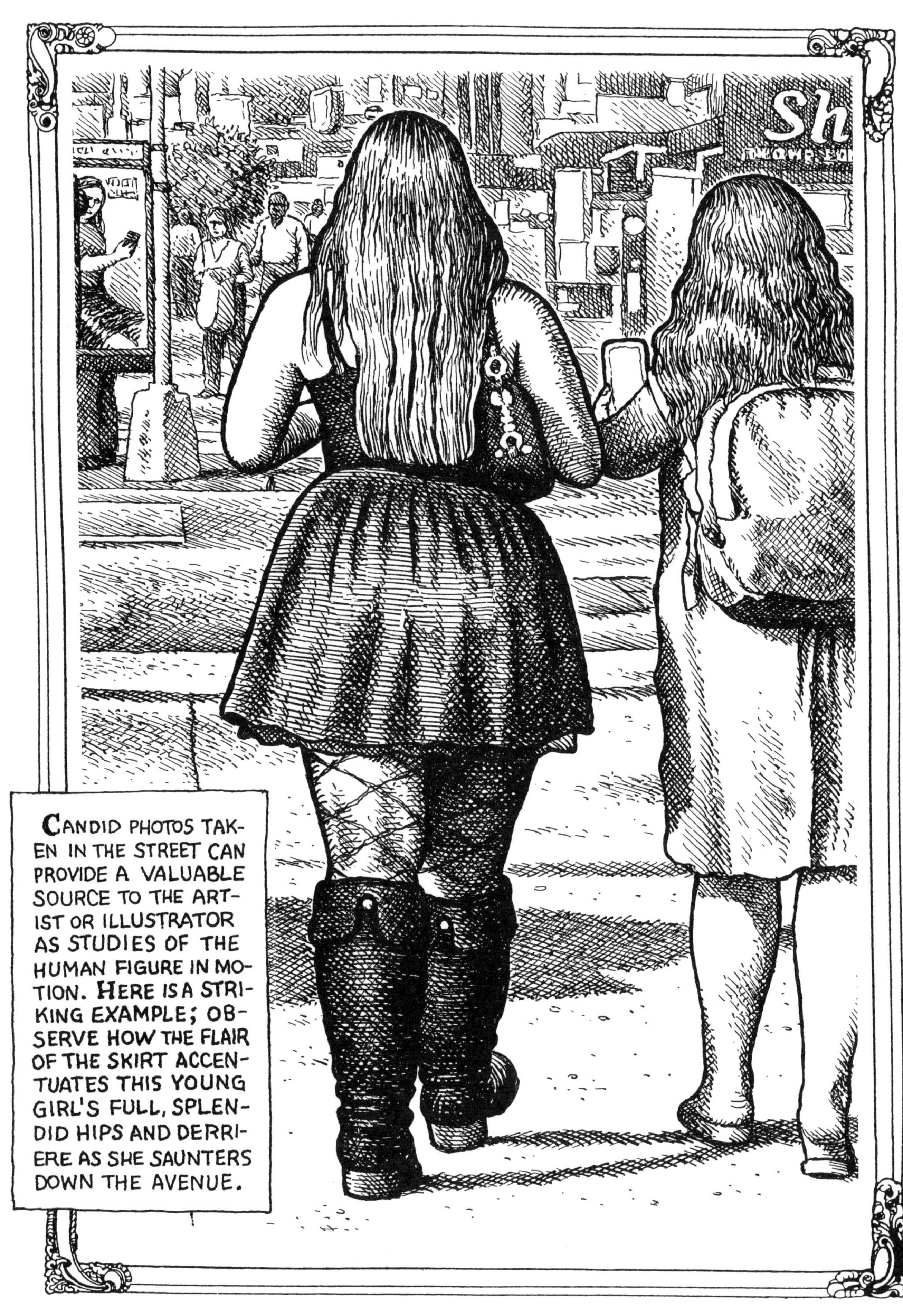
CANDID PHOTOS TAK-
EN IN THE STREET CAN
PROVIDE A VALUABLE
SOURCE TO THE ART-
IST OR ILLUSTRATOR
AS STUDIES OF THE
HUMAN FIGURE IN MO-
TION. HERE IS A STRI-
KING EXAMPLE; OB-
SERVE HOW THE FLAIR
OF THE SKIRT ACCEN-
TUATES THIS YOUNG
GIRL'S FULL, SPLEN-
DID HIPS AND DERRI-
ERE AS SHE SAUNTERS
DOWN THE AVENUE.

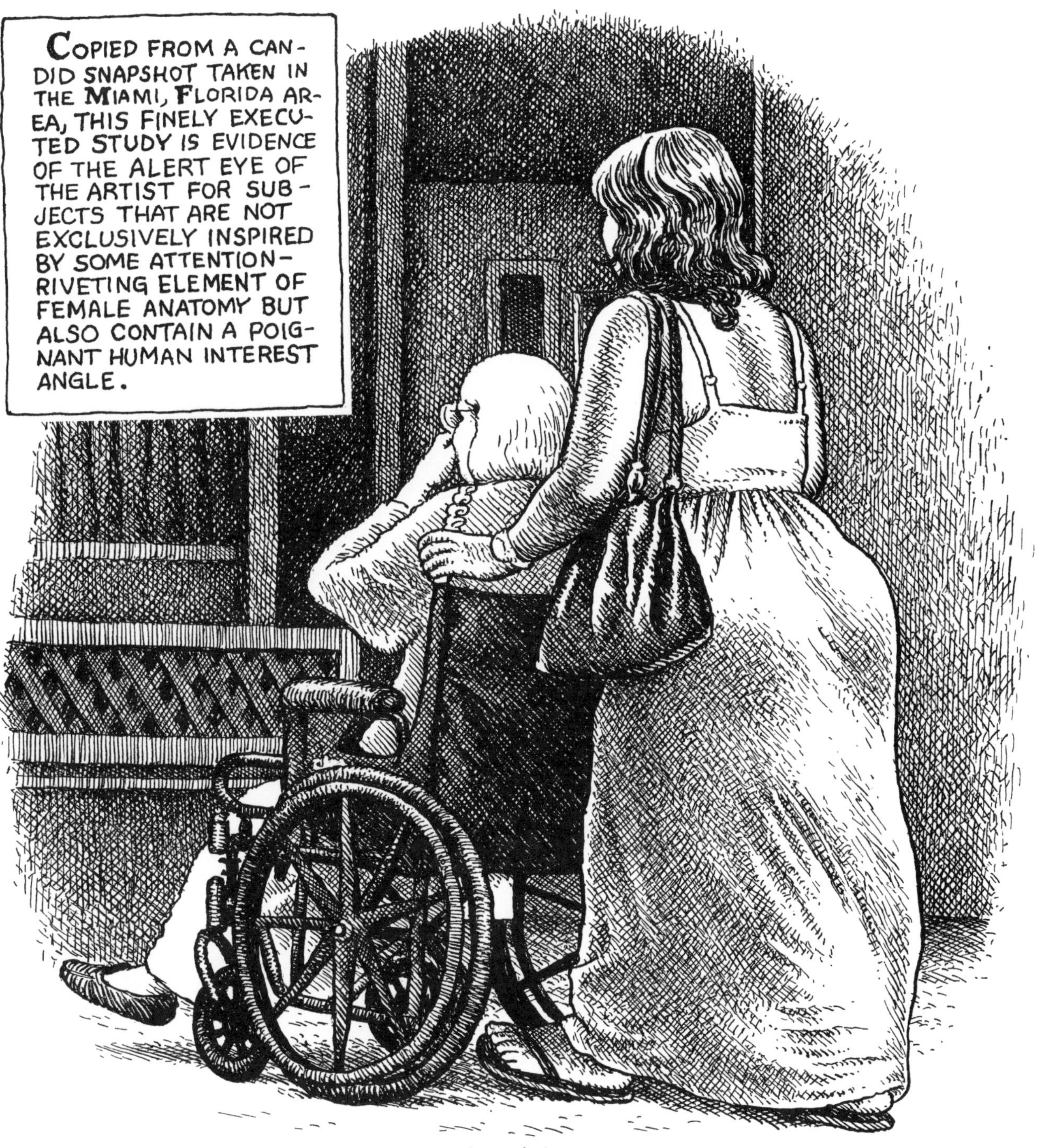

"Through my affirmation of the negation of the ideal and all that springs from the ideal I have arrived at the emancipation of the individual and finally at democracy. Realism is essentially the democratic art."
·····— Gustave Courbet

"To those who think painting is just about itself, I'm saying the exact opposite. The concreteness of a painting can't help but allude to a world of associations that may have a completely different face other than that of the image you are looking at."
·····— Julian Schnabel

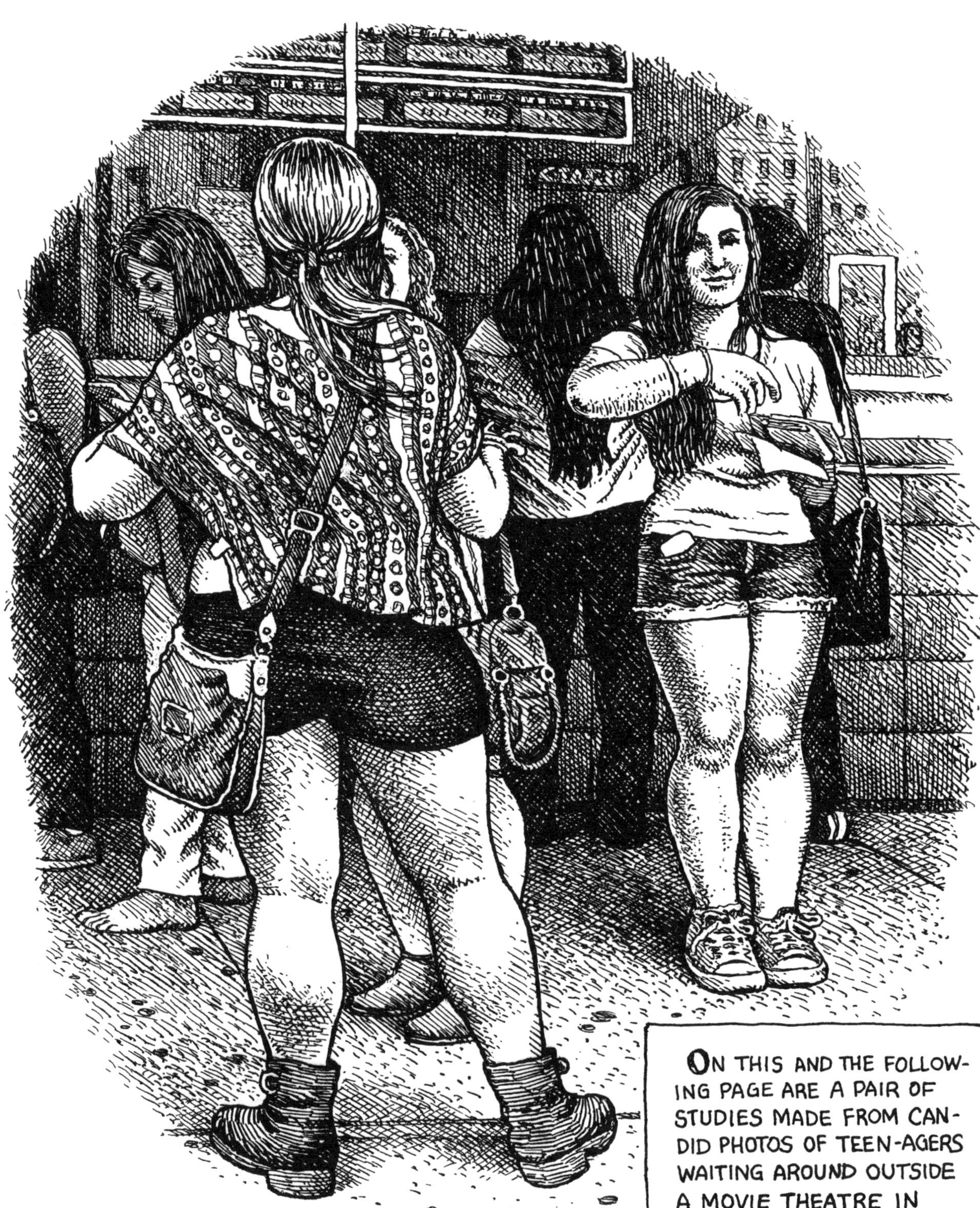

ON THIS AND THE FOLLOW-
ING PAGE ARE A PAIR OF
STUDIES MADE FROM CAN-
DID PHOTOS OF TEEN-AGERS
WAITING AROUND OUTSIDE
A MOVIE THEATRE IN
NEW YORK CITY WHERE
ON ANY GIVEN DAY IN WARM
WEATHER THE STREETS ARE
POPULATED WITH ATTRACT-
IVE GIRLS AND WOMEN IN
A VARIETY OF STYLES OF
BRIEF AND REVEALING AT-
TIRE.

"FOR ART TO BE SUCCESSFUL AND FOR
BEAUTY TO BE APPROACHED, IT HAS TO
BE CREATED OUT OF ONE'S TOTALITY—
THE LIGHT AND THE DARK PARTS, WITH
NOTHING HELD BACK." —STEPHEN DOBYNS

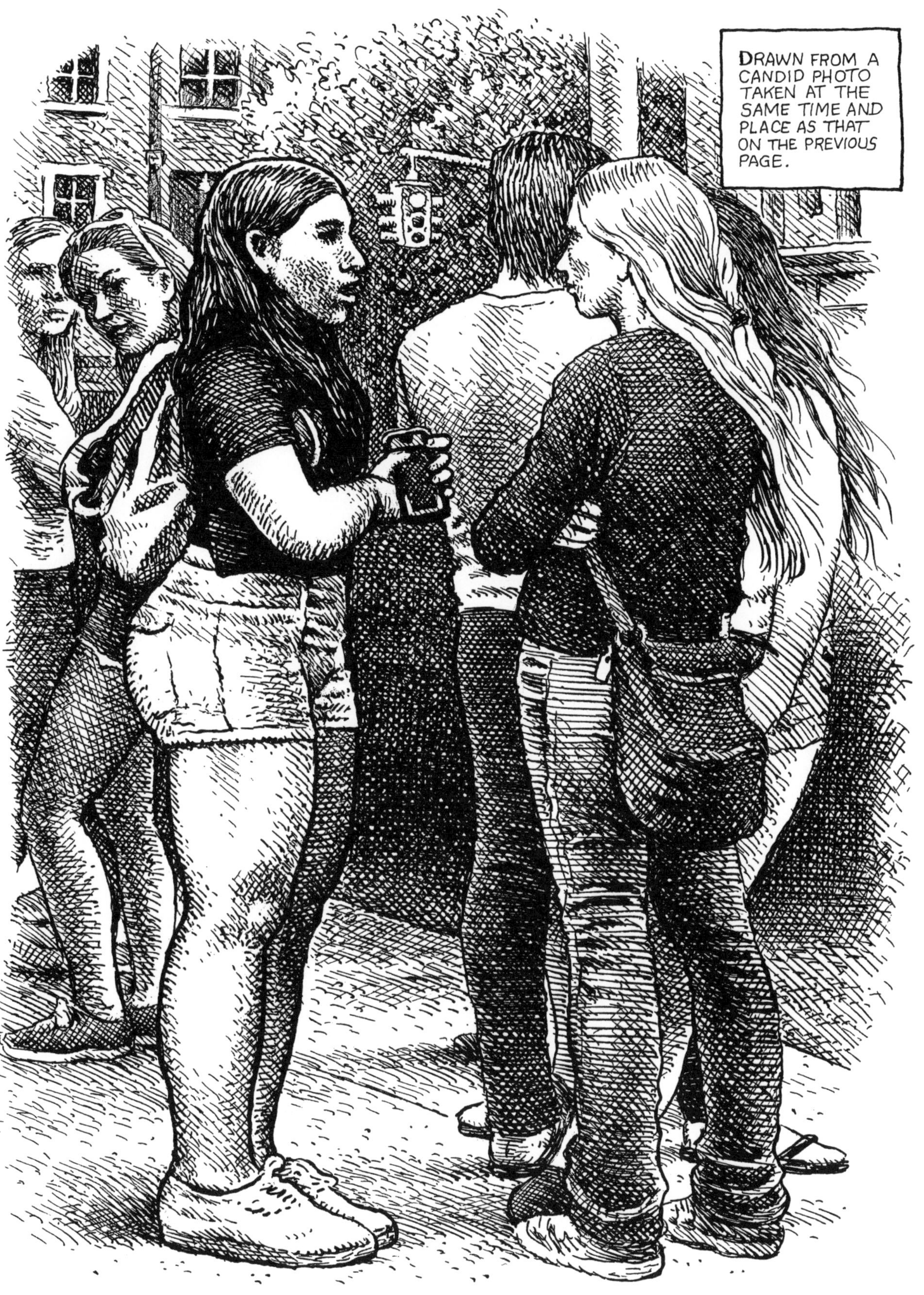

"THE PRODUCTION OF A WORK OF ART THROWS A LIGHT UPON THE MYSTERY OF HUMANITY." —— R.W. EMERSON on "NATURE AND REALITY"

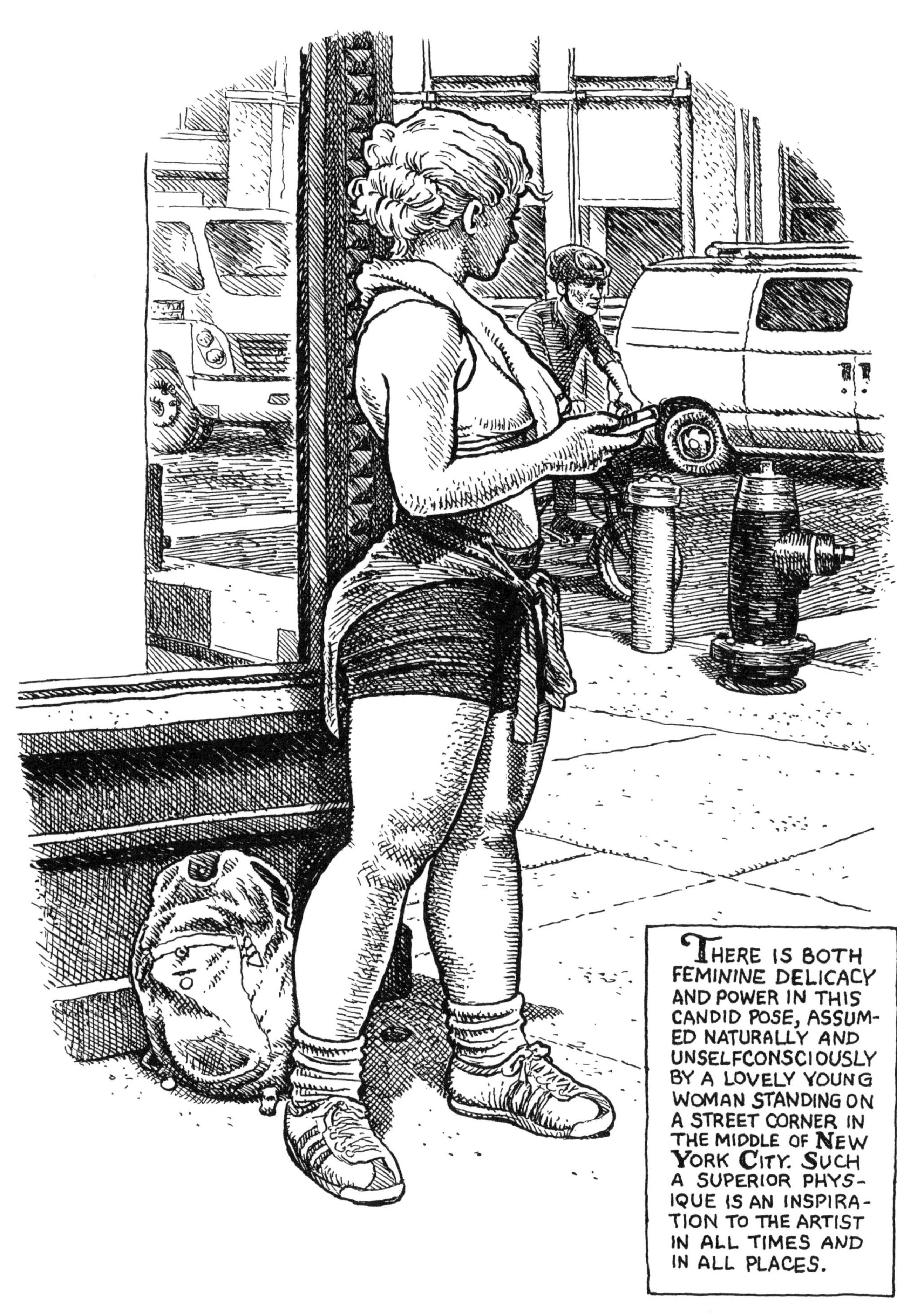

THERE IS BOTH FEMININE DELICACY AND POWER IN THIS CANDID POSE, ASSUMED NATURALLY AND UNSELFCONSCIOUSLY BY A LOVELY YOUNG WOMAN STANDING ON A STREET CORNER IN THE MIDDLE OF NEW YORK CITY. SUCH A SUPERIOR PHYSIQUE IS AN INSPIRATION TO THE ARTIST IN ALL TIMES AND IN ALL PLACES.

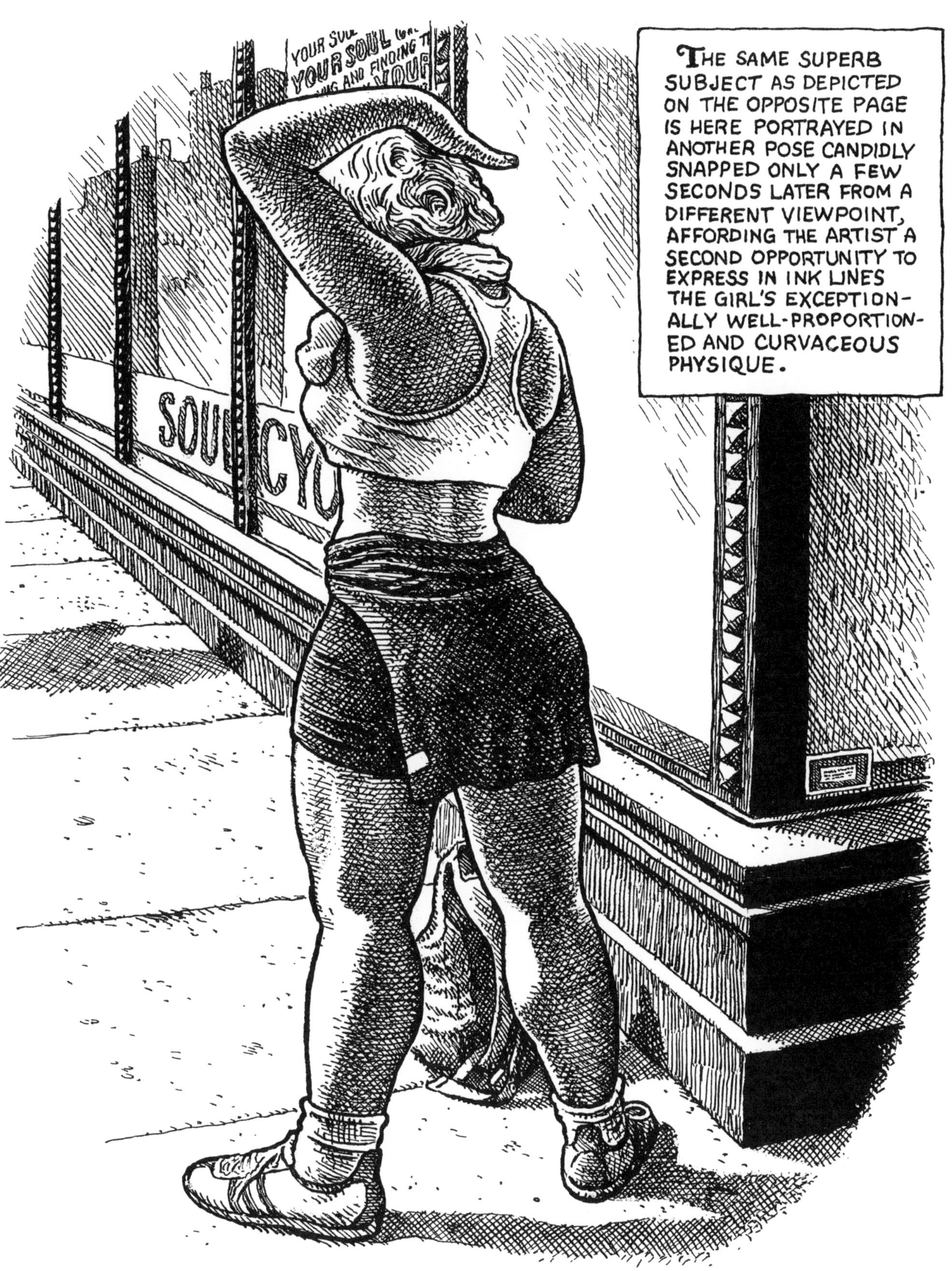

"REMEMBER THAT THE FIRST ESSENTIAL TO A GOOD ARTIST IS THAT HE BE A GOOD WORKMAN." ····—— SIR EDWARD POYNTER

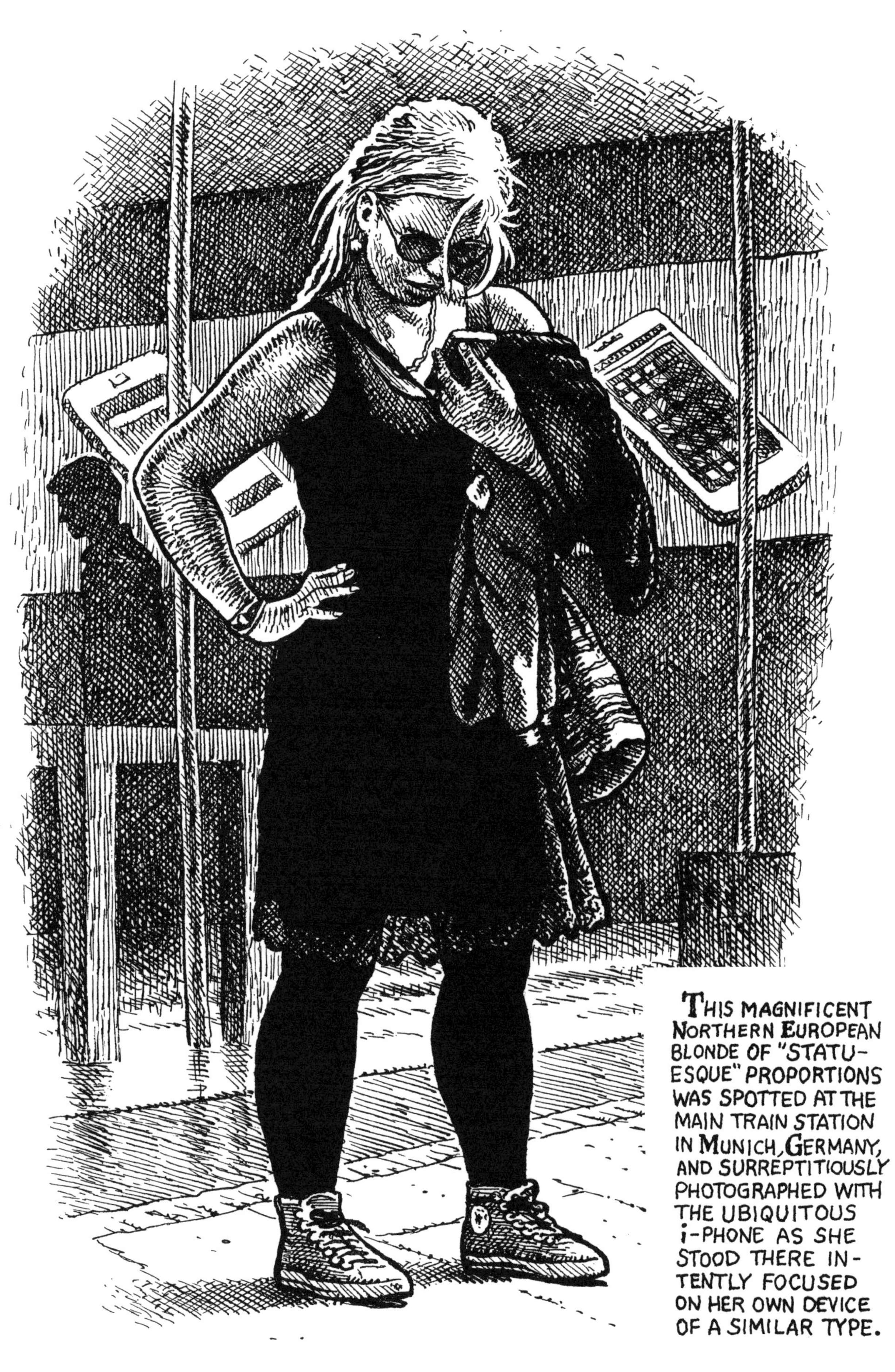

THIS MAGNIFICENT NORTHERN EUROPEAN BLONDE OF "STATU-ESQUE" PROPORTIONS WAS SPOTTED AT THE MAIN TRAIN STATION IN MUNICH, GERMANY, AND SURREPTITIOUSLY PHOTOGRAPHED WITH THE UBIQUITOUS i-PHONE AS SHE STOOD THERE IN-TENTLY FOCUSED ON HER OWN DEVICE OF A SIMILAR TYPE.

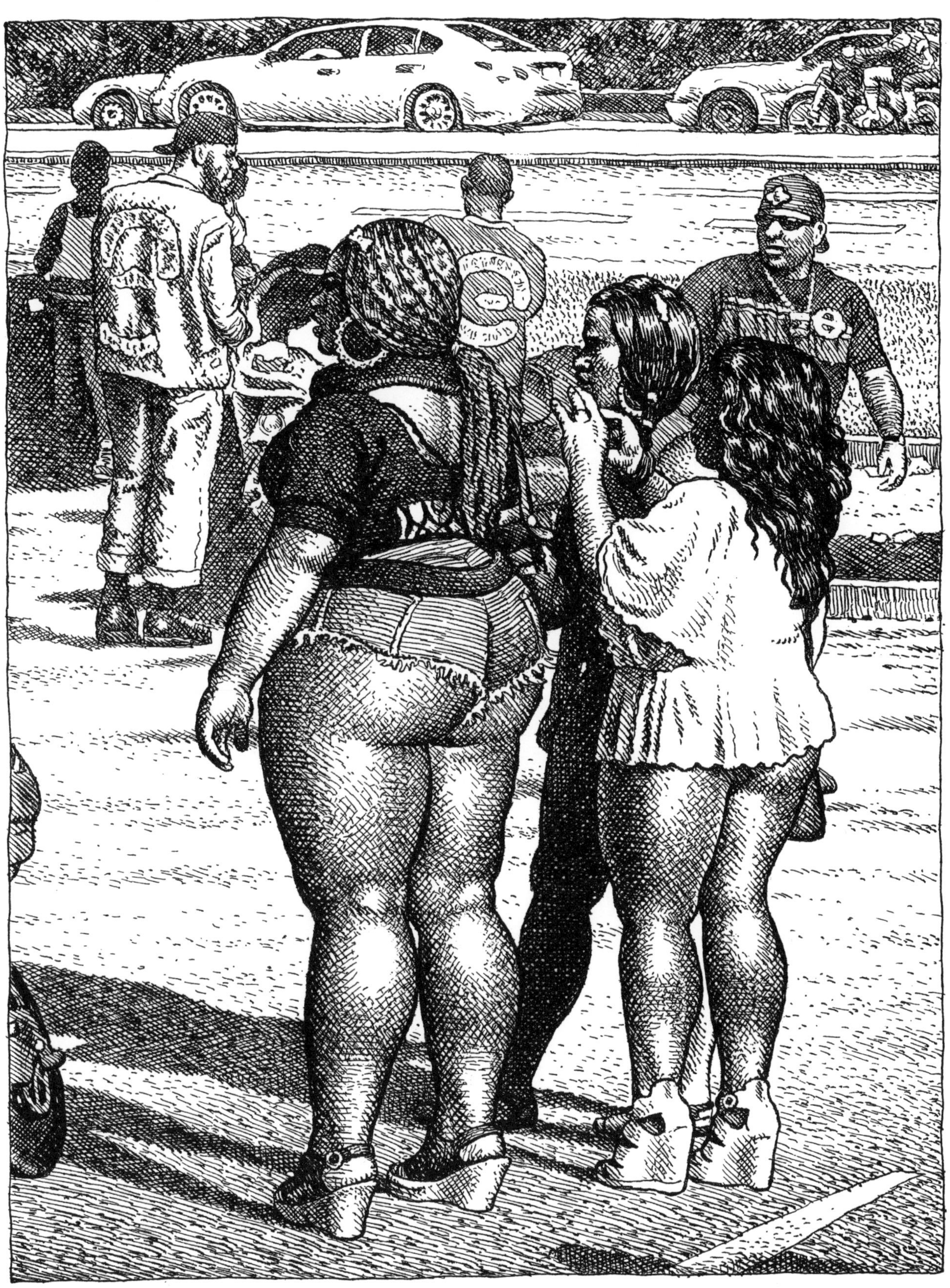

In this spectacular study the artist reveals his deep appreciation for that segment of African-American culture which encourages women of the physical type shown here to display their attributes in such brief and flamboyant costumes. This drawing was made from a photo taken at an African-American motorcycle gathering.

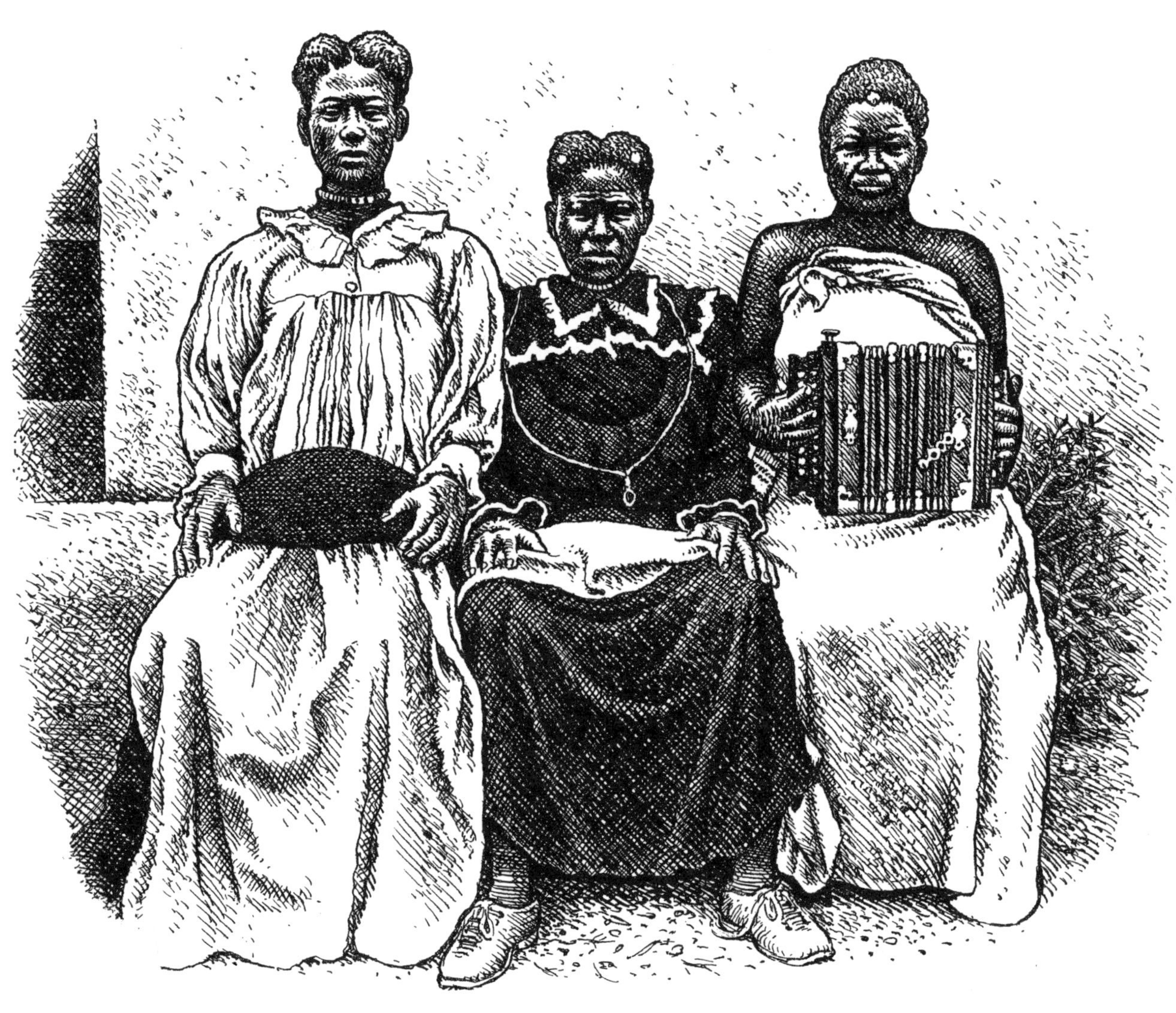

THREE AFRICAN WOMEN FROM BRAZZAVILLE, CONGO, FROM A PHOTO TAKEN A HUNDRED YEARS AGO. THE BEAUTY OF THESE WOMEN IS NOT ONE OF FINE OR LOVELY FEATURES, BUT OF CHARACTER, SOMETHING INEFFABLE. IT SEEMS LIKELY THAT THE THREE WOULD SING TOGETHER WHILE THE ONE EXERCISED THE SQUEEZE BOX. IT IS DEVOUTLY TO BE WISHED THAT WE COULD SOMEHOW LEND EAR TO THEIR MUSIC, NO DOUBT POWERFUL AND MOVING IN THE TRADITIONAL AFRICAN WAY.

"ALL EFFORTS AT SERIOUS ARTISTIC EXPRESSION SHOULD BE PRECEDED BY CAREFUL, THOROUGH PREPARATION. A PROFESSIONAL WOULD NOT FOR A MOMENT THINK OF DOING THE RASH THINGS AN AMATEUR ATTEMPTS WITH IMPUNITY."
—— H. L. McCLEOD

"A MASTERPIECE IS ABOVE ALL THE WORK OF AN ARTIST OF GENIUS WHO HAS BEEN ABSORBED BY THE SPIRIT OF THE TIME IN A WAY THAT HAS MADE HIS INDIVIDUAL EXPERIENCES UNIVERSAL."
—— KENNETH CLARK

"BE REGULAR AND ORDINARY IN YOUR LIFE, LIKE A BOURGEOIS, SO THAT YOU CAN BE VIOLENT AND ORIGINAL IN YOUR WORK."
—— GUSTAVE FLAUBERT

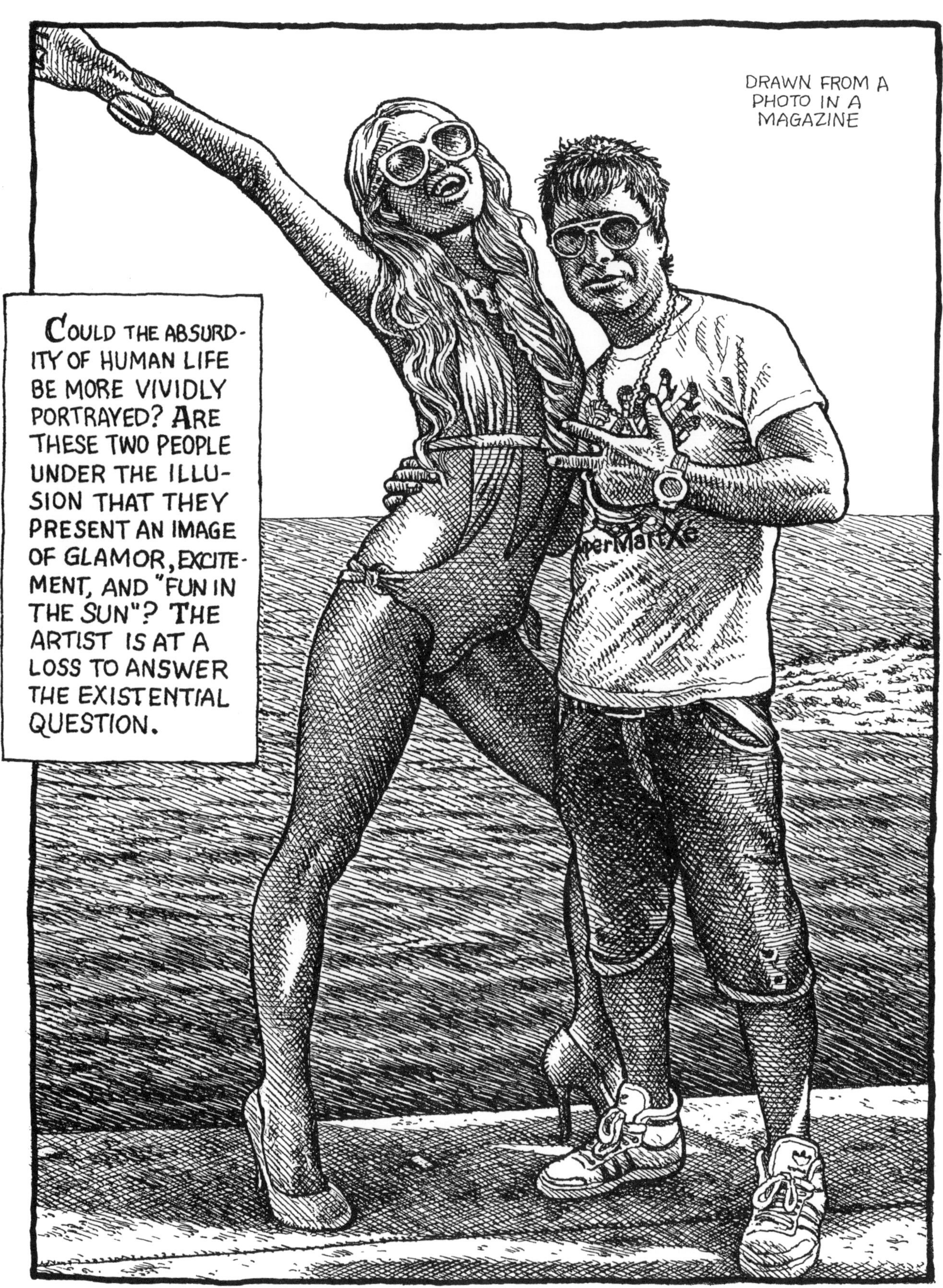

"*IN OTHER WORDS, AN EVOCATIVE ART IS THE MEANS AND RESULT OF GETTING IN TOUCH WITH THE POWERS OF OUR UNCONSCIOUS.*" ·····—JOHN GRAHAM, "*PRIMITIVE ART AND PICASSO*", 1937

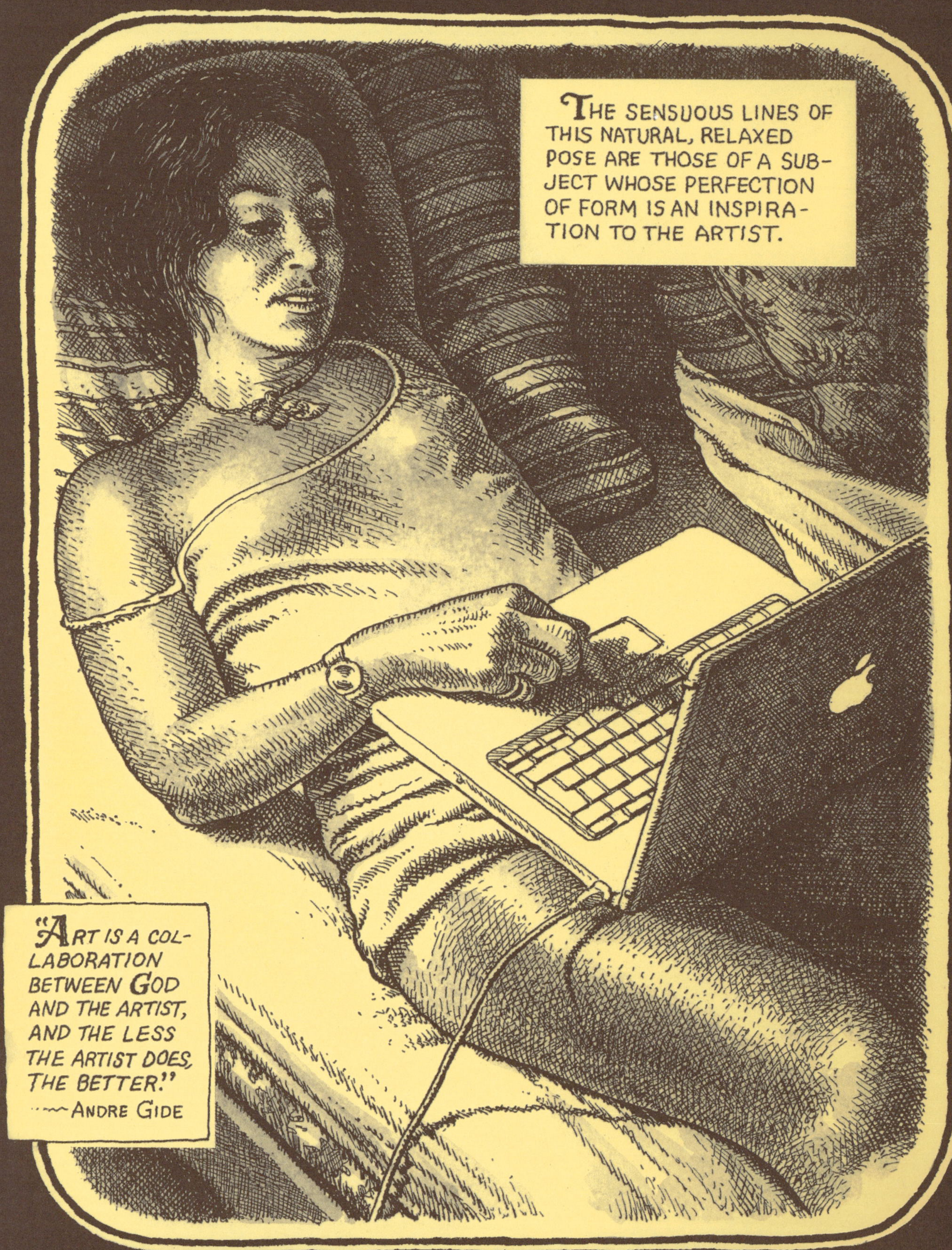

THE SENSUOUS LINES OF THIS NATURAL, RELAXED POSE ARE THOSE OF A SUBJECT WHOSE PERFECTION OF FORM IS AN INSPIRATION TO THE ARTIST.
"ART IS A COLLABORATION BETWEEN GOD AND THE ARTIST, AND THE LESS THE ARTIST DOES, THE BETTER." —ANDRE GIDE
$4.95
FANTAGRAPHICS BOOKS

Fantagraphics Editor: Gary Groth
Production: Paul Baresh
Associate Publisher: Eric Reynolds
Publisher: Gary Groth

Fantagraphics Books, Inc.
7563 Lake City Way NE
Seattle, WA 98115

www.fantagraphics.com
facebook.com/fantagraphics
@fantagraphics.com

ISBN: 979-8-8750-0072-0
Library of Congress Control Number: 2025942418
First Fantagraphics Books edition: February 2026
Printed in China